The Jewish Diaspora
in Latin America
and the Caribbean
Fragments of Memory

For Robert M. Levine

The Jewish Diaspora in Latin America and the Caribbean
Fragments of Memory

Edited by

Kristin Ruggiero

sussex
ACADEMIC
PRESS

Brighton • Portland

2 4 6 8 10 9 7 5 3 1

First published 2005 in Great Britain by
SUSSEX ACADEMIC PRESS
PO Box 2950
Brighton BN2 5SP

and in the United States of America by
SUSSEX ACADEMIC PRESS
920 NE 58th Ave   Suite 300
Portland, Oregon 97213–3786

British Library Cataloguing in Publication Data
A CIP catalogue record for this book is available from the British Library.

Library of Congress Cataloging-in-Publication Data
The Jewish diaspora in Latin America and the Caribbean : fragments
of memory / edited by Kristin Ruggiero.
    p. cm.
Includes bibliographical references and index.
ISBN 1-84519-061-0 (hardcover : alk. paper)
    1. Jews—Latin America—History—20th century. 2. Jews—
Caribbean Area—History—20th century. 3. Jews—Latin
America—Intellectual life—20th century. 4. Jews—Caribbean
Area—Intellectual life—20th century. 5. Latin America—Ethnic
relations. 6. Caribbean Area—Ethnic relations. I. Ruggiero,
Kristin.

F1419.J4J46 2005
980'.004924—dc22

                                                    2004026133
                                                    CIP

Typeset and designed by G&G Editorial, Brighton
Printed by MPG Books, Ltd, Bodmin, Cornwall
This book is printed on acid-free paper.

Contents

Contents

Acknowledgments

I would like to thank the contributors for their scholarship and commitment to this volume. Thanks to their enthusiasm – coming from Argentina, Israel, Canada, and the United States, the editorship of this endeavor has been a delight for me. Support for the project came from the College of Letters and Science, the Center for International Education, and the Center for Jewish Studies at the University of Wisconsin-Milwaukee; the US Department of Education's National Resource Center Title VI program; and the Wisconsin Society for Jewish Learning. A conference held at the University of Wisconsin-Milwaukee marked the venture's first stage in April 2001. I would like to thank all who were involved in that conference, especially the staff at the Center for Latin American and Caribbean Studies at UWM.

This book emerges from the people who have lived these lives and their families, friends, and communities. I and the contributors thank them for sharing their experiences with us.

Finally, this book is dedicated to Robert M. Levine, whose feelings for humanity made him a most valued and now greatly missed scholar, colleague, and friend.

Introduction

Kristin Ruggiero

A history that predates the encounter between the Old World and the New has shaped the experience of Jewish populations in Latin America and the Caribbean. Life for Jews in Spain changed in the year 1474, when the Catholic sovereigns Ferdinand and Isabel married, bringing together the kingdoms of Castile and Aragon, which unified much of what we know as today's Spain into the Spanish Empire. An essential part of this unification was a movement launched against Jews based on race and religion, which culminated in the expulsion of Jews in 1492.

In the same year, Columbus opened up the New World for colonization. Concerned about maintaining religious orthodoxy and racial purity in such a distant part of the empire, the Spanish monarchs decreed that only Christians were allowed to immigrate to the Americas. This included Jews who had converted to Christianity, who for centuries after figured among the colonists in the New World. Sometimes we see them pictured as mixed races in the uniquely Latin American genre called *casta* paintings. Other times we learn about them as victims of the Inquisition, the Catholic Church's tribunal to enforce orthodoxy that tracked people's ancestry and made sure that no converted Jews held public offices or joined the military. The Inquisition also concerned itself with inauthentic conversion, which was punished with imprisonment and confiscation of property. We also know about these Jews from their descendants, some of whose Christian families are only now beginning to realize that their ancestors were Crypto Jews, that is, Jews who secretly practiced Judaism centuries ago, bequeathing to their descendants customs that are actually Jewish in origin. The history of Jews in the colonial era is a fascinating one that forms an important part of the mix that makes up contemporary Latin American society and culture.

Independence for most Latin American and Caribbean countries from the Spanish Empire came within the first two decades of the nineteenth century. At this time, the newly constituted independent countries opened their borders to Jews in a spirit of religious toleration. Old World Jews from Eastern Europe and the Mediterranean region formed part of the alluvial European emigration movement that took place between the mid-nineteenth century and World War I. Jews, as well as Italians, Spaniards, Germans, French, and others, came to Latin America looking for a better life. Even though Jews were greatly outnumbered by other groups, they formed a significant minority, especially in Argentina and Uruguay. Here the larger Jewish communities developed strong organizations, neighborhoods, schools, and commercial enterprises. Argentine Jews also had an important benefactor in Baron Maurice de Hirsch, who undertook a colonization program specifically for Jews. His investment in an extensive agricultural colonization project in Argentina in the 1890s enabled many Russian Jews to immigrate to this country where they prospered as farmers and later as urban artisans and merchants.

Jews are today part of the vibrant urban life of most capitals and major cities in Latin American countries. The region contains approximately 500,000 Jews, which is the fifth largest concentration of Jewish population in the world. Argentina dominates with some 230,000 Jews (some reports are as high as 300,000), the majority located in Buenos Aires. Brazil follows with approximately 130,000 Jews; Mexico with over 40,000; and Uruguay with over 30,000. Although Jews with origins in the Iberian Peninsula, North Africa, and the Middle East – the Sephardim – had an easier time of integrating into Latin America than the Ashkenazim, whose origins were in Eastern Europe, it is today the Ashkenazim who constitute the majority of the Jews in the region. Dutch Jews also went to Latin America, many to Brazil and from there to the French Caribbean. Each group has its unique history and each destination has provided a special individual and collective space for Jewish settlement and assimilation, surviving and remembering. Since the 1970s, the Latin American Jewish Diaspora has been recognized as a unique phenomenon in diasporic studies. This is due in part to the development of diasporic studies itself, as well as to the development of new ways of thinking about internationalism and globalization.

This volume of essays is grounded in a substantial tradition established in the 1980s and 1990s by Judith Laikin Elkin in *The Jews of the Latin American Republics*, and by collections edited by J. L. Elkin and Gilbert W. Merkx, *The Jewish Presence in Latin America*, and by David Sheinin and Lois Baer Barr, *The Jewish Diaspora in Latin America*. These important works offer material that has established without a doubt the importance of Jews in Latin America. Essays in a more recent collection edited by Mieke Bal, Jonathan Crewe, and Leo Spitzer, *Acts of Memory: Cultural Recall in the Present*, contain examinations of the construction of memories by Jews, some of these in Latin America.[1] The present volume builds upon this previous work and furthers the interdisciplinary exploration of four themes prominent in Jewish history in Latin America and the Caribbean: memory, identity, anti-Semitism, and violence. The authors are from several different disciplines, including anthropology, art, history, literature, political science, and sociology, which underscores the variety of ways in which Jewish life can be and has been analyzed. The book makes no pretence to be "comprehensive"; rather, it provides suggestive new ways of talking about the Jewish Diasporas in Latin America through work done on the communities of Jews in six countries. Its importance also lies in the essays' engagement of twentieth-century history as seen through the intimate details of Jewish lives.

In **Part I**, *Relocation in the Nazi Years*, German literature professor Ruth Schwertfeger, linguistics professor Rosalie Sitman, and historian Jeffrey Lesser examine the relocation of European Jews, refugees from fascist Europe, and their identities and memories in Mexico, Argentina, and Brazil in the first half of the twentieth century. Latin American societal and governmental reactions to these immigrants differed. The Mexican government was receptive to Jews and thus German Jewish writer Anna Seghers made her way to Mexico during World War II where, argues Schwertfeger, she constructed a present from a Nazi past that could not be forgotten but that could not be integrated into her new life in Mexico either. Her story is the story of many immigrant Jews to the New World, who lived out a simultaneity of an "obtrusive past," a longing for their homeland, and a feeling of being bound to a new environment. In Argentina in this period, although the government refused refuge to Jews during the war, Sitman argues that individuals in literary circles risked censorship and agreed to publish Jewish testimonials of Eastern European concentration camps as well as Jorge Luis Borges' pro-Jewish short stories. Sitman's example, the literary circle surrounding the periodical *SUR*, saw themselves as providing a cultural bridge between the Americas and Europe, keeping ideas of liberal democracy alive in the face of fascism and denouncing the persecution of Jews. Even with the war over, *SUR* continued to bring the memories of anti-Semitism and violence to its audience. Finally, Lesser's contribution shows that, in spite of the collision of Brazilian nativism and Jewish immigration in the 1930s, Jewish leaders successfully manipulated ideas of Jewish identity and "otherness" to the benefit of the Jewish Diasporas in Brazil. Lesser suggests that in some respects the "Jewish Question" was part of a larger "Ethnic Question" in Brazil that included Brazilians of Asian and Middle Eastern descent.

In **Part II**, *Constructing Memory*, historians Raanan Rein and David Sheinin focus on the marked anti-Semitism and resulting violence against Jews in the second half of the twentieth century in Argentina. Although not the only Latin American country to witness these horrors, Argentina is one of the severest examples of anti-Semitism and violence against Jews in the region. Here, many Jews spent the 1950s to the early 1980s struggling to construct a community memory that involved an active forgetting. Argentine Jews did not want Holocaust memories to influence their integration into Argentine society. Committed to starting a new life in Argentina, Jews were reluctant to bring the baggage of a memory of persecution to the New World. Even in the face of anti-Semitism, Jews agonized over the origins and degree of violence against Jews in Argentina. The Argentine government and society had only reluctantly supported the establishment of the State of Israel and tolerated the Israeli kidnapping of Nazi criminal Adolf Eichmann in 1960 on Argentine soil. Nevertheless, many Jews agonized about whether this was really anti-Semitism.

This phenomenon resurfaced during the military dictatorship of 1976–83 when the military positioned Jews as a threat to Argentine sovereignty and to "Western Christian civilization." The military claimed that Israel had a plan to invade Patagonia, thus making attacks on Jews a matter of patriotism. Jews, however, expected that as good citizens they would be included and protected under the umbrella of the "civilized." They did not realize just how central anti-Semitism was to the military's internal war against civilians, and thus did not protest violence against Jews in the 1970s and 1980s. There was no way to have known at that point in the dictatorship that while Jews were only 2 percent of Argentina's population, they would account for as much as 10 percent of those "disappeared." Denials from both the government and the Jewish population that something unusual was happening to Jews in Argentina engendered a dissembling that completely negated the existence of anti-Semitism on Argentine soil, which may well have facilitated the bombings that took place at the Israeli Embassy in 1992 and the Jewish–Argentine Mutual Association (AMIA) in 1994. Attempts by Argentines, such as sociologist Beatriz Gurevich, to move toward transparency and accountability to uncover the identity of the perpetrators of the bombings and to not forget have been stonewalled, even by members of the Jewish community itself. So strong is the desire to not remember that even Jews reject investigation of the bombings. Interestingly, even with the site of the memory totally visible, that is, the Israeli Embassy, the AMIA building, and strong documentation, some Jews refused to let it influence them.

Part III, *Identity and Hybridity*, examines Jewish identity in the politically diverse and hybrid society of the Caribbean. In Cuba, documents reveal that Jews were much influenced by local politics. Historian Robert Levine explains that some Jews chose to remain in Cuba, to become part of Fidel Castro's revolution; some chose exile; and others just moved right on through to the US with minimal integration into the Cuban community. In anthropologist Ruth Behar's Cuba, her family left and never wanted to return to Cuba. Her video (and her description of it) illustrates how the next generation was able to recuperate a family memory as she struggles to get her father to be part of her video. In Martinique, historian William Miles uses interviews and documents to argue that Jews are unwilling to be identified with the island's increasingly hybrid population. He suggests that this might be because the anti-Semitic laws of 1940s Vichy France were also enforced in Martinique. It might also be due to the basic nature of contemporary Martinique, however, where Martinicans' creative energy goes into building a hybrid culture that is inattentive to Jewish issues or the population. Jews, however, do not feel a part of this vibrancy. Literature professor Ilán Stavans explores his grandmother's life as a Jew in Mexico through the Yiddish language and its effect on memory and identity. Like many immigrants, Stavans' grandmother carried a dual identity. This duality, argues Stavans, was and still is much more accentuated among Mexican Jews than in their counterparts in the US, and maybe even in Brazil and Argentina. His grandmother, although Yiddish was "the language of stomach and soul," wrote her diary in Spanish.

In **Part IV, *Poeticizing, Painting, Writing the Pain***, memory, identity, anti-Semitism, and violence are explored though the poems of literature professor Marjorie Agosín, the paintings of artist Raquel Partnoy, and the writings of literature professor Alicia Partnoy. These authors personally experienced the extension of Holocaust-level terror into Latin America's military regimes in Argentina and Chile. All remember the Holocaust; all remember the military regimes. They were affected deeply by both and struggle with how the two relate, how to explain their feelings, and how to make others feel them. Agosín explains that some memories, rather than being firm, are better described as traces, acts such as lighting a flame or picking a flower, acts that leave traces, "lucid testaments of history," like the memories of death at Auschwitz, able to be mentioned only in a poem, as a trace of memory, because spoken memories sometimes alienate people who do not share them. Raquel Partnoy struggles with this, searching for the images for paintings in the fragments of people's lives. Her painting series "Surviving Genocide" seeks to find the images that will explain that what happened in Argentina under the military regime was genocide. A decade after the anti-Semitic military government collapsed, the bombings took place at the Israeli Embassy and AMIA. These too were acts of violence and annihilation – and of fragmentation – especially of families, which is what her family experienced.

It is fitting to end this collection with an essay confirming Jewish identity by a survivor of the Argentine military's violence. Alicia Partnoy, a "disappeared" person for four years in Argentina, argues that Southern Cone torturers and prison authorities drew their inspiration from the Nazis as well as from the School of the Americas (now known as the Western Hemisphere Institute for Security Cooperation), and that similarities exist between Holocaust literature and the testimonial texts produced by victims in the Southern Cone. Many scholars of Latin American testimonial texts disagree and tend to highlight the differences between cultural productions under Nazis and under dictators. Partnoy argues that both Holocaust literature and Latin American writing were conceived as "instrument(s) to preserve the victim's moral and emotional integrity." As a "disappeared" person in Argentina herself, Partnoy understands the importance of this writing as a way for victims to recover voices fragmented by the pain of torture, as a tool for resistance while in prison, and as a way to chronicle these events for future generations. She explains that survivors' fear of speaking out is the fear that no one will listen: their voices and their agency shattered. Partnoy's goal has been to support victims' resistance to silence, and to construct a discourse of solidarity against the messianic discourse of power generated by the Nazis and Latin American dictators. She has endeavored to recover their integrity as human beings in control of their history and as people who belong to a world community that will hear their pain – and ultimately to privilege the collective experience over the individual drama. This is the goal of the collection as well, which aims to uncover and recover another story and history of the fragments of the Jewish experience.

Note

1   Judith Laikin Elkin, *Jews of the Latin American Republics* (Chapel Hill, NC: University of North Carolina Press, 1980; rev. edn., Holmes and Meier, 1998); *The Jewish Presence in Latin America*, eds., Judith Laikin Elkin and Gilbert W. Merkx (Boston: Allen and Unwin, 1987); *The Jewish Diaspora in Latin America: New Studies on History and Literature*, eds., David Sheinin and Lois Baer Barr (NY and London: Garland Publishing, Inc., 1996); *Acts of Memory: Cultural Recall in the Present*, eds., Mieke Bal, Jonathan Crewe, Leo Spitzer (Hanover, NH: University Press of New England, 1999). The current volume benefits from four essays foundational in this field of inquiry, two of which are based on chapters in books published by authors Jeffrey Lesser and Raanan Rein, and two that are reprinted here from other sources by Ruth Behar and Ilán Stavans. These essays provide valuable additions to the previously unpublished works presented here.

Part I

Relocation in the Nazi Years

Simultaneity of Past and Present in Mexico

Ruth Schwertfeger

The destiny of German Jews in flight from Nazi Germany, especially those who had initially found refuge in France, is often associated with the American Rescue Commission which sent Varian Fry to France in the summer of 1940 to save prominent European intellectuals – writers, artists, and scientists – from the escalating threat of being arrested in France by the occupying German army. What is less known is the fate of those who did not make that list, whether because of their affiliation with the Communist Party or sympathy with its tenets. The German Jewish writer Anna Seghers, winner of the prestigious Kleist prize for literature, honored speaker at international literary congresses in the thirties, member of the Communist Party since 1924, was one such person. She was among the several hundred German refugees who made their way to Mexico by the so-called Martinique route. This essay focuses on the short story "The Excursion of the Dead Girls," which Seghers wrote in 1943 in Mexico about the homeland – her German *Heimat*, locates it within the immediate frame of diaspora in Mexico, and finally in the broader context of memory – the vexing issue of German memory and the Holocaust.

German refugees who fled to Mexico in the thirties and early forties came in two waves. The first came after the Spanish Civil War when they were admitted as former combatants of the International Brigades by President Lázaro Cárdenas, whose liberal immigration policy provided protection for one hundred Germans, on the shirt tails, so to speak, of the ten thousand Spanish freedom fighters. The next wave also drew some of the Spanish contingent, but now included those who had been trapped in France after the outbreak of "the phony war" in September 1939 – "*la drôle de guerre*" – and especially after the armistice was signed nine months later. Fifth Column hysteria in France generated an internment policy that essentially detained anyone remotely German or "dangerous" in a foreign sort of way – German Jewish communists were fair game. Thus, Mexico was for them more than a destination; it was a country known for its liberal immigration policy. Many in flight from Nazi

Germany after 1933 had comfortably assumed that Czechoslovakia or above all France were destinations, but discovered otherwise, though for different reasons. Several prominent left-wing German Jewish intellectuals had done time in Le Vernet, the infamous internment camp, openly designated as "repressive" by the French, and they emerged from it toughened and hardened by the experience.

Seghers herself had spent over a year on the run in France, and considered herself fortunate to find shelter in a village near Le Vernet where her Hungarian husband Lzaslo Radvanyi was interned. After his release they waited for seven months in Marseilles, hoping for the coveted transit visa that would get them as quickly and efficiently as possible out of the country and to Mexico. For them, as for all refugees, the route was hardly direct. Many spent months trying to get to their destination; some were detained in North Africa, even in the dreaded camps of North Africa, or along the route in Cuba, Trinidad, or Santo Domingo.

Although there already existed a small politically diverse German community in Mexico City, which included some Nazi sympathizers, the newcomers were solidly anti-fascist. This is what had propelled or expelled them from Nazi Germany in the first place, and sustained and unified them in their exile in France. The Jewish Statutes of October 1940 passed by Vichy a mere four months after the armistice, however, targeted them specifically as Jews, even if they were not practicing Jews. Further, the Statutes targeted them as foreign Jews, putting them under the immediate threat of internment and by the summer of 1942 of deportation. Unable to travel directly from Marseilles to Mexico, since it was not until early 1941 that the Vichy government reinstated sailing routes to the Caribbean, refugees were forced to sit around waiting for transit visas, or stand in line with hundreds of fellow refugees at consular offices. In fact, the Mexican consulate in Marseilles is a presence in several works by German Jews fleeing from France, including Seghers who describes it in the novel *Transit* as "an immense house in which people live who were inviting her." Seghers and her family were finally able to leave Marseilles on March 24, 1941, sailed by way of Casablanca to Martinique, where they were detained for four weeks, then on to Santo Domingo for yet another detention, this time for two weeks.[1] In all, their journey took them three months before they landed in New York in June. She writes to a fellow exile, Bodo Uhse, "I have the feeling that I have been dead for a year."[2]

They were to spend the next six years in Mexico City as active members of the community of German refugees, which included some names known at least to Germanisten: Ludwig Renn, Bodo Uhse, Egon Erwin Kisch, Bruno Frei, Alexander Abusch, and Paul Merker. Communists were able to procure work, even in the government, but the others, especially those who did not speak Spanish, ended up teaching German. Without the financial support of refugees in the US and the Committee for Jewish Relief, which offered aid to *all* refugees, some would have been even worse off.

The most vital sign of German life was membership in cultural and political groups; several hundred people attended some events. There was a *Liga pro cultura alemana*, founded by the communists in 1937, and run by the writer and activist Ludwig Renn who later left to teach at the university in Morelia. Despite the efforts of some of the German refugees to adhere to a unifying agenda of anti-fascist policies, the league was sharply divided, so much so that the German communists left it to form their own group – the movement for a Free Germany, which they set up with Renn as the Minister of War, Seghers as the Minister of Culture, and Merker as the Prime Minister. The new organization was flanked by a publishing house – *El Libro libre* (*Das freie Buch*) and a monthly cultural and political journal called *Das Freie Deutschland*, founded in October 1941. The journal could not pay royalties, but was very influential and was able to attract the most prominent names in German letters – the Mann brothers (Heinrich and Thomas), Lion Feuchtwanger, and Hubertus Prinz zu Löwenstein. With a worldwide readership of 20,000, mostly German exiles, the journal lasted until 1946. In fact, its aim was to make Mexico the literary center for exile literature. The most influential German presence in Mexico, however, was the Heinrich Heine Club, which lasted from 1941 to 1946. Described as an "organization of anti-fascist intellectuals from different political camps," it offered literary readings, films, and theater productions that could draw an audience of four hundred to eight hundred for special events and two hundred for average evening events.[3]

Seghers' letters and notes from the first two years of her exile express both contentment with and affection for Mexico, a response that resonates in the narratives of the other German refugees. This was to change for her abruptly and dramatically in 1943, not as the result of the changing political situation after Cárdenas left office in 1940, and after Mexico had entered the war in May 1942, but because of a deep crisis in Seghers' life that became the catalyst for the story "The Excursion of the Dead Girls."[4] Crossing the busy street Paseo de la Reforma, Seghers was knocked down by a speeding car and lay unconscious for hours before she was transported to the hospital. For months she hovered between life and death, anxiously watched over by family and German friends. She later wrote: "For a long time I was in the hospital there. Artistically, it was excellent for me because in this way I got to know many people and talked with them. In this way I also came to understand the language."[5] Seghers' friend, Steffe Spira-Ruschin, herself a survivor of a French internment camp, writes about the time she spent at Seghers' bedside in the hospital during weeks of recuperation, or sitting outside in the sunny garden, talking about home. She wrote: "And now every day we could go for walks with her in the hospital garden, each day a little longer. The garden was not huge but the plants were luxurious and multi-colored in a way that you only see in gardens in southern regions. To us most of the trees and flowers were exotic. Bougainvillea, hibiscus, pepper trees and laurel trees. But in between were little strips of lawn and even daisies. There were benches and you could sit there and just look at the lawn in front of you. It was like you were at home. That's what we talked about – we talked about home."[6]

It was also in that year of crisis that Seghers finally learned about the fate of her mother in Germany, from whom she had not heard in months – she had perished in one of the camps of the east. News also reached her that allied bombs had flattened her beloved hometown of Mainz. This then from the first page of the story: "The bench on which I was resting was the farthest point on my journey thus far; in fact the most westerly point that I had reached in my life . . . Only one quest remained that could motivate me: the journey home."[7] Her point of departure is both a small Mexican village submerged in blazing heat, as well as the space between a coma and consciousness. It is here that she constructs a "site of memory" despite the encroaching fatigue. She writes: "I had just been through months of illness which had caught up with me here, even though the many dangers of the war had not been able to harm me. Although my eyes burned from the heat and from tiredness, I could follow the portion of road that led out of the village into the desert. The road was so white that it appeared etched on the inside of my eyelids as soon as I closed my eyes."[8] The desert landscape, punctuated by a burning bush, becomes the frame of her memory and the obligatory school essay describing the school excursion – arguably the lowest form of narration – becomes the vehicle of recapturing lost territory. Hitler's *Vaterland*, where mothers were taught not to mourn for lost sons, becomes in her narrative *Mutterland* represented by a group of teenage girls whose political choices, apathy or partners aligned them with either *Staat* - the Nazi state or Heimat.

Despite her fatigue, Seghers sees all the home – soberly, clearly, right down to the details of the teenage girls on the school trip, one with features "as finely chiseled as those of the medieval stone figures of young girls in Marburg cathedral," some of them clearly hormonally aware.[9] There is the elderly teacher called Fräulein Mees, with a big bottom and a large cross swinging across her bosom, shepherding her girls on their pre-First War Rhine excursion, yet in the same sentence defiantly collecting money years later for the Resistance. There is a young Jewish teacher, now adored on the school trip by the schoolgirl Nora, who in the same sentence is chased off a park bench by the same Nora because it was forbidden to Jews; and all that within the sparest of literary frames in which one lone Mexican, teetering perilously close to cliché, indolently observes the strange woman from the vantage point of his wall. "From Europe," she answers in the first sentence, apparently to his question of where she was from.

Yet despite the insistence on life, this is a story about a day in the lives of dead girls, summoned back to live on as German women, by a weary woman in 1943 – well before the belated confrontation of the Nazi past in narratives written mostly by men. "The Nazi past is too massive to be forgotten, and too repellent to be integrated into the 'normal' narrative of memory," writes the distinguished historian Saul Friedlander.[10] Seghers does not integrate the Nazi past into this narrative. Its power lies in a representation of a past that is defiantly obtrusive, that is forced to live side by side in the same sentence as the present with its pervasive fatigue and haze. The skill of her literary technique of simultaneity recedes before its effect – a powerful evocation of home, the banks of the Rhine, the portrait gallery of young Germans, flanked on that glorious late summer day by teachers, the elderly protestant who would become a resister and the young Jewish teacher, who would, in the words of Seghers "be transported to Poland by the Nazis, crammed into a sealed freight car" along with her student Sophie, who in the same sentence is being scolded for fooling around with one of the boys, Herbert Becker, and described thus by the narrator: "He still had the same bespectacled, sly, scampish face when I met him again just a few years ago in France, on his way back from the Spanish war."[11] The school excursion ends and the girls are returning home across the river:

> The little houses and a fisherman were reflected in the water, as was the village on the other side, which, with its rape and corn fields above a border of pink apple trees and its tumbled mass of gabled roofs right up to the tiny point of the church tower, rose up the mountain slope in a Gothic triangle. The late light shone first into a valley opening with a railroad spur, then against a distant chapel, and every-thing quickly peeped out of the Rhine once more before disappearing into the twilight.
>
> We had all grown still in the still light so that we heard the cawing of a few birds and the howling of the factory from Amöneburg. Even Lore had become completely silent. Marianne and Leni and I had all three intertwined our arms together in a union which simply belonged to the great union of all things earthly under the sun. Marianne was still resting her head against Leni's head. How then could a deception, a madness, later force its way into her thoughts, making her believe that she and her husband were the only ones who loved this land and therefore had every right to condemn and inform against the girl against whom she was now leaning. No one had ever reminded us, while there was still time, of this trip together. No matter how many essays were written about the Heimat, and the history of the Heimat, and the love for the Heimat, never was it mentioned that our group of girls especially, leaning one against the other, traveling upstream in the slanting afternoon light, belonged to the Heimat.[12]

What separates Seghers' story from other narratives of the diaspora is its relationship to time, space, and language. She in fact constructs a site of memory that stretches from a world of shadows and uncertainty – "I leant against the wall in the narrow shadows. One could not call this deliverance; sanctuary in this land was too questionable and too uncertain for that," she wrote in the first paragraph, to a place where "the villages and hills on the opposite bank, with their arable fields and forests, were reflected in a network of circles of sunlight . . . At the mere sight of that gently rolling landscape, my sadness was replaced by a serenity and a feeling of sheer joy at being alive, which sprang from my blood like a certain corn from a certain air and soil."[13] Alexander Stephan points to the fact that Seghers thus dared to reclaim language debased in Nazi Germany – blood, soil, Heimat, to embody them in a narrative that culminates at a personal level in her futile attempt to reach her mother at the end of her school excursion.[14]

Netty walked expectantly toward home, looking for her mother who typically was waiting for her on the balcony of their apartment after school trips. It is not that she is unable to see her – "She stood there cheerful and erect, intended for a hardworking family life, with the usual joys and burdens of everyday, not for an agonizing, cruel end in a remote village to which she had been banished by Hitler . . . My legs failed me . . . I (then) thought to myself weakly; What a pity, I would have liked so much for my mother to hold me in her arms."[15]

"The Excursion of the Dead Girls" is unashamedly a lament for Germany, written long before "the inability to mourn" was recognized in Holocaust discourse. The adumbration of her mother leaning over the balcony to greet her, her own inability to reach her is not an expression of incommensurability, because it shares the same space in her sentence, as in her memory with "banished by Hitler for an agonizing, cruel end in a remote village." Though still in the courtyard of her house in Mainz, she returns to the frame in Mexico, wondering to herself why turkeys are being raised there. She concludes: "I asked myself how I should spend the time, today and tomorrow, here and there, for I now sensed an immeasurable stream of time, unconquerable as the air. We have after all been trained from very young to somehow overcome time instead of meekly giving ourselves up to it. I suddenly remembered my teacher's assignment again, to carefully describe the school excursion. First thing tomorrow, or even this evening, if my tiredness had passed, I wanted to work on the assigned task."[16]

She had indeed been homesick, not in the tiresomely sentimental way of other exile writers. In 1933, shortly after she had fled from Germany, she once referred to the contents of her child's pocket – a few dried blades of grass, a *pfennig*, a ticket, a fir cone – as "half of Germany." She wrote in 1944 to Hermann Kesten that if she in fact had an old age she wanted to spend it in her hometown of Mainz, even drably, she writes, in the most boring of streets.[17] Seghers returned home to Germany from Mexico by way of Paris, from there to Mainz, her childhood town, arriving in Berlin on April 22, 1947. This is how she recalled those first hard days:

> For years we had imagined our homecoming. We had continually pictured our country, in flight and in questionable refuges, on ships in the war and in bombarded cities, in ruins and in books that others had written or we ourselves. Our imagination had uninterruptedly awakened to new life what was precious to us . . . We had longed for our language – it had become a hard, bare language. Abroad we had placed word next to word, so that their sound might never become lost to us. It had calmed our homesickness . . . The homeland had blossomed forth in our memory, and now in reality it was rough and gray. We thought that then in the dismal hotel room.[18]

It is significant that Seghers later thematized Mexico in Germany, not through the lens of memory, but as a projection of the motif of *die blaue Blume* (the blue flower), the quintessentially Romantic quest for the "ideal" taken from Novalis' *Heinrich von Ofterdingen*. Her story "Crisanta" is about a homeless girl who is searching for a blue hiding place, which in the end she finds. In 1965 she published a collection of stories called *Die Macht der Schwachen* (The Power of the Weak), one of which is set in Mexico with the title "Die Heimkehr des verlorenen Volkes" (The Return to Home of the Lost People) about the journey of a Yucatan Maya group into the twentieth century. In it she gives a role to Cárdenas as her tribute to the country where she found refuge and to the Mexican leader whom she greatly admired. Another figure from her Mexican exile is the painter Xavier Guerrero whom she also later fictionalized.

What is so important about the exile of German Jews in Mexico, Seghers included, is that as a group and individually they initiated a discourse that boldly confronted the political and moral crisis in Germany without recourse to mythologizing German culpability – the dark side of the German psyche. In their exile they already were dealing with the role they would play in rebuilding Germany's shattered structures. Merker, who was not Jewish, was one of the few German communists who insisted that one of the first tasks in rebuilding Germany was to deal with anti-Semitism. In November 1941, Seghers boldly wrote: "A people that sets upon other peoples, in order to exterminate them, is that still our people?"[19]

The legacy of Anna Seghers is among the most coveted treasures of German literary history of the twentieth century. "The Excursion of the Dead Girls" is the most autobiographical, possibly the only autobiographical narrative of that legacy. No writer in recent German history has elicited such lavish praise in both east and west for her representations of social and political repression in characters etched by a woman whose eye for detail was trained on Rembrandt's paintings before she began to write. She had written her doctoral dissertation on Rembrandt. And yet she was not without her critics and specifically by those who blamed her apparent heartlessness in remaining silent in the German Democratic Republic when younger writers were taken to task for criticizing the Marxist government. Yet she herself retained enough freedom to travel even during the most repressive years of the DDR, not only to approved destinations like China and the Soviet Union, but also to Chile and Brazil, where she was visiting the poet Jorge Amado in 1961 when the wall was erected. Over the years she maintained a long correspondence with Pablo Neruda. But she always returned to Berlin, far from her native Mainz.

Seghers had returned from her exile in Mexico with few illusions about the work that lay ahead, yet she clearly resisted the temptation that others fell prey to – an all-consuming *Antigermanisus*. Hans-Walter Albert writes of her: "In the danger laden hour of the German catastrophe Anne Seghers once more had seen farther and more clearly than the active politicians among her friends." She, even more so than the others, had been oriented to the future, to the day that Nazism would end, to a readership that needed the German language. Asked why she had chosen "sunny Mexico for the gray ruins of Berlin," Seghers replied: "I came back because I can do most for the language which I speak best, for the people whom I know best through good and bad." She went on to chide those who claimed to be democratic and were coming to conclusions that belonged in the repertoire of Goebbels.[21]

I close with the voices of exile, one Ilse Blumenthal-Weiss in the United States, for whom the Heimat and all that it represented was lost: "My belongings are a land/Where I no more belong/A language that no more belongs to me." In Mexico the poet Paul Meyer, who had survived Gurs and Le Vernet, heard in the summer of 1944 about the Allied invasion and wrote these lines in Mexico: "At this hour when the earth is screaming/At this hour let us feel, let us know. You bless the one who liberates your world." He thanked Mexico – "a cloudless sky where no contempt disturbs my dreams." But to return to Seghers for the final word, already cited: "We had longed for our language – it had become a hard, bare language. Abroad we had placed word next to word, so that their sound might never become lost to us. It had calmed our homesickness . . . The homeland had blossomed forth in our memory." In "Der Ausflug der toten Mädchen" she placed word next to word in both the present and past tense, in a powerful recuperation of the Heimat, sullied by ideology yet sustained by those who resisted, word next to word that blossomed on Mexican soil.

Notes

1   There were only a few hundred Jews who came by this route, according to David Wyman. Hans-Albert Walter, *Deutsche Exilliteratur*, Band 4, *Exilpresse* (Stuttgart: J.B. Metzlersche Verlagsbuchhandlung, 1978), 131.
2   Kathleen J. LaBahn, *Anna Seghers' Exile Literature: The Mexican Years (1941–1947)* (New York: Peter Lang, 1986), 3.
3   *Ibid.*, 6.
4   The translation I draw from, with some minor changes, was done by a former graduate student, Anne Willis, who worked with me in a seminar on translation. It is based on the text "Der Ausflug der toten Mädchen" in Anna Seghers, *Erzahlungen*, Band 1 (Berlin: Luchterhand Verlag, 1964).
5   Lowell A. Bangerter, *The Bourgeois Proletarian: A Study of Anna Seghers* (Bonn: Bouvier Verlag, 1980), 17.
6   *Über Anna Seghers: Ein Almanach zum 75. Geburtstag* (Berlin: Aufbau Verlag, 1975), 141.
7   Seghers, "Der ausflug der toten Mädchen," 1–2.
8   *Ibid.*, 1.
9   *Ibid.*, 4.
10 Saul Friedlander, *Memory, History, and the Extermination of the Jews of Europe* (Bloomington: Indiana University Press, 1993), 2.
11 Seghers, "Der ausflug der toten Mädchen," 15.
12 *Ibid.*, 17.
13 *Ibid.*, 1, 6.
14 Alexander Stephan, "'Ich habe das Gefühl, ich bin in die Eiszeit geraten...' Zur Rückkehr von Anna Seghers aus dem Exil," *Germanic Review* 3 (1987): 144.
15 Seghers, "Der ausflug der toten Mädchen," 21.
16 *Ibid.*, 22.
17 Stephan, "'Ich habe das Gefühl,'" 144.
18 Bangerter, *Bourgeois Proletarian*, 19–20.
19 Walter, *Deutsche Exilliteratur*, 303–4.
20 *Ibid.*, 305.
21 Ute Brandes, *Anna Seghers* (Berlin: Colloquium Verlag, 1992), 64; Stephan, "'Ich habe das Gefühl,'" 145.

2

Counter Discourse in Argentina

Victoria Ocampo and *SUR*'s Attitude toward the Jews during World War II

Rosalie Sitman

D ue to its neutrality during World War II, Argentina's image was – and probably still is – that of an anti-Semitic society. True, strong anti-Semitic currents have existed in Argentinean society since at least the late nineteenth century, and were particularly strong in the 1930s and 1940s, especially among the armed forces, the landed oligarchy, and the Catholic Church. However, at the same time, one should not ignore strong and manifest philo-Semitic currents which have coexisted in different sectors of Argentine society, and which have enabled, among other things, the integration of Jews into the economic, social, and cultural life of Argentina.

One of the leading exponents of Argentine culture in those critical years of the European débâcle was the literary review *SUR*, founded in 1931 by Victoria Ocampo, the eldest daughter of an established oligarchical family and therefore not exactly the kind of figure expected to be found at the helm of such an enterprise. But then the *"grupo SUR"* was unconventional in all sorts of ways, as evidenced in part by the attention and sympathy that these intellectuals gave to the plight of European Jewry at the same time as the government of Argentina closed the gates of the country to Jewish immigration during World War II. This essay suggests that by expressing their philo-Semitism, Ocampo and her group were in a way redefining themselves and carving for themselves a unique place in the Argentine intellectual field and culture. Moreover, the philo-Semitic manifestations published in *SUR* can be seen as a leitmotiv that not only highlighted their position and set them apart within the Argentine intellectual field, but also provided the common link that enabled them to express *simultaneously* their opposition to three pillars of the establishment, namely, the government, the Church, and the nationalists of the Argentine right, at the extreme end of the cultural spectrum. Therefore, *SUR*'s attitude toward the Jews should be viewed not only in the context of a humanitarian response to their plight during World War II, but also as an instrumental and discursive strategy within Argentine society and culture. With this in mind, we will broaden the scope of analysis to encompass the Jewish presence in *SUR* in the years immediately preceding the war in Europe and those that followed it as well.

SUR was born less than a year after General José Félix Uriburu's coup of 1930 rocked the foundations of Argentine society and inaugurated an "infamous decade" characterized by the curtailment of political freedom, economic difficulties in the wake of the Great Depression, growing conservatism and electoral fraud. During this period, the Catholic Church gained strength and influence in Argentina, as did the militant and xenophobic nationalist groups, whose pro-fascist sympathies and blatant anti-Semitism – largely inspired by the Church – did not bode well for the Jews already in Argentina nor for those fleeing Europe and seeking to enter the Latin American republic. These groups not only opposed what they saw as "the Semitic invasion of the country" – seeking to turn the clock back to the pre-immigration days of Argentina's glorious past – but they also applauded the open persecution of the Jews in Europe and readily accepted all Nazi propaganda against the Jews at face value. The close alliance between Church circles and the nationalists manifested itself most clearly in the right-wing Catholic press – *Criterio*, *El Pampero*, *Crisol*, *Pueblo*, *Sol y Luna* – that gave ample space to the anti-Semitic diatribes of activist clerics such as Gustavo Franceschi, Julio Meinvielle, and Virgilio Filippo, who basically blamed the Jews for the ills of the world, including Marxism, and for whom the Jewish presence in Argentina posed nothing less than a national threat. They, of course, welcomed all governmental measures that restricted immigration and kept undesirable elements such as Jews, "who did not adapt to the country in a positive way," out of Argentina.[1]

By contrast, *SUR*, originally conceived as a cultural bridge between the Americas and Europe, was cosmopolitan and firmly ensconced in the liberal democratic tradition that the nationalists rejected. Furthermore, the journal abhorred fascism, which it identified as a manifestation of "barbarian forces" that threatened intellectual freedom and the higher ideals of the human spirit that *SUR* was committed to defend and perpetuate.[2] Their paths were bound to collide. For a start, it cannot have escaped the nationalists' notice that there was *always* a Jewish presence in *SUR*, beginning with the foundational letter addressed to Waldo Frank, an American Jew often credited, in the journal's lore, with the idea of its inception.[3] Frank, whom *El Pampero* pejoratively dubbed "Yankee-Jew," not only became a regular contributor to *SUR* in the 1930s and 1940s, but worse, he proudly made frequent reference to his Semitic origins in his writings.[4] The appearance in 1934 of his essay, poignantly entitled "¿Por qué ha de sobrevivir el judío?" (Why Should the Jew Survive?), leaves little doubt as to the journal's attitude toward the Jews – a fact that acquires added significance, particularly concerning *SUR*'s position in the Argentine intellectual field at the time, in view of the publication in Argentina in 1935 of Hugo Wast's rabidly anti-Semitic *Kahal* and *Oro* shortly afterward.[5] *SUR*'s publication in the following years of Waldo Frank's essays denouncing fascism or extolling the Jews' contribution to America was equally eloquent, as were the positive reviews and articles written about the Jewish American intellectual by non-Jewish members of the group.[6] The Roumanian-born French Jewish writer and filmmaker Benjamin Fondane, a disciple of the Russian philosopher Leon Chestov, also appeared frequently in the pages of *SUR* during this period.[7] Moreover, in 1936 he was invited by Ocampo to visit Buenos Aires, where he spent several months making a film.[8]

The strategy of letting the texts speak for themselves – and therefore also for the magazine, without need for manifestos or lengthy editorials – would remain a favorite ploy of the journal. Determined to fulfill what they saw as the "civilizing" mission of their enterprise by "publishing the very best" – a task that they deemed incompatible with any form of political or partisan commitment – Ocampo and her group strove to remain outside the political fray. However, this was to prove impossible in the politically charged climate of the 1930s and 1940s. Soon, the clash with *Criterio*, avowedly the voice of Argentine Catholicism, over *SUR*'s endorsement of Jacques Maritain's integral humanism, against the background of the Spanish Civil War, would force *SUR* to make a stand and embark on a collision course with the nationalists, the Church, and to a lesser extent with the government. Maritain moreover was a Jewish sympathizer who championed the cause of the Jews during the war.

Incensed therefore by *SUR*'s publication of the "radical" French Catholic philosopher's "*Sobre la guerra santa*" (About the Holy War), which derogated Spain's fratricidal war as a horrible sacrilege and totally debunked the Spanish Church's justification of the atrocities under guise of a holy war, Monsignor Franceschi, editor of *Criterio* and an ardent supporter of Franco's rebellion and of the Spanish Church, launched a virulent attack on *SUR*, accusing it of being a leftist publication.[9] This time *SUR* chose to break its silence and published its position, borrowing heavily from Maritain, Nicholás Berdiaeff, and Emmanuel Mounier's unorthodox and personalist Christian discourse – a synthesis of religion and democracy – in a deliberate effort to combat the nationalists with their own arms.[10] Thus in August 1937 *SUR* wrote: "All sectarian persecutions – whether racial or political, or unjust persecutions couched in legal or codified forms – are equally odious and equally monstrous in our eyes."[11]

Obviously, *SUR*'s protest here is directed not just against the excesses of the Francoist Falange, but is intended to include the Nazi persecutions and the Stalinist purges as well, and on a different level, even the veiled abuses of President Agustín P. Justo's *Concordancia* in Argentina and certainly the relentless "persecution" of the Jews in the organs of the nationalist press.[12] Then a few lines further, in scarcely veiled reference to Franceschi's activities, came the journal's piercing indictment of the Church hierarchy: "We want a better clergy, a clergy who will be more concerned with spiritual matters of eternal salvation than with the transitory wheeling and dealing of politics."[13] From this point on, *SUR*'s political commitment would only grow stronger, culminating with the magazine's eventual positioning on the side of the Allies, in blatant defiance of the policy of neutrality doggedly espoused by the Argentine government.

SUR's opposition to all forms of oppression and authoritarian, dictatorial, or totalitarian regimes is crystal clear and was to remain a dominant theme throughout the journal's existence. In this context, the group's staunch anti-fascist line and sustained pro-Jewish stance are hardly surprising, and were to manifest themselves both within the magazine and outside, on a personal level. Thus, we find the names of leading members of the group swelling the ranks of the assorted organizations that were springing up as part of a wider, heterogeneous anti-fascist effort that banded together different sectors of the democratic and socialist opposition to the conservative government in what socialist leader Nicolás Repetto described ideally as "a movement of parties, groups and factions that would come to represent virtually the 'only party of Argentinean democracy.'"[14] For instance, Jorge Luis Borges, one of the more notable members of *SUR*, was among the signatories of the First Declaration of the Committee Against Racism and anti-Semitism, which was created in 1937 with the aim of rebutting Nazi racial propaganda and reaffirming the status of the Jewish community as an integral, and worthy, part of the Argentine nation.[15] Other signatures included those of prominent figures representative of the diverse elements comprising the anti-fascist camp: progressive democrats (Lisandro de la Torre), socialists (Américo Ghioldi and Carlos Sánchez Viamonte), radicals (future presidents Arturo Frondizi and Arturo Illia), university professors (Ernesto Laclau), communist sympathizers (Álvaro Yunque), and writers (César Tiempo).[16] Borges's name also appeared on the organizing committee of the First Congress Against Racism and anti-Semitism, held in Buenos Aires on August 2, 1938, which demanded that the gates of the country be opened to Jews fleeing persecution. The congress naturally aroused the ire of Monsignor Franceschi, who denounced the "violent Semitism of the Jews," comparing them with the Nazis, and blasted the organizers as *"judaizantes"* (Jewlovers).[17]

With the civil war raging in Spain and Europe headed for another all-encompassing war, *SUR* escalated its criticism of Nazism and fascism, and its indictment of the "crusader nationalism" of the Spanish Church and its supporters, that is, the Argentine Church and the pro-Francoist nationalists. "El Pastor Hall" (Pastor Hall), a play by the German Jewish writer Ernst Toller published in three consecutive installments in 1939, was a scathing condemnation of Nazi policies and practices in the Third Reich.[18] Below the title, in small print, it was written that the author dedicated the drama to the day when it could be performed in Germany. At the bottom of the same page, also in small print, a grim announcement informed *SUR*'s readers that after the issue had gone to press, word had arrived of Toller's suicide in New York's Mayflower Hotel, "by cruel coincidence, named after the ship that had brought to those same shores the first group of Pilgrims fleeing from the intolerance that reigned in their native land."[19] The allusion is unmistakable and a much more effective conduit for expressing condemnation than an impassioned declaration. This would become one of the group's preferred methods of protest, and it would prove particularly handy for *SUR* during the difficult years (for the journal) under the Peronist regime.

More importantly, issue after issue, in "Calendario," the new section devoted to current events that had been inaugurated in June 1937, *SUR* denounced the crimes and atrocities that were being perpetrated in Europe against both the Spanish Republicans and the Jews: the bombing of Durango and near destruction of Guernica went hand in hand with countless reports informing of the discrimination and persecution of the Jews by the German Nazis and Italian fascists.[20] Over the years, *SUR* made skillful use of "Calendario" to buttress its position on burning issues with carefully selected items extracted from speeches and magazines, interspersed with "innocent" disclaimers and asides: "We reproduce these sensible and lucid words" ([of] Léon-Paul Fargue on anti-Semitism); "Unless one has substituted faith for bad faith, that is: unless one is a Catholic-Nationalist" – which left little doubt as to *SUR*'s stance on anti-Semitism or its opinion of the nationalists' (mis)interpretation of Catholic teachings.[21]

This manipulative juxtaposition of Catholic/nationalist and Jewish for purposes of effect was a clever strategy used in "Calendario" that allowed the journal to convey its sympathies and antipathies in a subtle yet unequivocal way. A case in point is the "Calendario" for the month of August 1938 where declarations made by Pope Pius XI condemning both racism and nationalism, evidently aimed at the nationalists – "Catholic means universal. Therefore: neither racist, nor nationalist, nor separatist, but Catholic" – stand in sharp contrast to the fragment of a speech made by the interior minister of the Burgos government: "Jacques Maritain's wisdom has nuances which recall the lips of Israel, and he has the false mannerisms of a Jewish democrat."[22] No comment is necessary. Again in October 1938, Pius XI's words in the Belgian *L'avant garde*: "We call

Abraham our Patriarch, our forbear . . . Anti-Semitism is inadmissible . . . We, Catholics, are spiritually Semitic," are deliberately contrasted with *Arriba España*'s: "because the Spanish Civil War is also a battle against international Judaism. The Jews have always been the enemies of civilization." *SUR* asks: "Are the Phalangist Catholics in favor of Mussolini and against the Pope?"[23] The irony is inescapable. Not long afterward, *SUR* would underscore the contrast between this Pope's vocal commitment and the now controversial silence of his successor, Pius XII: "The authority of the Head of the Church has decreased in this world of infidels." Uncharacteristically, it was signed with the initials J. B., belonging to José Bianco, *SUR*'s editor-in-chief.[24]

The journal's continued endorsement of Christian humanists like the Belgian Georges Bernanos, whose pronouncements were anathema to the Argentine Catholic Church, traditionally of Spanish orientation, ensured that relations between the group and these circles remained strained.[25] Furthermore, the "established" Catholic press certainly cannot have regarded with benevolence *SUR*'s willingness to lend its pages to Christian democrats such as Rafael Pividal and Augusto Durelli, who were also associated with *Orden Cristiano*, the progressive Catholic publication that was eventually disavowed by the Argentine Church hierarchy.[26] Typically, in a contribution early in 1939, Durelli singled out the Jews as one of three martyred peoples, and in plain and simple terms drove home to *SUR*'s readers the desperate situation of European Jewry: "The Jew is a pariah. The Jew cannot write, speak, marry, or pray freely. The Jew cannot buy, nor sell, nor travel. The Jew cannot sit on park benches nor attend the cinema or the theatre. Hundreds of them have been murdered in concentration camps. Thousands are roaming the world, without a homeland and lawless, persecuted and hated." Not satisfied, Durelli proceeded to mock nationalist – "the new crusader or religion" – protestations that they did not hate Jews but drove them to desperation and suicide for their own good.[27]

The outbreak of the war in Europe forced *SUR* to make a second public stand in which it declared its alignment with the democracies and in theory exhorted the Argentine government to renounce the country's neutrality: "In such circumstances, nobody can remain morally neutral. We are not neutral."[28] Yet these words should be understood more as a show of solidarity and an expression of *moral* support for Great Britain and France than a call to belligerence.[29] It was not until the Japanese attack on Pearl Harbor brought the European war home to the shores of America that *SUR*'s tone changed dramatically, demanding intervention on behalf of the cause "that we would like to defend and for which others are spilling their blood." President Roberto Castillo, however, was unmoved and his stubborn determination to remain neutral was to cost his country dearly.

Meanwhile, the breach between the members of the group and the nationalists had become irreparable. The former regarded the latter as Nazi agents who *de facto* were pulling the strings of the government behind the scenes. Thus in 1940 the journal issued a resounding "Voice of Alert" in which it denounced Catholic nationalism for supporting totalitarian regimes and censured such a stance as being indecent, gangster-like, anti-Argentina, and anti-Christian.[30]

At the same time, *SUR* stepped up its unrelenting and stark reporting in "Calendario" – especially in the new subsection "Noticiario" – of European Jews' systematic extermination:

> The Committee of Interallied Information details the persecutions that the Semites have suffered in this war: in Yugoslavia, 99 percent have been killed; in Poland, chosen as the "central slaughterhouse" of the Jews, 2,000,000 have died and 5,000,000 are in the same danger; of the 52,000 Jews who lived in Belgium, half have been deported and the rest confined in concentration camps; in Czechoslovakia, 72,000 have been sent to Poland (. . .) It is said that in Poland, since August 17th, 10,000 Jews are taken daily from the ghettoes to their ultimate death.[31]

By highlighting the dimensions and the urgency of the plight of the Jews, *SUR* was not only raising consciousness regarding the fact that the Jewish problem was in fact of concern for all humanity, but was also, in a way, pressing the Argentine government again to abandon its neutrality and change its insensitive immigration policy and not turn the victims of Nazi persecution away. Back in 1939 *SUR* had despaired at President Roberto M. Ortiz's refusal to grant refuge to Spanish intellectuals in Argentina for fear that "underneath that mask, the journalist, the ideologue and the failed politician are hiding."[32] A few months earlier, very likely in protest over the government's imposition of increased restrictions on immigration limiting entry to certain selected groups from which Jews were excluded, *SUR* had published an impassioned analysis of the refugee problem by the Jewish Italian writer Gina Lombroso which refuted the arguments usually hurled against immigration and stressed the benefits that European refugees – and Jews in particular – might bring to the country that gave them asylum.[33]

The intense activity displayed by pro-fascist elements and increasing Nazi propaganda in Buenos Aires drove Ocampo, on a personal level, to join several protest groups. In June 1940 she was one of the founding members (and the only woman) of *Acción Argentina* (Argentine Action), a militant pro-Allied organization aimed at combating Nazi infiltration and fascism in the country, which strove to mobilize public opinion in order to force the government to change its international policy. Its roster boasted such names as finance minister Federico Pinedo, historian Emilio Ravignani, and the ubiquitous Nicolás Repetto, again illustrative of the wide demoliberal/socialist anti-fascist political spectrum. Later, upon learning of the invasion of Russia in 1941, Ocampo joined her friend María Rosa Oliver, also a close member of the group, at *Junta de la Victoria* (Victory Association), where former members of the relief operation for republican Spain now gathered to work on behalf of the Allied cause.

More poignantly, Ocampo also tried to use her resources to save Benjamin Fondane by securing a visa for him to leave Europe, but was unable to locate him. Turned in to the Gestapo by his concierge, Fondane and his sister were held for a while in the detention center at Drancy before being deported to Auschwitz, where he died in October 1944. Afterward, Ocampo wrote with obvious intent that Fondane "was punished for several crimes: for having been born a Jew, for being an intellectual, for owning nothing more precious than a handful of Chestov's letters and a pair of green woolen gloves . . . for being intelligent, laughing and knowing how to make others laugh. He was punished in the Nazi way, in the totalitarian way."[34]

Fortunately Ocampo fared better with the German Jewish photographer Gisèle Freund. Ocampo had met Freund on a visit to Europe before the war, at the French bookseller Adrienne Monnier's home, and invited her to visit Buenos Aires. While hiding from the Gestapo in France, Freund remembered Ocampo's invitation and cabled her for help. Ocampo immediately set about making the necessary financial arrangements and obtaining an Argentine visa for Freund. All told, it took about a year, but she finally succeeded in bringing Freund over to Buenos Aires in 1941, where Ocampo then harbored her in her own home until the photographer was able to make her own living.[35] At Freund's instigation, Ocampo established the Committee of Solidarity with French Writers and launched *Operación Encomiendas* (Operation Parcels) using Monnier's bookshop on the Left Bank of Paris to distribute relief packages to needy French intellectuals.[36]

Loyalty evidently was an outstanding feature of Ocampo's personality and it likely accounts for her refusal to renounce her friendship with the French writer Pierre Drieu La Rochelle, despite the latter's full-blown commitment to fascism during the war, which she concurred with Jean-Paul Sartre was attributable to some kind of death wish. She did however remove his name from the journal's International Editorial Board.[37] One of the few letters that La Rochelle left on his desk upon his suicide in 1945 was addressed to Ocampo, and in that letter he wrote that he had never actually hated the Jews. It is interesting that he had felt the need to tell her that just as he was about to take his own life. Ocampo was equally careful to single out this fact in an exculpatory essay she published, in which she attempted to fathom the ghosts that drove her erstwhile lover and friend of seventeen years.[38]

At the same time – again, mostly in "Calendario" – *SUR* consistently ridiculed the excesses of Nazi propaganda and the Nazi press, and denounced the activities of Nazi infiltrators, Nazi spies, and Nazi sympathizers in Argentina, who operated with the tacit complicity of the government. Thus in December 1939, *SUR* included a separate page with the translation of a Nazi propaganda text about the Russian–Finnish conflict that had appeared in the *Deutsche La Plata Zeitung* on the first of that month. Also the journal followed very closely the minutiae of the incident involving Frank's attack during his third visit to Buenos Aires on a conference tour under the auspices of the US government in 1942. Shortly before leaving for Chile, Frank published in an evening paper his "Farewell to Argentina," which was ill received in certain political circles. *El Pampero*, a major organ of Nazi propaganda reputedly financed by the German embassy, retaliated the following day with a "Farewell, Despicable Waldo Frank."[39] The matter did not stop there. In its "Calendario" for August 1942, it was reported that the Germans had arrested eighteen thousand Jews in Paris, who were to be sterilized, and announced that Frank had been declared persona non grata and subsequently been attacked by six armed thugs. In September *SUR* reported that Frank had declared in Rio de Janeiro that he was convinced that the German embassy was behind the attack, and he did not think that the perpetrators would be arrested. Finally in November an item in *SUR* coolly told readers that a certain Jorge Fernández Murray, one of Frank's attackers, had been brought before a judge, but immediately been set free for there was no reason to hold him. Readers were left to form their own conjectures.

Returning to the main section of the journal, Borges's contributions during this period are also paradigmatic of *SUR*'s anti-fascist and philo-Semitic discourse. In "Una pedagogía del odio" (A Pedagogy of Hatred) from 1937, for example, he vehemently condemned the demonization of Jews in the Third Reich as manifested in the virulently anti-Semitic Nazi literature to which schoolchildren were being exposed in Germany. Then four years later came his venomous attack on nationalist Nazi sympathizers in Argentina, "1941," in which he masterfully turned their own rhetoric against them: "Hitler's mercy is ecumenical; shortly (if undisturbed by traitors and Jews) we shall all enjoy the benefits of torture, sodomy, rape and mass executions."[40] Likewise, many of Borges's famous short stories, which he published in *SUR* during these years, were openly pro-Jewish or infused with explicit, and sometimes veiled, Jewish references. Clearly, as Edna Aizenberg has pointed out, when viewed in the context of *SUR*'s overall anti-fascist line, the philo-Semitism of Borges's stories assumes an added intensity. Thus, in "Tlön, Uqbar, Orbius, Tertius" (1940), "El milagro secreto" (1943), and "Deutsches Requiem" (1946), for example, totalitarianism, Nazism, and anti-Semitism are depicted as detestable abominations.[41] On a personal note, given Borges's amply demonstrated Jewish sympathies, it is fitting to find the names of two Jews – the Argentine playwright Samuel Eichelbaum and the Venezuelan philologist Ángel Rosenblat – in the roster of leading intellectuals that contributed to the special issue of *SUR* designed to indemnify Borges for having been denied the national prize for literature in 1942.[42]

Toward the end of the war and in the years immediately after, instead of waning, the Jewish presence in *SUR* was augmented with the publication of several important contributions on explicitly Jewish issues written by Máximo José Kahn. The titles speak for themselves: "La sinagoga" (The Synagogue, 1944); "'Mit Brennender Sorge.' La Contra Inquisición'" ('Mit Brennender Sorge.' The Counter-Inquisition, 1945) – a scathing indictment of national socialism and its persecution and extermination of six million Jews as well as an emotional vindication of Judaism's survival throughout history; "Judaísmo, sueño soñado por la deidad" (Judaism, A Dream Dreamed by the Deity, 1947); and "Los anti-judíos filosemitas" (The Philo-Semitic Anti-Jews, 1948) about covert anti-Semites posing as philo-Semites.[43] These texts kept the Jewish presence alive in *SUR* and acted as constant reminders of the evil that man could be capable of when blinded by pernicious ideologies such as anti-Semitism.

However, *SUR*'s publication of Kahn is significant from another perspective as well. A displaced German-born Jew who had lived for many years in Spain and Greece before finally settling in Argentina, Kahn epitomized the wandering Jew that was anathema to the nationalists and anti-Semitic officials in Juan Domingo Perón's government, like immigration director Santiago Peralta, who were bent on preventing the entrance of such "undesirable" elements to the country. By giving Kahn ample space in the journal, the group was ratifying what they perceived as the positive contribution of Jews to Western civilization and to Argentine culture in particular, and at the same time expressing their dissatisfaction with the Peronist government's immigration policies. Typically, upon Kahn's death in 1953, the journal published a moving eulogy by Rosa Chacel, herself a Spanish exile who had found refuge in Argentina, and in *SUR*.[44]

Once the magnitude of the Holocaust was known, *SUR* brought the overwhelming reality of it home to its readers by publishing various testimonies, among them the wrenching "Recuerdos de Auschwitz" (Memories of Auschwitz) of the Jewish Italian writer Giulianna Tedeschi, which tells of her despair at the indignities and tortures that her body and spirit endured in the subhuman conditions of the camp, as well as examples of supreme heroism and the triumph of the human spirit in the face of adversity. No less chilling was the account of the tragic fate suffered by Franz Kafka's sisters in the Nazi crematoria.[45]

Equal space was given to testimonies of non-Jews, which also told of the fate suffered by Jews that they had witnessed. Victoria Kent, formerly a republican deputy in the Spanish parliament, paints a dismal portrait of the routine of daily life for Jews at Drancy, the French detention center where Fondane and his sister had been interned. She writes for herself, she says, lest she forget, determined to record every minute detail of that grim existence, including the eighteen-month old baby registered as a "terrorist," so that one day others might judge. For his part, French resistance fighter Jean Bloch-Michel spares no stomach-churning detail in his account of the tortures to which he and the Jews confined with him were subjected at the hands of the Gestapo.[46]

Although the war was over, *SUR*'s refusal to let go of the Jewish question attests to the group's determination to ensure that such appalling crimes against humanity not be repeated, and not be forgotten. The journal's publication of Sartre's "Portrait of an Anti-Semite" (1946), together with Editorial *SUR*'s translation of his *Antisemite and Jew* by Pepe Bianco (1948), fit in nicely within this concerted effort. Ocampo's moving and perceptive account of her impressions of the Nuremberg trials, which she attended at the invitation of the British government, may well be construed as yet another warning to people not to fall prey to the same mistakes.[47] For anti-Semitism was still rife and the dangers very real; there was no doubt about it. In a survey carried out by *Lettres Françaises* and reported in "Calendario" for January 1949 under the heading "Malos y Buenos Judíos" (Bad and Good Jews), 548 anti-Semites were asked if some of their best friends were Jewish. All 548 answered affirmatively, and immediately added: "You know . . . he's not like the other Jews."[48]

In the course of its prolonged existence, the journal continued to publish Jewish authors and pay attention to Jewish and by now also Israeli matters. In 1948, a note entitled "Racism at UNESCO" informed readers that Lebanon had reneged on its promise not to discriminate between the delegates attending the UNESCO conference in Beirut and had refused to issue entry visas to the Israeli observers, who had been forced to withdraw. A year later, an entire issue of *SUR* was devoted to the literature of the State of Israel, and it opened with an "Argentinean Testimony" by Borges.[49]

Ocampo's stalwart adherence to anti-Semitism did not diminish with time. Upon hearing of Adolf Eichmann's capture and kidnapping in 1960, she had felt compelled to "shout," she confessed in an article she published on the subject in the Buenos Aires daily *La Prensa* a year later: "Everything connected with anti-Semitism, as with racism in general, provokes in me that reaction: the need to shout. I am not Jewish, as far as I know . . . but I feel the Jewish problem and the black problem with the same rebelliousness and indignation as a Semite or an African."[50] And here once again Ocampo's response to the issue of Israel's violation of

Argentine sovereignty during the abduction rings more like a denunciation of her own government, this time of its part in allowing the person responsible for the death of six million Jews to enter the country in the first place: "I ask, in my ignorance: 'Wasn't 'something' violated by welcoming or giving refuge to the criminal?' There must have been a moment when, I suspect, somebody realized, closed his eyes, compromised, was an accomplice in the end. Isn't it so?"[51] Eloquent indeed. Ocampo did feel, however, that since the inconceivable dimensions of the crime perpetrated by Eichmann rendered it of concern to mankind as a whole, Israel would be better advised to allow the United Nations to try him and not do so itself. History of course would prove otherwise.

No less eloquent, two years later, is Ocampo's response to the debate awakened by the performance of Rolf Hochhut's play "The Representative," a vicious indictment of the Vatican's Concordat with Nazi Germany and Pius XII's refusal to sever relations with Hitler despite the slaughter of the concentration camps. For Ocampo, the fact that the play had premiered precisely in East Berlin a year earlier in 1963, represented a form of closure, ending the cycle that had begun with the publication of " El Pastor Hall" in *SUR* in May 1939. Maybe the time had finally arrived when Ernst Toller's drama could be performed in Germany. After all, both plays were equally relevant to the times, since both explored the profound quandaries involved when an individual is faced with the need to make agonizingly difficult moral choices in extreme circumstances. After much painful soul searching of her own, Ocampo comes to the stark and simple conclusion that: "It was alright to speak of such things."[52]

True, the *SUR* group did not organize a committee for the defense of Jews as they had for the Spanish republican intellectuals.[53] They did something else. They brought Jews into the pages of the journal from day one and then kept the Jewish presence alive while it was being extinguished elsewhere. In the best Sarmientian tradition, they rose to the defense of "civilization" from the forces of "barbarism," and in so doing, they crafted a niche for themselves in the pantheon of Argentine letters as a liberal publication consecrated to the defense of the lofty ideals of the human spirit. Beyond that, there can be no doubt that *SUR*'s philo-Semitism was much more than simply a humanitarian response to one of the most horrific crimes ever committed against humankind, and formed part of the wider three-pronged strategy that allowed Victoria Ocampo and *SUR* to define themselves *vis-à-vis* the Argentine political, religious, and cultural establishment.

Notes

1 Quoted in Graciela Ben-Dror, "La conferencia de Evian: el periodismo católico argentino y la conformación de la opinion pública," in *Judaica*

Latinoamericana. Estudios Histórico-Sociales 2 (Jerusalem: Editorial Universitaria Magnes, Hebrew University, 1993), 87–97.

2   The antithetical "civilization and barbarism," immortalized by the liberal nineteenth-century statesman, Domingo Faustino Sarmiento, in his *Vida de Juan Facundo Quiroga; civilización y barbarie* (1845), constitutes a key concept in Argentine history. The terms referred to the need to populate, and thus vanquish, the vast expanses of Argentina with desirable white immigrants, preferably northern European. The *SUR* people saw themselves as heirs of the Sarmientian tradition and therefore defenders of the lofty values of civilization that were being threatened by the barbarous forces of fascism and totalitarianism.

3   Victoria Ocampo, "Carta a Waldo Frank," *SUR* 1 (Summer 1931): 7–18.

4   Sandra McGee Deutsch and Ronald H. Dolkart, eds, *The Argentine Right: Its Historical and Intellectual Origins, 1910 to the Present* (Buenos Aires: Editorial Sudamericana, 1987), 91.

5   *SUR* 9 (July 1934), 152–70. Hugo Wast was the pseudonym of Gabriel Martínez Zuviría, an extreme right-wing nationalist who was appointed director of the National Library by the Uriburu government in 1931 and later became minister of education and justice during the military regime that came to power in the coup of 1943.

6   Waldo Frank, "Nuestra culpa en el fascismo," *SUR* 69 (June 1940): 7–26 and "El judío en el futuro de América," *SUR* 77 (February 1941): 12–20. An example of an essay written by a non-Jew is Carlos Alberto Erro, "Un filósofo americano: Waldo Frank (Con motivo de 'América Hispana')," *SUR* 7 (April 1933): 45–95. Patricio Canto, in his review of 'Chart for rough water,' highlighted Frank's typically Jewish *joie de vivre* and a certain quality reminiscent of a biblical prophet: "Waldo Frank: 'Chart for rough water,'" *SUR* 73 (October 1940): 77.

7   Benjamin Fondane, "El cinema en el atolladero," *SUR* 1 (Summer 1931): 158–65; "Prefacio para el presente," *SUR* 21 (June 1936): 72–86; "Nietzsche y los problemas 'repugnantes,'" *SUR* 42 (March 1938): 53–60; "Lévy-Brühl o el metafísico a pesar suyo," *SUR* 57 (June 1939): 65–75.

8   Laura Ayerza de Castilho and Odile Felgine, *Victoria Ocampo* (Barcelona: Circe Ediciones, 1993), 170–1.

9   *SUR* 35 (August 1937): 98–117.

10 "Posición de *SUR*," 7–9. On the *Criterio*-Maritain controversy see Marcelo Monserrat, "La polémica doctrinaria: el caso Maritain," in *Usos de la memoria* (Buenos Aires: Editorial Sudamericana, Universidad de San Andrés, 1996), 186–96; Mark Falcoff, "Argentina," in Mark Falcoff and Frederick B. Pike, eds, *The Spanish Civil War, 1936–39: American Hemispheric Perspectives* (Lincoln and London: University of Nebraska Press, 1982), 291–348; John King, *Sur. A Study of the Argentine Literary Journal and Its Role in the Development of a Culture, 1931–1970* (Cambridge: Cambridge University Press, 1986), 86–9. For a definition of personalism see Nicolás Berdiaeff, "Personalismo y marxismo," *SUR* 13 (1935): 7–39, and Emmanuel Mounier, *Manifeste au service du personalisme* (Paris, 1936) and Mounier, "Inteligencia y personalismo," *SUR* 46 (July 1938): 38–42.

11 "Posición de *SUR*," 8. All translations are the author's.

12 As described in Graciela Ben-Dror, "Posturas del catolicismo argentino durante los primeros años de la Segunda Guerra Mundial," *Estudios Interdisciplinarios de América Latina y el Caribe (EIAL)* 7 (July–December 1966): 101–32 and "La conferencia de Evián."

13 "Posición de *SUR*," 8.

14 *La Vanguardia* (December 17, 1937): 3, quoted in Andrés Bisso, "La recepción de la tradición liberal por parte del antifascismo argentino," *EIAL* 12 (July–December 2001): 85–113. Although united around a common objective, this was not, however, a monolithic bloc. Leonardo Senkman has ably exposed the cracks in this demoliberal front in "El nacionalismo y el campo liberal argentinos ante el neutralismo: 1939–1943," *EIAL* 6 (January–June 1995): 23–50. See also Andrés Bisso, "La división de la comunidad antifascista argentina (1939–1941)," *Reflejos* 9 (2000–2001): 88–99.

15 This was almost to be expected. Already in 1934, Borges's philo-Semitism had caused the nationalist publication *Crisol* to accuse him of being secretly Jewish. Borges retorted by publishing in *Megáfono* his "Yo, judío," a masterpiece of irony, in which he wrote that it would not displease him to be Jewish and that his surname Borges-Acevedo was of Jewish-Portuguese origin. In later years, he would often reiterate that he would consider it an honor to belong to one of the most civilized races in the world. See María Esther Vázquez, *Borges. Esplendor y derrota* (Barcelona: Tusquets Editores, 1996), 66; Gustavo Daniel Perednik, "La judeidad entre las ideas de la narrativa de Borges," *Reflejos* 2 (August 1993): 39.

16 Pseudonym of the Jewish writer Israel Zeitlin, whose magazine *Columna* and various ancillary publications also evidenced a manifest preoccupation with the fate of European Jews and concern over the phenomenon of growing anti-Semitism worldwide; Naomi Lindstrom, "The Role of Jewish Editors in Argentine Publishing, 1920–1940," in *Judaica Latinoamericana. Estudios Histórico-Sociales* 3 (Jerusalem: Editorial Universitaria Magnes, Universidad Hebrea, 1997), 371–83.

17 Ben-Dror, "Conferencia de Evián," 92–3.

18 *SUR* 56 (May 1939): 39–69; *SUR* 57 (June 1939): 43–64; *SUR* 58 (July 1939): 21–34.

19 Signed with the initials M.R.O. (María Rosa Oliver), *SUR* 56 (May 1939): 40.

20 Nidia Burgos, "La repercusión de la Guerra Civil Española en la sección 'Calendario' de la revista *SUR*," *Cuadernos Americanos* 74 (March–April 1999): 72–84.

21 Calendario, *SUR* 53 (February 1939): 81–2; Calendario, *SUR* 68 (May 1940): 78.

22 *SUR* 47 (August 1938): 91, 88.

23 *SUR* 49 (October 1938): 90.

24 Calendario, *SUR* 68 (May 1940): 79.

25 For example, Georges Bernanos, "Georges Bernanos escribe para 'SUR,'" *SUR* 48 (September 1938): 7–19 and Robert Weibel-Richard, "El testimonio de Bernanos y la responsabilidad del cristianismo," *SUR* 47 (August 1938): 64–9.

26 As illustration see Rafael Pividal, "Católicos fascistas y católicos personal-

istas," *SUR* 35 (August 1937): 87–97 and "Un ministro nacionalista insulta a Maritain," *SUR* 47 (August 1938): 70–2; Augusto J. Durelli, "La unidad entre los católicos," *SUR* 47 (August 1938): 72–80 and "Los cristianos y el reposo," *SUR* 60 (September 1939): 74–80.

27 Augusto Durelli, "Tres pueblos mártires," *SUR* 52 (January 1939): 64–5.

28 "Nuestra Actitud," *SUR* 60 (September 1939): 8.

29 In fact, at this point *SUR* published several contributions that appeared to endorse the policy of neutrality which Argentina still shared with the US and the other Latin American nations, in accordance with the agreements reached at the meeting of foreign ministers that President Franklin D. Roosevelt had convened in Panama shortly after the outbreak of the war in 1939. See for example Carlos Alberto Erro, "La Argentina frente a la nueva guerra," *SUR* 60 (September 1939): 13–15; Eduardo González Lanuza, "Posición del escritor frente a la actual guerra europea," *SUR* 61 (October 1939): 30–5 and Enrique Anderson Imbert, "Hitler corre el amok," *SUR* 61 (October 1939): 41–5.

30 "Voz de alerta," signed 15 May 1940, *SUR* 67 (April 1940), n/p.

31 *SUR* 99 (December 1942): 104. Ernesto Sábato, whose biting sarcasm added a razor-sharp edge to the political commentary, took over Calendario in 1942.

32 Calendario, *SUR* 57 (June 1939): 110. Ortiz's declarations had been in response to a petition he had received signed by leading French intellectuals, among them André Gide, Nobel Prize recipients Fréderic Joliot and Jean Perrin, Jacques Maritain, and François Mauriac from the French Academy.

33 Gina Lombroso, "El problema de los refugiados," *SUR* 55 (April 1939): 60–9.

34 Reproduced in Ayerza de Castilho and Felgine, *Victoria Ocampo*, 283.

35 Gisèle Freund, "Reina Victoria," *La Prensa* (June 10, 1979). See also Ayerza de Castilho and Felgine, *Victoria Ocampo*, 188–90.

36 *Ibid.*, 221–5. Both André Gide and Paul Valéry wrote letters expressing their gratitude to Ocampo for her efforts on their behalf during the war: "Correspondencia," *SUR* 347 (July–December 1980): 37 and "Lettres de Paul Valéry à Victoria Ocampo," *SUR* 132 (October 1945): 80–104.

37 Victoria Ocampo, "El caso de Drieu La Rochelle," *Soledad sonora* (Buenos Aires: Editorial Sudamericana, 1950), 30. Not long before, a similar incident involving *SUR*'s publication of "Capricho español" (Calendario, *SUR* 59 [July 1939]: 70–1), in which the journal ridiculed Franco and rejected the "*hispanidad retinta*" (rabid Hispanism) of the nationalist *Sol y Luna*, had forced Ocampo to remove the name of her good friend, the Spanish philosopher José Ortega y Gasset, from *SUR*'s international editorial board; Tzvi Medin, *Ortega y Gasset en la cultura hispanoamericana* (México, D.F.: Fondo de Cultura Económica, 1994), 31.

38 Ocampo, "El caso de Drieu La Rochelle." In her biography of Borges, María Esther Vázquez is similarly perplexed by the fact that Borges, as much an anti-fascist as Ocampo, likewise would never condemn La Rochelle, whom he had admired since the early days of their friendship, forged during the Frenchman's visit to Buenos Aires in May 1933, invited by *SUR*, that is, by Campo: Vázquez, *Borges*, 136–8.

39 Victoria Ocampo, *Testimonios. Séptima Serie (1962–1967)* (Buenos Aires: Editorial Sur, 1967), 185–8.

40 *SUR* 32 (May 1937): 80–1; *SUR* 87 (December 1941): 22.

41 Perednik, "La judeidad," 38–41; Jaime Alazraki, *Borges and the Kabbalah. And Other Essays on his Fiction and Poetry* (Cambridge: Cambridge University Press, 1988); Edna Aizenberg, *Borges, el tejedor del Aleph y otros ensayos* (Madrid: Iberoamericana, 1997), 37–41; *SUR* 86 (May 1940): 30–46; *SUR* 101 (February 1943): 13–20; *SUR* 136 (February 1946): 7–14.

42 "Desagravio a Borges," *SUR* 94 (July 1942).

43 *SUR* 117 (July 1944): 48–61; *SUR* 133 (November 1945): 44–61 ["Mit Brennender Sorge" is an obvious reference to Pope Pius XI's encyclical condemning the religious situation under the Third Reich.]; *SUR* 152 (June 1947): 59–75; *SUR* 160 (February 1948): 48–57.

44 Rosa Chacel, "Una palabra de adios; Máximo José Kahn, 1897–1953," *SUR* 224 (September–October 1953): 124–9.

45 Published in two installments in *SUR* 140 (June 1946): 44–60 and *SUR* 151 (May 1947): 69–90. H. Zylberger, "El trágico fin de las tres hermanas de Kafka," *SUR* 145 (November 1946): 73–6.

46 Victoria Kent, "Cuatro años en París," *SUR* 150 (April 1947): 32–7; Jean Bloch-Michel, "La prisión," *SUR* 145 (November 1946): 62–73.

47 *SUR* 138 (April 1946): 7–41; Victoria Ocampo, "Impresiones de Nuremberg," *Soledad sonora*, 41–61.

48 Roger Caillois started the magazine and collection of titles in French under *SUR*'s aegis, during the French sociologist's stay in Buenos Aires as a protegé of Ocampo in the war years. *SUR* 171 (January 1949): 84.

49 *SUR* 170 (December 1948): 95; *SUR* 254 (September–October 1958).

50 Victoria Ocampo, "Karl Jaspers habla de Eichmann," *La Prensa* (May 29, 1961), reproduced in *Testimonios, Séptima Serie*: 201–4.

51 *Ibid.*, 202.

52 Victoria Ocampo, "El vicario," in *Testimonios. Séptima Serie*, 211.

53 "Comisión Argentina de Ayuda a los Intelectuales Españoles," *SUR* 56 (October 1939): 103.

3 Imagining Otherness

The Jewish Question in Brazil, 1930–1940

Jeffrey Lesser

The late 1920s were among the most tumultuous in Brazilian history. As the coffee economy declined the federal government came under increasing fire from regional elites allied with the military officers whose army revolt had been aborted mid-decade. The presidential campaign that began in 1929 reflected these problems, creating bitter political infighting. In the midst of the violence-marred electioneering a series of economic crises hit Brazil. In early March 1930, Júlio Prestes was declared the winner amid accusations of widespread fraud. In early October, losing candidate Getúlio Vargas proclaimed the vote a sham and his troops began to agitate. The Revolution of 1930 had begun. On November 4, the generals made Vargas "Provisional President" of a "Provisional Government." The Revolution of 1930 was over.[1]

One area where Vargas's appointment led to change was in the attitude toward immigrants and their descendants, most notably Jews, Japanese, and Middle Easterners. After 1930 the government and its supporters increasingly used the discussion of immigration to express nationalist and nativist positions. Many members of the new regime were attracted to certain racist forms of national regeneration popular in Europe at the time and thus had ideological reasons for limiting foreign entry. These leanings dovetailed with the attitudes of a small but growing urban middle class, most noticeably in São Paulo and Rio de Janeiro but to some extent in Brazil's other large cities as well, that desired economic and social mobility without immigrant competition. Thus, as urban unemployment grew in the early 1930s, immigrants, many of whom had worked extremely hard to become moderately successful, became easy scapegoats. It took only a few years for political attacks on foreigners to be transformed into policies based on the commonly held notion that "one of the causes of unemployment is found in the free entry of foreigners . . . [who]

frequently contribute to an increase in economic disorder and social insecurity."[2] Anti-immigrant rhetoric was aimed at those who might settle in urban areas and whose occupations revolved around the distribution, and not the production, of important goods.

It was in this highly charged atmosphere that Brazilian politicians shifted their discourse on immigration and immigrants in dramatic ways between 1930 and 1935. New strains of nationalism would transform old ideas about the "racial whitening" of Brazil into federal policies aimed at "Brazilianization." This helped to encourage an anti-foreigner movement among many federal and state officials. At its start, however, nativist movements targeted only groups that, while not banned from entering Brazil, did not fit "European" ideals. Jews (including those from Europe), along with those from the Middle East and Asia, were increasingly defined as problematic. The anti-immigrant rhetoric so prevalent in the cities, however, was not hegemonic. Indeed, the image of immigrants as a positive force for development continued among many large landowners who remained committed to non-Brazilian labor. Whatever political cachet nativism had, it was of only moderate concern to *fazendeiros* (large landowners) worried about maintaining their social status, harvesting their crops, and rounding up their cattle.

The positions in the immigration battle were plainly staked out, although not always clearly articulated. Large landowners and their representatives wanted to guarantee the continued entry of agricultural workers. Many urban politicians, on the other hand, argued that most immigrants should be banned, especially those who did not fit into the "European" category. The Vargas regime was squarely in the middle, encouraging the tension between competing political forces as a means of enhancing and consolidating its own power. This placed Jewish immigrants and refugees in a particularly precarious position. Jewish immigrants to Brazil after the 1920s rarely settled in rural areas and thus had no support from large landowners. Urban nativists, generally at odds with the fazendeiros over immigration policy, also viewed Jews negatively, considering them an insidious non-white race whose racial difference was dangerously invisible. The undesirability of Jews became one of the few areas of agreement among urban and rural politicians.

The growth of nativism among local rural and urban politicians forced the federal government to reevaluate its traditional promotion of immigration. Brazil's long tradition of European-influenced racialist thought provided the xenophobic rhetoric with which to target immigrant Jews who entered in growing numbers and often settled in urban areas.[3] Jews posed a particular challenge since they were considered racially distinct yet seemed to insult nativists by not pressing their physical advantage and choosing to maintain their culture by dressing and worshipping differently.

35

With already established presences in Brazil, Jews, along with Japanese and Middle Easterners (from various religious and ethnic backgrounds), became the most important target of nativists. The Japanese, however, had two important defenders: large landowners who desired the presumed agricultural orientation of most Japanese immigrants, and the federal government, which realized that the economic, political, and military might of Japan demanded respect.[4] Targeting Jewish (or Middle Eastern) immigration, on the other hand, had comparatively few pitfalls. Jewish immigrants had little international diplomatic support, and those arriving to Brazil in the 1920s rarely played the agricultural roles demanded of immigrants. This allowed politicians who represented powerful landowners to participate in the anti-immigrant movement without fear of arousing the wrath of their sponsors. At the same time, Jews made up an increasing percentage of the expanding East European migratory stream, representing almost 42 percent of all Poles who emigrated to Brazil between 1926 and 1937 and a remarkable 77.7 percent between 1931 and 1935.[5]

Brazilian nativism and Jewish immigration collided in the realm of formal policy in the 1930s. On June 7, 1937, following two years of informal restriction and five months before the establishment of the fascist-inspired *Estado Novo* (New State), Brazil's Ministry of Foreign Relations (known as Itamaraty) issued a secret circular that prohibited visas to all persons of "Semitic origin." Why did Jews, a small part of the large immigrant stream from Europe to Brazil, cause such consternation that they were eventually banned from entering Brazil? And how, just one year after the ban was in place, did more Jews enter Brazil legally than at any time in the previous twenty years?

The answer to these two questions involved a change in the way a small but extraordinarily powerful group of intellectuals and politicians were convinced by leaders of Jewish organizations to revise their attitudes about otherness and its relation to Brazilian national identity. Put differently, leaders of Brazil's Jewish community, along with influential members of international refugee relief organizations, successfully manipulated the content of many of the images that Brazilian policymakers and intellectuals had about Jews, transforming negative stereotypes into positive ones. This was possible only because the stereotypes were devoid of content.

Beginning in the mid-1930s, Brazilian nativists regularly targeted Jews, whose economic success led to great visibility, as an enemy of the urban middle class. Such bigoted attitudes, however, were not always mirrored by national leaders who stereotypically viewed Jews as rich, intelligent, and industrially oriented. For the Vargas regime that had come to power in 1930, Jews were as economically desirable as they were politically inexpedient. This contradiction between economic needs and political desires meant Jews were simultaneously viewed in a positive and negative light.[6] As a result, during the late 1930s, Jewish immigration became an integral part of a political debate that sought to reconcile the growing movement for immigrant restriction with an awareness that some immigrants might bring much needed skills and capital to Brazil.

Many influential members of the Vargas government believed that Jewish immigrants could foster economic growth. Thus a tension existed between restrictive immigration policies deemed necessary for maintaining urban middle-class support and more open policies aimed at promoting economic development. This contradiction was resolved in 1938 when policymakers began to systematically ignore or modify restrictions on Jewish immigration. Probing the contradictory ideological and political attitudes surrounding an immigration policy that simultaneously banned and permitted Jewish entry demonstrates how notions about the desirability of Jewish immigration to Brazil changed from anti-Semitism to philo-Semitism during the World War II era.

Few intra-governmental conflicts aroused as much political passion, or focused as much public attention, as Jewish immigration did during 1939. Over four thousand Jews entered Brazil legally and openly in that year, more than in any since 1929. The marked increase should not suggest a shift in images of Jews. Indeed the very notions – that Jews were urban, financially oriented, and internationally powerful – that had been the basis for so much Jew-hatred were, in late 1938 and early 1939, increasingly viewed as indicators of the usefulness of Jews for Brazil's economic development. In other words, images about Jews that had been interpreted as negative came to be regarded by some important decision makers as positive attributes. There were numerous reasons for this change. Jewish relief groups actively put positive twists on old stereotypes. The US, itself unwilling to make a major commitment toward accepting Jewish refugees, put pressure on others to do so. Furthermore, important Brazilian federal politicians were convinced, usually by leaders of Jewish relief organizations, that refugees from Italy, Austria, and Germany had the occupational experience needed to aid Brazil's industrializing economy and urbanizing society. The relaxation of the absolute ban on Jewish entry thus did not signal so much a change in attitude as a change of interpretation. This reimagination of what it meant to be an "other" gave almost ten thousand Jewish refugees a chance to survive.

From 1930 to 1937 anti-Jewish stereotypes, when held by those making crucial decisions on immigration policy, worked to the disadvantage of Jewish immigrants and refugees. In 1938, however, this had begun to change. This was related directly to the appointment of Oswaldo Aranha, at the time Brazil's ambassador to the US, as foreign minister. Aranha, it must be emphasized, adhered to many of the same anti-Jewish stereotypes held by other politicians in the Americas.[7] He often tied Jews to an alleged world communist conspiracy, believed they were "radically averse to agriculture," and that "en masse they would constitute an obvious danger to the future homogeneity of Brazil."[8] Aranha was not, however, a Judeophobe. There was an important philo-Semitic component in his conceptions. Jews, in the view of the new foreign minister, were rich, skilled, and influential and thus useful for Brazil's economic development. Moreover, Aranha recognized that Brazil's response to the refugee question would have an impact on relations with the US, a country he admired greatly.[9] As early as 1937 he had worried, as ambassador to the US, that Brazil's ban on Jewish entry had to avoid provoking "the immense and powerful Jewish colony" in the United States.[10]

At first glance a policy shift allowing Jews considered useful for national development to enter Brazil seems simply rational. Since few Brazilians were trained industrial managers or skilled technicians, the undesirability of certain immigrants could be overlooked if they delivered needed economic or political benefits. Many German and Austrian Jewish refugees were in fact capitalists or industrialists, giving a factual basis of the stereotype.[11] Italian Jewish refugees, whose pre-migratory support of fascism led them to call themselves the "colônia Mussolini," were almost universally administrators, academics, businesspeople, and members of the liberal professions. While a desire for development seemed more important than banning refugees, a sense still remained that Jews were unable to guard "what is most sacred to us, the basis of our institutions: Country, Religion, Family."[12] Yet something had changed. Starting in 1938 influential politicians began to imply, using that most Christian of metaphors, that certain Jews did not carry the stigma of being Jewish. This helps to explain why so many Jews were allowed into Brazil even while anti-Semitic images remained so preponderant. Ideas about Jews never changed, only ideas about who fit the category.

The most important reason that the images of Jews began to change in Brazil in the 1930s was related to the way in which Brazilian anti-Semitic stereotypes were conceived and discussed. By maintaining the traditional stereotypes and simply modifying their assessment of them, international relief organizations could turn accepted stereotypes to the advantage of refugees. One image of Jews, for example, involved money and economic success. Rich Jews could thus be constructed as part of an international conspiracy to force national wealth to the exterior *or* glorified for their ability to help domestic industrial development by injecting capital into Brazil. Influential Jews, such as world famous intellectuals Giorgio Mortara and Stefan Zweig, were hailed for the propaganda opportunities they represented, not the inassimilable foreign culture they had been accused of maintaining in the past. Negative stereotypes of "Jewish millionaires . . . [who] flee from their various European homelands, come to Brazil, and leave their capital in the United States or bring it to Argentina" were transformed into positive ones of Jews as accountants, bookkeepers, and financial planners.[13] By promoting the existence of "Jewish " wealth and industriousness, past accusations of communist activity were dismissed. In a moment of crisis, Jews used anti-Semitic stereotypes against the anti-Semites.

Critical in convincing Brazilian leaders that some Jews were acceptable immigrants was the influence – both informal and formal – of the United States. Old stereotypes took on new meanings when Jewish relief agency representatives and US diplomats disingenuously overstated the leverage of Jews in the US political, economic, and journalistic spheres. Notions of Jewish influence were encouraged when relief officials offered financial schemes that would benefit Brazil's economy in exchange for visas. In March 1939 Aranha arrived in the US to negotiate a series of trade and loan agreements. While attending a dinner at New York's Council of Foreign Relations, the foreign minister was asked by a director of the stock firm Bendix, Lutweiler and Company if Brazil "was prepared to accept Jewish emigrants of a type and training to be readily assimilated and having sufficient financial resources." Perhaps visas might be tied to reducing Brazil's foreign debt. Aranha seemed interested and the following day learned that an "American group interested in the problems of Jewish emigration from Germany" was prepared to accept "a substantial amount" of Brazilian currency as repayment for debt contracted in dollars. Deposits to a fund to help refugees would be accepted as payback for certain debt obligations, having "a most salutary effect upon the standing and credit of Brazil."[14] There is no evidence that the plan would have been accepted by Brazil, or enacted if it had. Even so, the contents of the scheme played on a strong image held by Brazilian authorities: that international Jewish power and wealth existed and was committed to helping refugees.

The tension between traditional anti-Semitic images and less negative judgments of Jews led some policymakers simultaneously to favor and to oppose Jewish immigration. On any given day immediate political pressure, be it domestic or international, affected the implementation of immigration policy. Correspondence sent by Aranha to various European diplomatic posts indicates the swings. On August 9, 1939, Itamaraty ordered H. Pinheiro de Vasconcelos, consul general in London, to give permanent visas to a number of Polish Jewish refugees.[15] These visas were issued a few months later. In mid-October 1939, on the other hand, the following orders were received by Brazil's legation in Helsinki: "The legation should stamp visas in passports of refugees as long as they are not Jews."[16] Seemingly contradictory memos granting visas to some refugees and denying them to others followed an internal logic based on the dual images of Jews in Brazil.

Politicians in Rio were not the only ones revising their estimations of Jews; requests for exceptions to the anti-Jewish orders also arrived from Brazil's consulates and embassies in Europe. A diplomat in Paris, although believing in principle that Jews should not be allowed permanently into Brazil, wondered if it "would be prudent to persevere on the path" of absolute bans.[17] French Jews, he claimed, made up 75 percent of all French commercial interests and applied for Brazilian visas only for business purposes. Pedro Leão Veloso, who considered himself "one of the few in our country who is not a declared enemy of the Jews," pointed out to Aranha that "the Banco do Brasil can inform you that, thanks to the entrance of seventy capitalist Jews, the national economy benefited by thirty-five million milreis [US $2 million]. Imagine what [all the others] brought?"[18] Jewish refugees, according to Leão Veloso, brought far more capital to Brazil than Argentine tourists, who were allowed to enter without question, presumably as long as they were not Jews.

Others wondered if visas for renowned Jews might promote Brazil's international image and help the country progress. Mortara, the Italian Jewish intellectual and editor of the prestigious *Giornale degli Economisti e Rivista di Statistica* was dismissed from his post in 1938. Almost immediately he was invited to Brazil by the director of the Instituto Brasileiro de Geografia e Estatística (Brazilian Institute of Geography and Statistics), the former foreign minister José Carlos Macedo Soares. Soon after arriving in Rio in early 1939 with his wife and four children, Mortara was appointed coordinator of the 1940 national census. The French playwright Hénri-Leon (Henry) Bernstein, living as a refugee in the US, was rumored to believe that an extended visit to Brazil would inspire a new theater piece. In spite of Bernstein's well-known condemnation of anti-Semitism in his play *Israël*, a diplomat asked "What reasons could be invoked to refuse him a visa?" and worried that "our nation will lose an extraordinary propaganda opportunity."[19] Although Bernstein never pursued his desire for tropical inspiration, the Austrian-Jewish novelist Stefan Zweig did. The grant of a life-saving visa to Zweig may well have influenced his decision to write the propagandistic *Brazil: Land of the Future*. Zweig's presence in Brazil was even used by the Department of Press and Propaganda to promote such unlikely ventures as municipal government organization.[20]

In 1939 more than four thousand Jews entered Brazil with permanent or temporary visas.[21] Jews received more than 60 percent of the permanent visas and almost 45 percent of the temporary visas given to Germans and Poles.[22] Almost 9 percent of all those with permanent visas and more than 14 percent of those with temporary visas were Jews.[23] One reason for the high numbers was the pressure the US put on friendly nations to allow Jewish refugees to enter, a regular topic of correspondence between the Brazilian and US governments. The US desired to "take an increased part in the establishment and settlement of Jewish immigrants in the Latin American countries," and regularly played on stereotypes of Jewish refugees as having capital and skills.[24] Jews were also a topic in meetings of the Conselho de Imigração e Colonização (Council of Immigration and Colonization), which tried to moderate between those who believed that some refugees should be allowed to enter if they would aid Brazil's economic development and others who viewed all Jews as social dangers and wanted the absolute ban reinstated.

The fears of an increased number of Jews in Brazil collided head-on with both new positive interpretations of stereotypes and US diplomatic pressure leaving an impression on some foreign diplomats that the Brazilian government, "while feeling sympathetic toward the plight of Jewish refugees, will continue to be extremely cautious about receiving additional numbers."[25] This gave Itamaraty officials the latitude to interpret visa regulations in light of their own opinions on Jewish immigration. Some individual consular officers gave visas to large numbers of Jews. In most German, Austrian, and East European consulates, however, visa applications were often rebuffed on the basis of the first secret circular. Itamaraty sometimes approved visas directly from Rio, while at other times rejecting them.[26] While almost forty-five hundred refugees legally entered Brazil in 1939, many others were turned away.[27]

Nothing illustrates the shifting interpretations of policy more clearly than a situation involving Albert Einstein, who visited Brazil twice in 1925. Those voyages had been arranged by the Jewish Colonization Association, eager to "demonstrate to the people of Brazil that Jews are not only peddlers but that among them one may find world famous scientists."[28] The plan was a success. Brazil's most noted scientists formed a welcoming committee, important members of the Jewish community courted Einstein, and journalists printed long interviews with the scientist.[29] Over a decade later, Einstein's fame in Brazil and his warm feelings for the country encouraged him to approach Brazilian officials for help in getting visas for refugee Jews. In 1938 an old friend of Einstein, Dr. Hans George Katz, a German Jew living in São Paulo with a permanent visa, contacted the scientist about his sister Helene Fabian-Katz. Katz was desperately worried since Helene was in Nazi Berlin, frantic to leave and unable to get a visa. Einstein supported her application for a US visa, but this was rejected. Finally the scientist suggested that Brazil might have visas available.[30] On January 23, 1939, Einstein wrote directly to Aranha, noting that there was "no risk of Mrs. Fabian-Katz ever becoming a public charge" and requesting that her visa application be approved.[31]

Aranha apparently never received the letter. In early February Dr. Katz again wrote Einstein, complaining that Itamaraty had taken no action and that the situation in Germany was becoming increasingly difficult.[32] Katz however had discovered that Aranha would be in the US and wondered if Einstein could somehow contact the foreign minister while he was in Washington. The suggestion was a good one. Einstein wrote to Aranha in care of the US State Department and had a copy delivered in person to Itamaraty in Rio by Cecilia Razovsky, the executive director of the National Coordinating Committee for Aid to Refugees and Emigrants Coming from Germany.[33] The request was received, held for three months, and then sent to the Council of Immigration and Colonization.[34] The visa for Fabian-Katz was then apparently granted as, some months later, Einstein again wrote to Aranha asking for a visa for another family friend, noting that "your kind assistance in a previous case encourages me."[35] Typed in the corner of the letter is a note from Einstein's secretary explaining that the "previous case" was that of Helene Fabian-Katz. Indeed she and the scientist were in correspondence between São Paulo and Princeton as late as 1953.[36]

In spite of its restrictions on Jewish immigration, Brazil established a relatively liberal attitude toward resident refugees. The refusal to institutionalize anti-Semitism in domestic policy was part of Brazil's continued desire to portray itself in a positive light to the world. Refusing entry to Jews on the basis of immigration law was much easier than attacking refugees already in Brazil. Furthermore, by blaming general immigration law for the refusal of visas to Jews, important politicians could still claim a willingness to make exceptions. In this regard, Brazil's policy was much like that of the US. In 1940, for example, Vargas and Aranha met with a World Jewish Congress/American Jewish Congress study group traveling through South America.[37] The group also met with João Carlos Muniz, who, in spite of his regular attacks on Jewish immigrants and immigration, "expressed himself as highly gratified with the valuable contribution the Jewish community was making ... [as] the refugees who had come in recent years had ... brought new industries, supplementing their limited financial capital with large technical and intellectual capital [and provided] work opportunities for native Brazilians."[38] In late 1940 a firm in Porto Alegre requested diamond cutters and a group of French-Jewish refugees experienced in the trade were given visas as technical experts.[39] The almost twenty-five hundred visas given to Jews in 1940 led refugee organizations to believe that "Brazil still continues to accept a great many [Jewish] immigrants."[40]

In January 1942 Brazil severed relations with the Axis and Japan; in August Brazil entered the war on the side of the Allies. This gave Jews an opportunity to be "good" citizens and residents of Brazil, show solidarity with the plight of European Jewry, and battle anti-Semitism, all at the same time. Later that year a group of Jews presented five military training planes to Vargas "as a gesture of solidarity in the war." A few days later a fast day was observed in protest against the Nazi murders taking place in concentration camps.[41] Many young Jews joined the Brazilian armed forces, including, to the surprise of a journalist in Rio, a German Jew living in the city of Belém do Pará at the mouth of the Amazon.[42] Others contributed money to Brazilian relief organizations.[43] This situation was mirrored in Brazil's Japanese-Brazilian community where Brazil's entry into the war led many *Nikkei* to volunteer to fight fascism, in part to prove their own Brazilianness.[44]

With Brazil a member of the Allied camp, much of the antagonism directed at Jewish refugees seemed to subside. This was certainly related to a drop in Nazi propaganda in the Brazilian press. Furthermore, the resignations of three of the most powerful nationalist-authoritarians in the Vargas regime, Justice Minister Francisco Campos, Police Chief Felinto Müller, and Department of Press and Propaganda head Lourival Fontes, the latter two open Axis supporters, further lowered the priority given to discussion of Jews. The press now glorified the position of Jews in Brazil. The *Correio de Manhã* reported with excitement that Brazilian Jews and Jewish refugees attended a special religious service in Rio to "thank President Getúlio Vargas for saving their children."[45] Journalists began portraying Jews as successful farmers and a *Diário de Notícias* editorial commented that "the activities of the Jews are not limited exclusively to city trade. Actually they are capable of engaging in other spheres of work that are certainly more useful to the country that did not deny them shelter."[46] Niteroi's *Diário da Manhã* echoed the praise, reflecting that Jewish children in the small Jewish Colonization Association colony of Quatro Irmãos spoke Portuguese "and are masters of the history, geography and economics of Brazil, (unlike) Aryan races where thousands of Brazilians do not speak [Portuguese]."[47] *O Globo* hailed Brazil's treatment of "Jewish victims of Nazi-Fascism," suggesting that "a huge group of Israelites . . . [now] believe in our glorious flag" and were volunteering for military service. This article was even reprinted in *Nação Armada*, a military journal that had regularly attacked Jews since its inception in 1939.[48]

Why did the Vargas regime concern itself with writing secret circulars that were modified or left unenforced? It would be a mistake to place the blame on bureaucratic incompetence. Rather, the shifting immigration policy reflected how images of otherness were malleable with regard to Jews and the role they might play in Brazil's development. This did not happen by accident. Rather, leaders of formal Jewish institutions manipulated ideas of Jewish difference to their own advantage in a moment of crisis. Policies banning the entry of Jewish refugees at first presented Brazil's government with an easy way to gain nationalist credentials and silence critics of its immigration policy. Nazi economic and ideological relations with Brazil prior to the outbreak of World War II certainly encouraged the Vargas regime to take this position. Yet negative international response to Brazil's denial of visas to *all* Jews coincided with

Aranha's return from Washington and his new power as foreign minister. Aranha's acceptance of Jewish otherness as simultaneously advantageous and problematic led him and other important Estado Novo policymakers to be convinced that Jews were critical to bringing capital and skills to Brazil and to maintaining good relations with the US. Combined with pressure from the US and Great Britain, Brazil's eventual diplomatic and military allies and the only war-time buyers of Brazilian cotton and coffee, this made absolute restriction unviable.

In World War II era Brazil, Jew-hatred and philo-Semitism existed side by side. Jewish relief organizations realized that complicated and contradictory images of otherness could thus be manipulated to pry open Brazil's doors. Jews were able to exploit the vacuous nature of stereotypes to save more than ten thousand lives.

Notes

This chapter is based in large part on the author's *Welcoming the Undesirables: Brazil and the Jewish Question* (Berkeley: University of California Press, 1994).

1   Boris Fausto, *A Revolução de 1930: Historiografia e História* (São Paulo: Brasiliense, 1986); Thomas E. Skidmore, *Politics in Brazil, 1930–1964: An Experiment in Democracy* (New York: Oxford University Press, 1967); Jordan M. Young, *The Brazilian Revolution of 1930 and the Aftermath* (New Brunswick: Rutgers University Press, 1967), 30–54.

2   Decree 19.482 (December 12, 1930). *Colecção da leis da República dos Estados Unidos do Brasil de 1930*, vol. 2, *Actos da Junta Governativa Provisoria e do Governo Provisório (Outubro a Dezembro)* (Rio de Janeiro: Imprensa Nacional, 1931), 82.

3   Thomas E. Skidmore, *Black into White: Race and Nationality in Brazilian Thought* (New York: Oxford University Press, 1974), 38.

4   Hiroshi Saito, *O Japonês no Brasil* (São Paulo: Editora Sociologia e Política, 1962), 23; Jeffrey Lesser, *Negotiating National Identity: Immigrants, Minorities and the Struggle for Ethnicity in Brazil* (Durham: Duke University Press, 1999).

5   Jacob Lestschinsky, "National Groups in Polish Emigration," *Jewish Social Studies* 5 (April 1943): 110–11; C. R. Cameron, "Immigration into São Paulo: Parts II and III" (April 14, 1931), 832.55/78, National Archives and Record Center, Washington, D.C., USA (hereafter NARC-W).

6   Commercial Attaché to Octavio Mangabeira (April 17, 1930), Maço 29.625/29 (1291), Arquivo Histórico Itamaraty, Rio de Janeiro (hereafter AHI-R).

7   David S. Wyman, *The Abandonment of the Jews: America and the Holocaust, 1941–1945* (New York: Pantheon Books, 1984), 178–92; Irving Abella and Harold Troper, *None is Too Many: Canada and the Jews of Europe 1933–1948* (New York: Random House, 1982), 101–26; Michael Blakeney, *Australia and the Jewish Refugees 1933–1948* (Sydney: Croom Helm Australia, 1985), 101–21.

8   Oswaldo Aranha to Adhemar de Barros (October 20, 1938), Maço 9601

(612), AHI-R. The anti-Semitic component to Aranha's thought has been examined briefly by Theodore Michael Berson, "A Political Biography of Dr. Oswaldo Aranha of Brazil, 1930–1937" (doctoral dissertation, New York University, 1971), 265, and more currently by Maria Luiza Tucci Carneiro, *O Anti-Semitismo na Era Vargas: Fantasmas de uma Geração* (São Paulo: Brasiliense, 1988), 258–95.

9 Aranha, for example, proposed that a US public relations firm be hired and that journalists be paid for image-enhancing stories. Aranha to Vargas (May 19, June 4, September 24, and November 27, 1937), OA 37.19.5, OA 37.4.6, OA 37.24.9, OA 37.11.27, Centro de Pesquisa e Documentação de História Contemporânea do Brasil, Fundação Getúlio Vargas, Rio de Janeiro (hereafter CPDOC-R).

10 Aranha to Vargas (November 30, 1937), EM/30/30/XI/37, Maço 9857 (660), AHI-R.

11 Alfred Hirschberg, "The Economic Adjustment of Jewish Refugees in São Paulo," *Jewish Social Studies* 7 (January 1945): 37.

12 Vargas (April 11, 1939) attached to Scotten to Hull (April 14, 1939), 832.00/1253, NARC-W.

13 Rosalina Coelho Lisboa to Vargas (no date), GV 40.09.00/4, CPDOC-R.

14 Illegible to Aranha (March 8, 1939), Maço 10.561 (741), AHI-R.

15 511.14 (547)/324 (November 9, 1939) and 511.14 (547)/326 (November 13, 1939), Maço 29.630 (1291), AHI-R.

16 Itamaraty to Legation in Helsinki (October 13, 1939), 558 (72), 511.14 (457), Maço 29.630 (1291), AHI-R.

17 Cônsul General (Paris) to Aranha (June 13, 1939), Maço 10.561 (741), AHI-R.

18 Pedro Leão Veloso to Aranha (January 26, 1940), OA 40.02.01/1, p. 3, CPDOC-R.

19 Cônsul General (Paris) to Aranha (June 13, 1939), Maço 10.561 (741), AHI-R.

20 Cândido Duarte, *A Organização Municipal no Governo Getúlio Vargas* (Rio de Janeiro: Departamento de Emprensa e Propaganda, 1942), 213.

21 According to HIAS the number was 4,601. "Rapport D'activité Pendant la Periode 1933–1942," HIAS NY-Folder 1, Archives of the YIVO Institute for Jewish Research, New York (hereafter YIVO-NY). According to the Conselho de Imigração e Colonização the number was 4,223 (*Diário Official*, November 27, 1940, 22135) and *Revista de Imigração e Colonização* 3 (April 1942): 184–94.

22 *Revista de Imigração e Colonização* 1 (October 1940): 123–4 (misprinted).

23 *Ibid.*

24 Morris C. Troper (Joint) to HIAS-JCA Emigration Association (January 11, 1939), SCA 2 (February 10–11, 1939): 136, Archives of the Jewish Colonization Association, London (hereafter JCA-L). Achilles to Robert Pell (March 20, 1939), 832.55 J/3; and Achilles to Briggs (March 13, 1939), 832.55 J/2, NARC-W.

25 Scotten to Welles (March 10, 1939), 832.55 J/3, p.4, NARC-W.

26 Raphael Fernandes to Aranha (April 13, 1939), OA 39.05.15/2; Aranha to Fernandes (May 15, 1939), OA 39.05.15/2, CPDOC-R.

27 US Department of State, Division of European Affairs, Memorandum (March 13, 1939), 832.55 J/2, NARC-W. In March 1939, for example, the steamship San Martín, carrying twenty-one Jewish refugees from Germany and Italy, requested permission to disembark at Recife after being refused at Montevideo. Telegrams of support from around the world were of no help since Itamaraty claimed, untruthfully, not to have received any visa requests until four days after the ship had left Recife in search of another port. Passport Division to Secretary of the President of the Republic, March 24, 1939. Fundo Secretaria da Presidência da República - Relações Exteriors (hereafter PRRE), Box 27.586, Documents 7241 and 7341, Arquivo Nacional, Rio de Janeiro (hereafter AN-R). Alfred Rothschild to Vargas (April 15, 1939), PRRE, Box 27.586, Document 9768, AN-R.

28 Isaiah Raffalovich, *Tsiyunim ve-tamrurim be-Shiv'im shenot nedudim. Otobayografiya* (Landmarks and Milestones during Seventy Years of Wanderings: An Autobiography) (Tel Aviv: Defus Sho-Shani, 1952), 200–3.

29 *A Noite* (Rio de Janeiro) (March 21, 1925) and *O Jornal* (Rio de Janeiro) (March 22, 1925).

30 Einstein to Katz (December 12, 1938) and Katz to Einstein (December 24, 1938), Einstein Duplicate Archives, 53602, 53604, Seeley G. Mudd Manuscript Library, Princeton University Archives (New Jersey) (hereafter SMML-NJ). Nachman Falbel, *Estudos sobre a comunidade judaica no Brasil* (São Paulo: Federação Israelita de São Paulo, 1984), 134–9.

31 Einstein to Aranha (January 23, 1939), Einstein Duplicate Archive, 53607, SMML-NJ.

32 Katz to Einstein (February 4, 1939), Einstein Duplicate Archives, 53608, SMML-NJ.

33 Einstein to Aranha (February 14, 1939) and Einstein to Katz (February 14, 1939), Einstein Duplicate Archive, 53609, 53610, SMML-NJ. Einstein to Aranha (February 24, 1939), SP/SN/558/Anexo único, Maço 9857 (660), AHI-R.

34 Itamaraty memo to CIC (May 11, 1938), Labienne Salgado dos Santos to Einstein (May 11, 1939), Salgado dos Santos to Razovsky (May 11, 1939), Maço 9857 (660), AHI-R.

35 Einstein to Aranha (December 3, 1940), Einstein Duplicate Archive, 54769, SMML-NJ.

36 Fabian-Katz to Einstein (September 18, 1953) and Einstein to Fabian-Katz (September 25, 1953), Einstein Duplicate Archive, 59627, 59629, SMML-NJ.

37 Jacob X. Cohen, *Jewish Life in South America: A Survey Study for the American Jewish Congress* (New York: Bloch Publishing, 1941), 3. In all the other nations the study group visited, they gained access only to low-level officials.

38 Cohen, *Jewish Life*, 12.

39 Dr. A. d'Esaguy (HICEM) to Mr. Baumgold (NY) (December 18, 1940), HIAS/NY, Folder 37, YIVO-NY.

40 Oungre to Gottschalk (HIAS) (November 28, 1941), HIAS/NY, Folder 10, p. 2, YIVO-NY.

41 *The New York Times* (December 24 and 29, 1942).

42 *Diário de Notícias* (Rio de Janeiro) (October 27, 1942).
43 Memorandum of D. Bloomingdale attached to Duggan to James W. Wise (October 26, 1942), 840.48 Refugees/3421, NARC-W.
44 See Massaki Udihara, *Um medico brasileiro no front: Diário de Massaki Udihara na II Guerra Mundial* (São Paulo: Hacker Editores; Narrativa Um; Imprensa Oficial do Estado; Museu Histórico da Imigração Japonesa no Brasil, 2002).
45 *Correio da Manhã* (Rio de Janeiro) (September 5, 1942).
46 *Diário de Notícias* (Rio de Janeiro) (October 27, 1942).
47 *Diário da Manhã* (Niteroi) (November 24, 1943).
48 *O Globo* (Rio de Janeiro) (September 18, 1942); *Nação Armada* 35 (October 1942): 143–4.

Part II

Constructing Memory

Argentine Jews and the Accusation of "Dual Loyalty," 1960–1962

4

Raanan Rein

Although the State of Israel had defined itself from the very beginning as a Jewish state and declared its commitment to defending the interests of all Jews, the interests of Israeli foreign policy were not always congruent with those of local Jewish communities. The dynamics at each of these levels were different. Moshe Sharett, the first foreign minister of Israel, met Argentine president Juan Perón (1946–1955) in 1953 and expressed his satisfaction at "the existence of a triangular harmony: between the Argentine government and its Jewish citizens; between Argentine Jews and Israel; and between the Argentine government and its Israeli counterpart." In practice, of course, the situation was more complex.[1] This explains why, for example, Perón could succeed in cultivating close relations with the State of Israel while failing to mobilize any significant support in the Argentine Jewish community.

The disparity between Israel's interests and those of Argentine Jews was also notable during the presidency of Arturo Frondizi, leader of the centrist Radical Party, whose democratic credentials and sympathy for the Jewish minority were never in doubt. Frondizi's election in February 1958 was welcomed by both the Israeli embassy in Buenos Aires and the leaders of the organized Jewish community. Soon after the new president took office, their expectations seemed to have been justified. Argentine Jews felt an increasing sense of security and well being, in part because several Jews had been appointed to high posts in the government – posts that Jews had never held before in Argentina. Relations with Israel too grew closer. Foreign minister Golda Meir's visit to Buenos Aires in 1959, for example, allowed the Frondizi government to display its sympathy for Israel publicly.

A year later however all this changed. In May 1960, at the height of the celebrations to mark a hundred and fifty years of Argentine independence and the Republic's liberation from the yoke of Spanish colonialism,

Mossad agents kidnapped the Nazi criminal Adolf Eichmann and took him to Israel for trial.[2] In Buenos Aires this violation of Argentina's national sovereignty aroused great anger. Although various foreign policy considerations ensured that the ensuing diplomatic crisis was resolved within a few weeks and relations with Israel quickly returned to normal, violent manifestations of anti-Semitism brought a substantial deterioration in the position of Argentine Jews, whose number at the time was estimated at more than three hundred thousand out of a population of about twenty-one million – in other words, less than two percent of the total population.[3] The Argentine Jewish community, just then marking the hundredth anniversary of its existence, became the target of a wave of anti-Semitic terror and nationalist attacks that, among other things, did their best to cast doubt on the Jewish citizens' loyalty to the Argentine Republic.

Paying the Price for the Kidnapping of Eichmann

On 19 May 1960, the Jews of Argentina enthusiastically greeted the Israeli delegation, headed by Abba Eban, that had just arrived for Argentina's independence day celebrations. A week later, while the delegation was still in Buenos Aires, the leaders of the Jewish community were astonished to read in the evening paper *La Razón* that the Nazi criminal Adolf Eichmann, whose kidnapping and transfer to Israel had already been announced to the Israeli parliament by prime minister David Ben-Gurion, had in fact been captured in Argentina.[4] Argentine Jews had mixed feelings – happiness and satisfaction that Eichmann had been caught interlaced with strong anxiety about how the Argentine government and public opinion were likely to react toward Israel and the local Jewish community. None of the Jewish organizations in Argentina made any public demur to the kidnapping of Eichmann, and some Jewish public figures even helped resolve the crisis in relations between Israel and Argentina. Others urged friends in the major political parties and the press to try to give the incident a positive aspect by emphasizing the monstrosity of Eichmann's crimes against humanity.[5]

Nonetheless, certain circles in the Jewish community were definitely uncomfortable with the way Israel had carried out its operation. According to a representative of the American Jewish Committee in Buenos Aires, the leaders of the community came close to panic in the first days after Eichmann's capture was reported. They feared that tension between Israel and Argentina would affect the local Jewish community: that there would be direct anti-Semitic attacks and Argentine Jews would be accused of dual loyalty, or greater loyalty to Israel than to their own country.[6] In contrast, Natan Lerner, vice president of the *Delegación de*

Asociaciones Israelitas Argentinas (Delegation of Argentine Jewish Associations, DAIA) in the years 1957–1958, explained: "There were mixed feelings. In the first place, we all supported the action . . . some of us were worried about the possible consequences. Some said it was an illegal act. Some said it could hurt [Israel's] relations with Argentina . . . But there wasn't any alarm among the Jewish leadership." Years later, Marcos Korenhendler, one of the editors of *Di Idishe Tzaitung*, recalled the way many had felt: "There was understanding of Israel's position and also understanding of Frondizi's anger when he said, as president of the country: 'Why didn't they talk to me? I am not the president of some African jungle state. They could have come and talked to me.' No one could say that Frondizi had the slightest fascist or anti-Semitic tendencies."[7]

At the height of the crisis, the *Ha'aretz* correspondent in Buenos Aires wrote even more forthrightly about a certain uneasiness:

> The public had the feeling of having been knifed in the back; on the one hand festive appearances and demonstrations of friendship, on the other a violation of state sovereignty. In the Jewish street they are saying that the government of Israel showed a lack of understanding concerning a sensitive point in these [Latin American] countries. The wording of the Israeli communiqués and explanations did not seem in keeping with either the Jewish public's status, which is closely linked to Israel's position, or [Israel's] friendly relationship with Argentina. The Argentines, including the Jews among them, consider themselves insulted by the snub to their country that in their view was implied in the wording of that first announcement. Confusion shows also in the views of a man like Dr. [Gregorio] Topolevsky, the (Jewish) former Argentine ambassador to Israel, who moves in Israeli circles here, and who initially expressed the view that Eichmann should be returned to Argentina. Later Dr. Topolevsky changed his mind.[8]

Dr. Mario Schteingart, president of the Argentine Jewish Institute believed that it would be better for both Israel and the Jews of Argentina if an international court rather than an Israeli one were appointed to try Eichmann.[9] He was not the only one.

The two years between Eichmann's kidnapping in May 1960 and his execution in June 1962 were the hardest that the Jews of Argentina had known since the *Semana Trágica* (Tragic Week) pogrom in January 1919.[10] Although the dark wave of anti-Semitism might have been expected to exhaust itself within a few months after the kidnapping and the resolution of the diplomatic conflict, the beginning of Eichmann's trial in Jerusalem in April 1961 and the wide press coverage it received all over the world, including Argentina, kept the anti-Semitic campaign alive. During the four months of the trial, which revealed what Hanna Arendt termed "the banality of evil," people all over the world were transfixed by the drama unfolding in Jerusalem, as the man in the glass booth faced the chilling testimony of Holocaust survivors. Eichmann pleaded not guilty on the grounds that he had only been following orders handed down from above, but he was convicted of "crimes against the Jewish people."[11] On December 11, the president of the court pronounced the sentence: death by hanging.

Argentine nationalist groups sought to exploit Eichmann's kidnapping and trial and the infringement of Argentine sovereignty in order to attack the Jews in their country. The surge of anti-Semitism that occurred at this time is also attributable to Argentine political culture and the prevailing socioeconomic conditions, notably a difficult economic situation, the alienation felt by the supporters of Peronism, and widespread disappointment in Frondizi, who did not keep even part of the promises he had strewn around during his presidential campaign. The combination of a political crisis and a series of strikes and demonstrations created frustration – and an environment that encouraged anti-Semitic manifestations, as well as growing pressure on the government by the military.[12]

Tacuara: The Spearhead of the Anti-Semitic Offensive

During the ten years of Perón's regime most anti-Semitic publications and nationalist organizations had gradually faded from view, but after Perón's overthrow they sprang to life again. The campaign against the Jews was spearheaded by the extreme right-wing organization *Movimiento Nacionalista Tacuara*, which first appeared on the scene in 1957. This quasi-military organization was constituted by a new generation of nationalist activists, most of them educated, middle- or upper-class young males in their late teens or early twenties.[13] The organization included no women in the 1960s. Many of them were the offspring of veteran anti-Semitic nationalists from respected oligarchic families, bearing such surnames as Guevara Lynch, Quintana Martínez Zuviría, Sánchez Sorondo, and Díaz de Vivar.[14]

Tacuara's primary goals focused first on the struggle to reinstitute religious instruction in the public schools – abolished by Perón just before his ouster – and the campaign to establish Catholic universities. Even in its early days it was already physically attacking leftists, reformists, and Jews. Tacuara was headed by Alberto Ezcurra Uriburu, a nationalist from a respected upper-class family who was both a descendant of Juan Manuel de Rosas, the nineteenth-century Argentine dictator, and a relative of General José Félix Uriburu, the officer who had seized power in a military coup in September 1930.

The nationalist right-wing organizations turned Argentine Jews – some of whom were already the third generation in the country – into scapegoats to be blamed for the ills of the era. Their extremist concept of Argentina as a melting pot in which all immigrant communities had to assimilate marked Jews as foreigners and separatists, and therefore dangerous. At the same time, their anti-Semitic struggle was a tool used to challenge the parliamentary political system and Frondizi's elected regime. At one of Tacuara's political rallies, after attacking "the dirty Jews living on Libertad [street] and in [the neighborhood of] Villa Crespo" and calling for their elimination, Ezcurra Uriburu declared:

> We repeat that we have no faith in our false liberal democracy made up of corrupt institutions which are tumbling down. Yes, comrades, the system is collapsing and it must be thoroughly cleaned up, with violence and bloodshed even if we must do so against opposition thereto, for this is the only solution . . . we want a country free of politicians, free of demagogues and of Jews . . . we are ready to do whatever may be necessary to have them disappear . . . but we insist that we do not want to change one set of governing members for another, one clown for another; we want the whole circus to go away . . .[15]

For some of the Catholic nationalists, Frondizi was a "Menshevic politician" whose anti-nationalist economic policy, inclusion of leftists in his government, and conciliatory policy toward the Castro regime in Cuba were paving the way to Bolshevism in Argentina.

One of Tacuara's spiritual mentors was the Jesuit priest Julio Meinvielle, who saw Jews and Communists as a threat to Western Christian civilization. Meinvielle's views were a hodgepodge of ideas derived from both medieval Christian sources and the opinions of prominent figures of the modern Catholic European right. In his view, liberalism and socialism were secular, materialistic ideologies which Jews had helped to develop.[16] Meinvielle's book *El judío* (The Jew), published for the first time in 1936, was reissued in 1959 under the title *El judío en el misterio de la historia* (The Jew in the Mystery of History), and since then has been reprinted a number of times.

Between 1960 and 1963, Tacuara underwent a number of divisions and schisms as a result of personal rivalries, ideological differences, and quarrels over strategy and the implications of the Cuban Revolution and the Algerian liberation struggle. In November 1960, Tacuara's right wing left the organization and adopted the name *Guardia Restauradora Nacionalista* (GRN). The GRN was an active participant in the anti-Jewish offensive of the early 1960s. This offshoot of Tacuara was apparently in contact with Jordán Bruno Genta, who in 1960 became the Argentine air force's "advisor on educational policy." Genta, a former Marxist and Freemason who had become an extremist militant nationalist, had won some notoriety in the early 1940s for his speeches to senior army officers encouraging them to get involved in political life, since "the warriors represent the most esteemed class of the state, [because] the nation enters into political existence by virtue of war and preserves its right to exist in war."[17] Genta called for the defense of the Western Christian order, claiming: "Jews, Masonry, and Communism are the three ideological manifestations of the negation of the Divine Redeemer."[18]

In the 1960s Tacuara drew additional inspiration for its anti-Semitic and anti-Israel views from contacts with both neo-Nazi organizations in other countries and Hussein Triki, the Arab League's representative in Buenos Aires, who promoted anti-Semitism under cover of anti-Zionism and as part of the anti-colonialist, anti-imperialist struggle. Triki explained to Argentine nationalists that "if the State of Israel did not exist, Argentina would not be in the deplorable conditions it is in now."[19] He argued that it was necessary to "fight international Zionism, the common enemy of the Argentines and the Arabs," and portrayed Tacuara and the GRN as Argentine forces that were building a dam to contain the violent action of the Zionist force.

In one of Tacuara's press conferences, Ezcurra Uriburu declared that the organization would "defend Catholic views against Marxist-Jewish-liberal-Masonic-capitalist imperialism. We are not anti-Semites with racialist aims, but we are enemies of Jewry. In Argentina the Jews are the servants of Israeli imperialism [who violated] our national sovereignty when [their agents] arrested Adolph Eichmann. In this struggle we have much in common with [the Egyptian president Gamal Abdel] Nasser."[20]

In the wake of the Eichmann kidnapping, various nationalist publications began to shake accusing fingers at Argentine Jews. Notable among them were *El Pampero*, *Cabildo*, and *Azul y Blanco*. All these periodicals frequently asserted that Jews bore no loyalty to Argentina, or that their divided loyalties made them support Israel in moments of crisis instead of remaining faithful to the Argentine Republic, whose sovereignty had been violated by the Zionists.

Jewish Solidarity and Self-Defense

Nationalist hostility was not confined to propaganda against the "Jewish fifth column" – articles, posters, and anti-Semitic slogans and swastikas painted on the walls of buildings in Jewish neighborhoods; it encompassed actual violence: vandalism against Jewish institutions and attacks on Jewish schoolchildren and university students. At the beginning of July 1960, nationalist and liberal students clashed in front of the faculty of medicine at the University of Buenos Aires. Some right-wing students shouted, "We want Eichmann back," "Death to Jews," or "Jews, go to Israel." Swastikas were painted on university buildings and others in the vicinity. In the scuffle two nationalist students and four others were seriously injured.

However, such clashes were in fact more frequent in the high schools. One of the most notorious incidents occurred at Sarmiento High School in Buenos Aires. During a ceremony in honor of the national hero General José de San Martín on August 17, 1960, Tacuara thugs attacked a few Jewish pupils. One of them, fifteen-year-old Edgardo Manuel Trilnik, was shot and seriously wounded, and several other Jewish pupils were lightly injured.[21] This was one more link in a chain of similar incidents that had taken place in previous weeks at the Sarmiento, Urquiza, and Mitre schools, incidents during which the attackers had shouted "Long live Eichmann, death to Jews!"

These incidents must also be viewed in the context of the struggle then dividing Argentine society between those who favored liberal, secular education and those who favored nationalist Catholic education.[22] Against this background, it is even easier to understand the flood of protests that were expressed in newspaper articles and statements by government officials, political figures, and student and teacher organizations.[23] The minister of the interior, Alfredo Vítolo, declared that the police would take firm measures to prevent anti-Semitic incidents of this kind, including patrols around the school. In practice, however, the police did not take any serious action against Tacuara.

An editorial in the Jewish weekly *Mundo Israelita* expressed the rage and frustration Jews felt over the impunity of the perpetrators of anti-Semitic attacks: "The police never finds them out, never punishes them, They know who they are, who commands them, where they meet . . . their signals. They make no mystery of their intentions, they even announce in advance the base deeds they plan to carry out, but no one bothers them. On the contrary, the police authorizes their public meetings, and the press, misinterpreting its mission, divulges them."[24]

On August 25 pupils from Sarmiento and other high schools in the capital participated in a march to protest anti-Semitic violence. Police and US embassy reports emphasized the fact that "Communist elements joined the act of protest at an early stage," as though this lessened the seriousness of the acts being protested. One of the arguments used by a number of spokespeople of the nationalist right, and adopted by the federal police as well as some American diplomats during the Cold War era, was that the anti-Semitic aspect of right-wing violence was connected with the prominent Jewish presence among radical students and in organizations of the extreme left.[25] A senior government source explained to Rabbi Guillermo Schlesinger that the government could not concern itself with Tacuara's anti-Semitic activity because the organization was needed for the war on communism, and everything else was secondary to that need. Diplomats in the US embassy went on to say that

Frondizi would never initiate conflict with the army over its sympathy for Tacuara, as long as his silence would help maintain the delicate balance of power on which his regime was based. "This is simply one of the unavoidable concessions that the feeble Frondizi administration has to make in order to assure the support of the military," said Irving Salert, first secretary at the embassy, to Abraham Monk, a representative of the American Jewish Committee.[26]

In the following weeks parents from Sarmiento met with Frondizi to discuss Tacuara's provocations, while the leaders of the Jewish community met with the interior minister, members of the national committee of the ruling party, and the rector of the University of Buenos Aires, Risieri Frondizi, the president's brother, who linked the anti-Semitic attacks with the Catholic nationalists' campaign against secular universities.[27]

Over the next months, almost every week brought new reports of anti-Semitic incidents, some more serious than others, including the placement of bombs in synagogues and community institutions. The next major outrage was an attack in August 1961 on participants in a Jewish agricultural training course in the province of Buenos Aires, while the young people were sleeping. Some of them were badly injured and the camp was destroyed. The press gave the incident wide coverage, and DAIA immediately registered protests with interior minister Vítolo and the governor of Buenos Aires province, Oscar Alende. This series of attacks was part of what Jacob Blaustein, honorary president of the American Jewish Committee, described as an "extensive campaign of anti-Semitic vandalism by Argentine neo-fascist terrorist groups."[28]

The anti-Semitic incidents that occurred throughout the years 1960–1961 created a sense of solidarity among the beleaguered Jews and prompted two initiatives of great significance to the Jewish community. In the first place, Jewish parents joined forces to set up a Jewish day school where pupils would not be vulnerable to anti-Semitic attacks. The result was the *Tarbut* (Culture) school in Buenos Aires, for which the founding meeting took place July 26, 1960, in Florida, in the province of Buenos Aires.

The second initiative was the formation of Jewish self-defense organizations in the capital, where some eighty percent of Argentine Jews made their home.[29] Many Jews felt that even under a friendly government such as Frondizi's the authorities did not have the power to confront the anti-Semitic, Catholic, and nationalist right-wing groups head-on.[30] The early 1960s therefore saw spontaneous organization by young Jews who had begun to practice judo, boxing, and various other means of self-defense in order to cope with the provocations of anti-Semitic bullies. The Israeli embassy and various Israeli emissaries assisted in this organization. Some groups even considered undertaking retaliatory operations if necessary. The members of these groups talked of the need to challenge the stereotype of Jews as timid and cowardly which was prevalent among nationalist right-wing circles.[31]

The Argentine authorities began to receive exaggerated reports concerning such plans for self-defense, and were concerned – especially after shots were exchanged in mid-1962 between a group of young Jews and members of the federal police. Since the police officers were dressed in civilian clothes, were driving a Volkswagen rather than a police car, and did not identify themselves, the young Jews believed that the men were Tacuara thugs, and opened fire. One police officer was seriously wounded in the incident, two young Jews suffered light injuries, and seven were arrested.[32]

Jewish organizations in the US watched the anti-Semitic trend in Argentina with concern. The American Jewish Committee began to publish and denounce each anti-Semitic incident that occurred in the South American republic. From 1960 on, the Committee systematically briefed the State Department on anti-Jewish manifestations, and asked the US administration to try, through the medium of its diplomatic representatives and military attachés, to persuade the Argentine authorities to take active measures against anti-Semitism. The heads of the Committee also met with Argentine diplomats in Washington to discuss the problem. Representatives of the World Jewish Congress took similar action during 1962, and Rabbi Israel Goldstein of New York met with the US ambassador in Buenos Aires, Robert McClintock, for the same purpose.[33]

Senator Jacob K. Javits and Congressman Leonard Farbstein, the latter a member of the foreign affairs committee of the House of Representatives and of the subcommittee on inter-American affairs, soon joined them in their efforts. Both men expressed their concern about what was happening in Argentina and demanded action from US diplomacy. "There are times," wrote Farbstein, "when intervention [in the internal affairs of another country] is not only justified, but highly necessary."[34] In fact, toward the end of 1961 the State Department instructed the embassy in Buenos Aires to track the anti-Semitic incidents, brief officials in Washington, and make discreet use of this information whenever possible in order to show the Argentine authorities the negative international response that would be engendered by any increase in anti-Semitic activity by gangs such as Tacuara.[35]

The Sirota Affair and the Beginning of Large-Scale Emigration to Israel

Frondizi's feeble handling of nationalist activity did not help him politically. His enemies in the armed forces and the political right were merely waiting for the best moment to topple him. In the elections of March

1962, the Peronists, finally allowed to participate, made an impressive showing. They won a majority in ten provinces, including Buenos Aires, proving that they were still a political force to be reckoned with. The military, unable to tolerate the resurgence of Peronism, demanded that Frondizi void the elections. Initially refusing, he eventually intervened in five provinces, including Buenos Aires. However, the officers were not satisfied, and after bickering among themselves for a week, they finally deposed him. In his place they put the senate president, José María Guido, as interim president until general elections were held a year later.[36] The delight this caused the nationalist groups was apparent in the pages of *La Segunda República*, edited by Marcelo Sánchez Sorondo, and the articles by Father Meinvielle that appeared in the periodical *La Grande Argentina*.

Reports from the Israeli ambassador in Buenos Aires, Yosef Avidar, painted the picture of a new government struggling ineffectually with social and economic problems. At the same time a struggle was being waged within the army between two factions, the "Blues" (Azules) and the "Reds" (Colorados), the latter strongly anti-Peronist, suspecting that Guido meant to maintain Frondizi's policies. Thus, Guido's government lacked a civil and popular base of support, a socioeconomic program, or political legitimacy. However, what worried the Israeli ambassador still more was the fact that "with the new regime a number of reactionary, nationalist, and anti-Semitic personalities and elements have risen to key positions."[37] Indeed, the government leadership now included such nationalists as José María Astigueta, the education minister, and General Enrique Rauch, the interior minister.

Under these circumstances it was not to be expected that Guido's interim government would display any more efficiency than its predecessor in dealing with the organizations of the nationalist right, especially since some of their members had personal and family ties with senior army officers and government officials. Indeed the anti-Semitic wave did not subside. Time after time DAIA sent telegrams of protest to President Guido and the interior minister, Jorge Walter Perkins, and the latter met with the leaders of the Jewish community. However, the steps that the Guido temporary administration eventually took against the organizations of the extreme right fell for the most part into the category of too little and too late.

According to Ambassador Avidar, "It is clear that the nationalist anti-Semitic organizations, which guessed or even knew that the government or elements in it would be sympathetic to them as nationalists and anti-communists and would not oppress them, saw the right moment to begin a series of anti-Jewish attacks." In an interview with a reporter from the English-language daily *Buenos Aires Herald*, the leader of Tacuara, Alberto Ezcurra, said that the police did not bother his organization at all, and stated explicitly, "Under the present government we have been treated much better than under the Frondizi regime."[38]

A new anti-Semitic outburst followed Eichmann's execution in Israel around midnight between May 31 and June 1, 1962. The organs of the nationalist right used an extreme language to attack Israel and the Jews. For example, "a most extreme anti-Israeli article, with clear Nazi elements, worthy of the *Stürmer* tradition," appeared in Marcelo Sánchez Sorondo's *La Segunda República*.[39] But the nationalists went beyond newspaper articles. During that month about thirty anti-Semitic incidents were recorded in Argentina: demonstrations, telephone threats, terror attacks against Jewish institutions. The most serious incident was an assault on a nineteen-year-old student by the name of Graciela Narcisa Sirota on June 21. Sirota was kidnapped in the street while waiting for a bus to the University of Buenos Aires. A gray car containing three young men stopped beside her, whereupon one of the men got out, clubbed her, and dragged her into the car. They took her to a place where she was beaten and brutally tortured; her assailants burned different parts of her body with lighted cigarettes and tattooed a swastika on her chest. "This is in revenge for Eichmann," the kidnappers told her.[40]

When Sirota's father went to lodge a complaint with the police, he was treated with contempt and the investigation was conducted with an alarming lack of alacrity. Although the three kidnappers were quickly identified, and one of them even boasted of the revenge he had taken for Eichmann's kidnapping, the federal police chief, Horacio Enrique Green, suggested that the attack had been nothing more than an act of provocation by leftist Jews trying to undermine the social order in Argentina. He claimed that there were no grounds for exaggerated talk of anti-Semitism in Argentina, and that complaints of this sort were merely exploited by the communists. This was a new stage in the campaign to identify the Jewish community in general and DAIA in particular with communism.

Leaflets distributed by nationalist organizations questioned the tattoo on Sirota's chest. The heads of DAIA had foreseen this. Upon hearing of the iniquitous deed, they had immediately summoned a photographer to document the scar on the young woman's chest, and two psychologists, one Jewish and one Catholic, to talk with her, in order to forestall future claims that she was not sane or any other argument that sought to undermine the credibility of her testimony.[41]

Police commander Green explained his view that "the execution [of Eichmann] caused a reaction – justified or not – by a certain sector of the people, moved by a deep and purely nationalistic sentiment which assumed the form of hurt pride and was evidenced by means of a few anti-Semitic incidents." He also argued that too many people confused nationalism with fascism. "I myself am a nationalist. My country comes first even before my personal well-being. But I am not a fascist."[42] Other people claimed that "the Jewish organizations exploited these [anti-Semitic] attacks and made a big fuss about them in order to cover up the shady deals and economic crimes against the state that have been committed by Jews." This was again part of the effort to blame Jews for the economic crisis then prevailing in Argentina.[43] Speaking with President Guido, Green avoided denouncing the anti-Semitic thugs, and warned that DAIA and Maccabi should not "take the law into their own hands," since this would lead to "a confrontation with the racist groups," which would in turn result in "a serious breach of the peace."[44]

The press office in the presidential palace did hurry to publish, on June 25, a trenchant condemnation of the abominable act against Sirota in the name of the government, which undertook to use its legal powers to suppress incidents of this kind, since they damaged the social structure of the nation. Once again the old claim was trotted out that anti-Semitism was alien to Argentina and its tradition.[45] However, Tacuara was apparently a useful tool not only to the nationalists, but also to state bodies interested in suppressing communist and student activity – hence the indulgence shown it. The minister of defense himself, Leopoldo Suárez, declared in April 1964 that Tacuara enjoyed the support of elements in the police department and defense organizations.[46] "The expectations of the anti-Semitic organizations were justified," wrote Ambassador Avidar. "The authorities did their best to whitewash their actions, and to this day have not lifted a finger to bring those responsible to justice."[47]

The Argentine Jewish community was galvanized into angry, firm, and unified action by the appalling attack on Sirota and the police's indifference to violent acts committed against Jews. This action was the result of pressure from various elements in the community who were no longer willing to settle for quiet lobbying and requests for government protection, and who found added support in the public storm aroused by the despicable deed.[48] Others opposed the adoption of militant strategies in response, but they were now the weaker camp. The disputes as to what the Jewish response should be were complicated by the fact that some of those injured in the anti-Semitic attacks of the 1960s, such as Sirota, were communists or communist supporters. Some people said then that DAIA did not have to defend communists. However, most people believed that all Jews in Argentina should be protected regardless of their political views.[49] DAIA published sterner public declarations denouncing anti-Semitism; it sent telegrams to President Guido and to the interior minister Carlos Adrogué – who himself had once been a victim of nationalist right-wing violence – demanding that the government guarantee the safety of its Jewish citizens; it asked the Jewish communities and various institutions in the US and Europe for solidarity; and it organized a series of protests.

On June 28 a commercial strike lasting several hours was declared throughout the Republic, and many businesses bore signs reading, "Closed in protest over Nazi aggression in Argentina." Most of the Jews in Buenos Aires left their workplaces and closed their shops. Although the Jewish protest had been anticipated, the strike turned into an impressive show of strength, since, to the surprise of DAIA leaders themselves, the response extended far beyond the limits of the Jewish community; "Businesses closed not only in Villa Crespo, but throughout the Argentine Republic, from one end to the other."[50] Many secondary school students, Jewish and gentile alike, were absent from classes that afternoon. Political, student, intellectual, occupational, economic, and religious organizations, as well as many public figures, expressed solidarity with Argentine Jews in their struggle for a democratic regime and against racism and violence. The leaders of the community, wrote Ambassador Avidar, "stood their ground in the difficult and tense struggle against the chief of police and . . . the entire community showed unusual unity on the day of the strike."[51] Indeed, such a display of Jewish power had never been seen before, and would not be seen again for another thirty years.

Representatives of Jewish organizations all over the world increased their pressure on the Argentine government to put a stop to anti-Semitic thuggery. A B'nai B'rith delegation arrived in Buenos Aires in October and met with Guido and the ministers of the economy, the interior, and foreign affairs. The US embassy, which usually tended to downplay the extent and significance of anti-Semitism in Argentina, also approached the foreign minister in this matter. Efforts to organize self-defense increased, and dozens of young Jews carried handguns with them to the university lecture halls in case of violent clashes with young nationalists. In various community centers Jews organized systems of constant alert to guard against possible terrorist attacks.

Tacuara responded to the Jewish protest by publishing a pamphlet that was sold at newspaper stands in October 1962 in Buenos Aires, designed to prove "the provocation of the Jewish community," which had planned the Sirota affair in order to attack Argentine nationalism. In this publication Jews were presented as trouble-making leftists or avaricious merchants – in both cases dividing their loyalties and serving Zionist interests. In a well planned pincer movement, the pamphlet said, the leftist Jews would take control of Argentine universities and intellectual life, while the Jewish capitalists would take over the country's trade and financial life.[52]

Israeli diplomats expressed concern that the anti-Semitic propaganda was being absorbed by members of the government, army officers, and many others, adding: "Today we received the news that this argument, and the consequent anti-Semitic atmosphere, are gaining currency in the poor neighborhoods of Buenos Aires, which are populated mainly by the 'lumpen proletariat' that came to the capital from the northern regions."[53]

A study by the well-known Argentine sociologist Gino Germani, based on a sample of 2,078 male respondents in greater Buenos Aires, did in fact show that anti-Semitism was greater among the lower classes in Argentina than among the upper classes. This is not the place to address the validity of this sociological study, which contradicted previously accepted assumptions, but Germani's data indicate that some degree of anti-Semitism, whether "traditional" or "ideological," was detectable in all social classes in Argentina in 1962. These figures worried the leaders of the Jewish community, who tended to see anti-Semitism as a phenomenon that was limited to Catholic aristocratic circles. However, Germani emphasized that upper-class anti-Semites were ideologically motivated, and accordingly more likely to translate their views into actions. In the lower classes, in contrast, anti-Semitism was mostly traditional – a passive acceptance of stereotypes that did not necessarily have the same psychological significance as upper-class anti-Semitism did. Germani wrote about the fear that upper-class anti-Semites would try to exploit this "dangerous reservoir" of traditional anti-Semitism in the working classes.

The authorities finally began to rein in the nationalists to some degree just before the Argentine finance minister, Alvaro Alsogaray, went to the US to negotiate credit from US banks.[54] In an effort to improve Argentina's image in the US and to ensure a favorable atmosphere for its aid requests, the government pressed the extreme right-wing organizations to moderate their activity. Gradually the Guido government also began to arrest activists of the anti-Semitic right wing and to break up their demonstrations, in order to restrain their activity or at least create such an impression.

Yet contrary to the impression that the US embassy in Buenos Aires was (for reasons of its own, trying to create), the wave of anti-Semitism did not abate, as can be seen from DAIA's annual report to its board of directors.[55] By the end of October not even the US diplomats could deny the Guido government's weakness in dealing with anti-Semitic violence. Three attacks took place simultaneously on synagogues in Buenos Aires. Nationalists threw incendiary bombs and Molotov cocktails. Shots fired from a moving car, apparently carrying members of GRN, injured two young girls aged eleven and thirteen at the entrance to one of the synagogues. Ironically enough, these incidents occurred a few days after the Argentine government had assured the president of B'nai B'rith, Label A. Katz, that groups such as Tacuara would be outlawed, and just at the same time that the Argentine delegation was telling the UN General Assembly that the publicity concerning anti-Semitism in Argentina had been "grossly exaggerated."[56]

In any case, the multitude of anti-Semitic attacks in 1960–1962, coming on top of an economic crisis that injured the middle classes to which most Jews belonged, caused a considerable shock to the large Argentine Jewish community:

> The psychological implications of the events were much stronger than any political or practical aspect of the question . . . Among the elements which constituted that feeling were rage, bitterness, physical fear, disappointment, surprise, and also combativeness. The Sirota case, as well as several other events that followed later, was a tremendous shock, particularly to those Argentinean Jews born in the country and sometimes sons of native parents, for many of whom this was the first occasion on which they were compelled to meditate and ponder on their destiny as Jews and as individuals.[57]

The bi-weekly *La Luz* wrote in a similar vein in October 1962 in an issue marking the Jewish new year:

> For Argentine Jewry, the stormy year we have just left behind us was the saddest of the hundred years of its existence in this country. This intolerable situation has caused Jews in some circles to think that Jewish life may be impossible in Argentina . . . One thing is clear now: The beautiful ideal, enveloped in rosy expectations concerning the future, which the Jewish settlers brought with them . . . began to crumble with each Jewish child slashed with swastikas, each Jewish institution shot at . . . The painful dilemma is posed: Does the Jewish community have a future here, and is it worth it for Jews to continue living in Argentina?[58]

In the short term there was an increase in applications to the Israeli embassy and the *aliyah* (immigration) department of the Jewish Agency requesting information about emigrating to Israel. During the month of July 1962, following the Sirota affair, the number of applicants was much larger than in the entire first six months of the year. The same jump could be seen in the number of people who actually registered to emigrate to Israel.[59] After a mission to Argentina on behalf of the Jewish Agency, Moshe Kitron wrote:

> When the economic and social crises in this country escalated, giving rise to an outbreak of active anti-Semitism without any pacifying response from the authorities and democratic circles, the Zionist Jewish community's response was clear: increase *aliyah*, and put the *aliyah* process at the center of the public's concerns, in both theory and practice. Of course, the motive was not only Zionist awareness. At a time when reports were arriving from Israel about full employment and prosperity, the economic crisis in Argentina worsened; disappointment with the political parties and the government made the younger generation despair; emotional confusion and social disparities created a feeling of suffocation with no relief in sight in the near future; . . . the expansion of Hebrew education stimulated, for a

certain number of young people, the need for a full Jewish life that could be lived only in Israel.[60]

In the middle and long term the anti-Semitic incidents of the 1960s constituted a watershed in all sorts of trends in the Jewish community. Emigration to Israel became a permanent, practical option that Argentine Jews weighed and still weigh, and a growing need was felt to establish frameworks that strengthened Jewish identity. The year 1963, following the 1960–1962 wave of anti-Semitism sparked by the Eichmann affair and Argentina's economic crises, was a peak year in Jewish aliyah from Argentina. From the establishment of the State of Israel up to the year 1983, no other year brought such a large number of immigrants from this South American country.[61] The phenomenon of Jews leaving Argentina was even more striking if we include figures for Jews departing for destinations other than Israel. In the five-year period from 1960 to 1965, 12,900 Jews left Argentina. There had never been another period in the history of Argentine Jewry when emigration was so much greater than immigration.[62]

Thus the wave of anti-Semitism that washed over Argentina in the early 1960s actually became a unifying factor in the life of the Jewish community. It helped strengthen Argentine Jews' identification with the State of Israel, prompted an expansion of Jewish education and the creation of separate frameworks for it, stimulated organization for self-defense, enlisted general public opinion in a protest that went beyond the limits of the Jewish community, and increased emigration to Israel. These were the Jewish community's responses to the brutal offensive launched by Tacuara and the other nationalist and anti-Semitic forces that exploited Eichmann's kidnapping and the violation of their country's sovereignty as ideological justification for their own iniquitous actions.

Notes

This chapter is based on chapter seven of the author's *Argentina, Israel, and the Jews* (Bethesda, MD: University Press of Maryland, 2002).

1 *Documents on the Foreign Policy of Israel* 8 (1953) (Jerusalem: Israel State Archives, 1995), 248. On the Jewish aspect of Israel's foreign policy and on the intrinsic tension between the definition of Israel as a Jewish state and its role in the international arena as a state like any other that wanted to promote and safeguard specific interests see Michael Brecher, *The Foreign Policy System of Israel* (New Haven: Yale University Press, 1972), 233–44; Shmuel Sandler, "Is There a Jewish Foreign Policy?" *The Jewish Journal of Sociology* 29 (December 1987): 115–22.

2 On the kidnapping operation see the book by the former head of the Israeli secret service (the Mossad), Isser Harel, *The House on Garibaldi Street* (London: Frank Cass, 1997), as well as Zvi Aharoni and Wilhelm Dietl,

Operation Eichmann: The Truth about the Pursuit, Capture and Trial (New York: J. Wiley, 1997) and Peter Z. Malkin, *Eichmann in My Hands* (New York: Warner Books, 1990).

3 *American Jewish Year Book* (hereafter *AJYB*) 63 (1962): 474. On the characteristics and structure of the Jewish community in those days see Haim Avni, *Argentine Jewry: Social Status and Organizational Profile* [Hebrew] (Jerusalem: Ministry of Education, 1972); Irving Louis Horowitz, "The Jewish Community of Buenos Aires," *Jewish Social Studies* 24 (October 1962): 195–222; Daniel J. Elazar and Peter Medding, *Jewish Communities in Frontier Societies: Argentina, Australia and South Africa* (New York: Holmes and Meier, 1983), part two. For a pioneering study of the Jewish leadership in Argentina in that period see Haim Avni, "Jewish Leadership in Times of Crisis: Argentina During the Eichmann Affair (1960–1962)," *Studies in Contemporary Jewry* 11 (1995): 117–35.

4 Testimonies by Arye Levavi, Joel Barromi, and Natan Lerner, Oral History Division, Institute of Contemporary Jewry, Hebrew University of Jerusalem (hereafter ICJ/OHD).

5 Natan Lerner's testimony, ICJ/OHD, 10,21; and author's interview with him (Herzliyah, August 22, 2000); DAIA, *Informe de actividades realizadas por el Consejo Directivo (June 1961–July 1962)* (Buenos Aires: DAIA, 1962), 18; Confidential Memo, July 1, 1960, American Jewish Committee Files, Archives of the YIVO Institute for Jewish Research, New York (hereafter, YIVO-NY, AJC files), box 1; and Naomi W. Cohen, *Not Free to Desist: The American Jewish Committee, 1906–1966* (Philadelphia: Jewish Publication Society of America, 1972), 547–8.

6 Memo by Ralph Friedman (July 1, 1960), YIVO-NY, AJC files, box 1.

7 Author's interview with Korenhendler (Tel Aviv: August 21, 2000).

8 Eliahu Arel, "Public Reactions in Argentina in the Eichmann Affair," [Hebrew] *Ha'aretz* (June 15, 1960).

9 Confidential Memo (July 1, 1960), YIVO-NY, AJC files, box 1.

10 On the events of the Tragic Week see Victor Mirelman, "The Semana Trágica of 1919 and the Jews in Argentina," *Jewish Social Studies* 37 (January 1975): 61–73; Victor Mirelman, *Jewish Buenos Aires 1890–1930: In Search of Identity* (Detroit: Wayne State University Press, 1990), 61–7; Eugene F. Sofer, *From Pale to Pampa: A Social History of the Jews of Buenos Aires* (New York: Holmes and Meier, 1982), 42–8; and Beatriz Seibel, *Crónicas de la Semana Trágica* (Buenos Aires: Corregidor, 1999).

11 On the Eichmann trial see Hanna Yablonka, *The State of Israel vs. Adolf Eichmann* [Hebrew] (Tel Aviv: Yedioth Acharonot, 2001); Tom Segev, *The Seventh Million: The Israelis and the Holocaust* (New York: Henry Holt, 2000), part one, chapter one; *AJYB* 63 (1962): 3–131; Hanna Arendt, *Eichmann in Jerusalem: A Report on the Banality of Evil* (New York: Viking Press, 1963); and Gideon Hausner, *Justice in Jerusalem* (New York: Harper and Row, 1966).

12 On Frondizi's presidency see for example Celia Szusterman, *Frondizi and the Politics of Developmentalism in Argentina, 1955–62* (Pittsburgh: University of Pittsburgh Press, 1993); Daniel Rodríguez Lamas, *La presidencia de Frondizi* (Buenos Aires: CEAL, 1984); Isidro J. L. Odena, *Libertadores y*

desarrollistas (Buenos Aires: La Bastilla, 1977); and Emilia Menotti, *Frondizi: Una biografía* (Buenos Aires: Planeta, 1998). On the factors of anti-Semitism during those years see David Schers, "Anti-Semitism in Latin America," in *Violence and Defense in the Jewish Experience*, eds, Salo W. Baron and George S. Wise (Philadelphia: Jewish Publication Society of America, 1977), 247.

13 On Tacuara, its organizational roots and ideological characteristics, see McClintock to US State Department (April 18, 1962) National Archives and Record Center, Washington, D.C., USA, documents of the US Department of State, record group 59, College Park, MD (hereafter NARC-W), 735.00/4-1862; Hoyt to US State Department (June 13, 1962) NARC-W, 735.00/6-1362; *Mundo Israelita* (May 5, 1962); *Primera Plana* (Buenos Aires: December 4, 1962); Leonardo Senkman, "The Right and Civilian Regimes, 1955–1976," in *The Argentine Right*, eds, Sandra McGee Deutsch and Ronald H. Dolkart (Wilmington, DE: Scholarly Resources Books, 1993), 126–8; and David Rock, *Authoritarian Argentina* (Berkeley: University of California Press, 1993), 205–9.

14 Hoyt to US State Department (December 1, 1961) NARC-W, 735.00/12-161; and Juan José Sebreli, *La cuestión judía en la Argentina* (Buenos Aires: Editorial Tiempo Contemporáneo, 1973), 244.

15 Quoted in McClintock to US State Department (April 18, 1962) NARC-W, 735.00/4-1862.

16 On Julio Meinvielle see Graciela Ben-Dror, "Three Anti-Semitic Priests in the Catholic Church: Deviation or Norm?" [Hebrew], in *Society and Identity in Argentina* [Hebrew], eds, Tzvi Medin and Raanan Rein (Tel Aviv: University Publishing Projects, 1997), 231–67; Christián Buchrucker, *Nacionalismo y peronismo* (Buenos Aires: Sudamericana, 1987), 123ff.; and *New York Times* (August 21, 1962).

17 Jordán Bruno Genta, *Acerca de la libertad de enseñar y de la enseñanza de la libertad* (Buenos Aires: Ediciones Dictio, 1976), 36.

18 *Ibid.*, 286.

19 Quoted in Sebreli, *La cuestión judía*, 245; Yehuda Adin, "Nationalism and Neo-Nazism in Argentina" [Hebrew], *Be-tefutzot Ha-gola* 7 (1965): 75–9.

20 Quoted in Rock, *Authoritarian Argentina*, 206.

21 Weekly Report by the US Embassy in Buenos Aires (August 23, 1960) NARC-W, 735.00(w)/8-2360; *AJYB* 62 (1961): 216; *La Luz* (September 9, 1960); and *Chicago Tribune* (August 19, 1960).

22 Mónica Esti Rein, *Politics and Education in Argentina, 1946–1962* (Armonk, NY: M.E. Sharpe, 1998), chapter eight.

23 *El Mundo* (August 24, 1960); *La Vanguardia* (August 31, 1960); *Noticias Gráficas* (August 31, 1960); *La Luz* (September 9, 1960); and *Mundo Israelita* (September 10, 1960).

24 "Ante la indignación del país y la indiferencia de las autoridades," *Mundo Israelita* (August 20, 1960).

25 Weekly Report by the US Embassy in Buenos Aires (September 21, 1960) NARC-W, 735.00(w)/9-2160; McClintock to US State Department (September 18, 1962) 735.00/9-1862.

26 A. Monk, "The New Wave of Anti-Semitism in Argentina," (October 25,

1961), YIVO-NY, AJC files, box 3; Monk to Segal (January 11, 1962), YIVO-NY, AJC files, box 3; and Hoyt to US State Department (December 1, 1961), NARC-W, 735.00/12-161.

27 *Mundo Israelita* (December 2, 1960).

28 *Ha'aretz* (January 19, 1962). See also contemporary accounts in Jacob Beller, *Jews in Latin America* (New York: J. David, 1969), 179–81.

29 This concentration in Buenos Aires led to an extreme expression of both Jewish and Argentine living patterns, which influenced the development of organized Jewish life in Argentina. In general Jews tend to congregate in urban areas more than the general population in the country in which they are living, whereas in Argentina a substantial part of the population notably tended to concentrate specifically in the federal capital and its environs. See Elazar and Medding, *Jewish Communities*, 99.

30 Avni, "Jewish Leadership," 124–5.

31 Author's interview with Jacobo Kovadloff, who during the 1960s was vice president and later president of the Hebraica Club in Buenos Aires (Washington, June 14, 2000). This trend toward organizing for self-defense may have contributed to a certain drop in anti-Semitic attacks, as the perpetrators feared an escalation of violence in which they themselves might be attacked. See Schers, "Anti-Semitism in Latin America," 251.

32 Monk to Slawson (July 1, 1962), YIVO-NY, AJC files, box 3.

33 See Cohen, *Not Free to Desist*, 549; Rubin to Thomas C. Mann (August 29, 1960), YIVO-NY, AJC files, box 2; "Memorandum on Anti-Semitism in Argentina," presented to Woodward (November 13, 1961), YIVO-NY, AJC files, box 3; McClintock to US State Department (June 30, 1962), NARC-W, 735.00/6-3062; and Memorandum (August 22, 1962), NARC-W, 735.00/7-2662.

34 See Farbstein to Edwin M. Martin (July 19, 1962), NARC-W, 735.00/7-1962; Javits to Dean Rusk (July 27, 1962), NARC-W, 735.00/7-2762; Martin to Farbstein (July 31, 1962), NARC-W, 735.00/7-1962; and Dutton to Javits (July 26, 1962), NARC-W, 735.00/7-2662.

35 See Hoyt to US State Department (December 1, 1962), NARC-W, 735.00/12-161.

36 On Guido's nineteen-month term as president see Robert A. Potash, *The Army and Politics in Argentina 1962–1973* (Stanford: Stanford University Press, 1996), chapters 1 and 2; and Eduardo Crawley, *A House Divided: Argentina, 1880–1980* (London: C. Hurst, 1984), chapter 14.

37 Avidar to Israeli Foreign Ministry (July 27, 1962), Documents of the Ministry of Foreign Affairs, in Israel State Archives, Jerusalem (hereafter ISA), 103/1.

38 *Buenos Aires Herald* (August 29, 1962); *New York Times* (September 16, 1962); and McClintock to US State Department (September 1, 1962), NARC-W, 735.00/9-162.

39 Anug to Israeli Foreign Ministry (June 9, 1962), ISA, 103/1.

40 McClintock to US State Department (June 27, 1962), NARC-W, 735.00/6-2762; *Time* (July 6, 1962), 21; *Primera Plana* (March 10, 1964); DAIA, *DAIA, medio siglo de lucha por una argentina sin discriminaciones* (Buenos Aires: DAIA, 1985), 14; Leonardo Senkman, "El antisemitismo bajo dos experiencias democráticas," in *El antisemitismo en la Argentina*, ed., L. Senkman, vol. 1, 2nd edn (Buenos Aires: CEAL, 1989), 37–43.

41 Testimony by Gregorio Feigon, ICJ/OHD, 12–13; and Monk to Slawson (July 2, 1962), YIVO-NY, AJC files, box 3.

42 *Buenos Aires Herald* (September 5, 1962); *New York Times* (September 16, 1962); *Nueva Sión* (June 29, 1962); and McClintock to US State Department (September 10, 1962), NARC-W, 735.00/9-1062.

43 Avidar to Israeli Foreign Ministry (July 27, 1962), ISA. See the accusations by Brigadier Gilberto Hidalgo Oliva and the Peronist congressional deputy Juan Carlos Cornejo Linares, in Cornejo Linares, *El Nuevo orden sionista*, 24–5. The financial scandal linked to the Jews that received the greatest public attention involved the Banco Popular Israelita and the Todres brothers at the end of 1959. Máximo Yagupsky compared it to the Stavisky affair in France in the 1930s. See Yagupsky to Segal (November 25, 1959) and Yagupsky to Desser (December 16, 23, and 31, 1959, and January 9, 1960), YIVO-NY, AJC files, box 1. In 1962 the Central Bank of Argentina discovered irregularities in the granting of loans during the period of May 1961 through January 1962 when José Mazar Barnett was president of the bank, and again it provided fodder for anti-Semitic propaganda. See Monk to Slawson (July 3, 1962), YIVO-NY, AJC files, box 3.

44 *La Nación* (June 28, 1962); and "Cronología de la comunidad judía en la Argentina," *Todo es Historia* 179 (April 1982): 43.

45 Monk to Slawson (July 2, 1962), YIVO-NY, AJC files, box 2.

46 *Nueva Sión* (April 11, 1964).

47 Avidar to Israeli Foreign Ministry (July 27, 1962), ISA, 103/1.

48 *La Razón* (June 27 and 30, 1962); *La Prensa, La Nación,* and *El Mundo* (June 28, 1962); and *La Luz* (June 29, 1962).

49 Schers, "Anti-Semitism in Latin America," 250.

50 See interview with Gregorio Feigon, a leader of DAIA, in ICJ/OHD, especially 12–14; and DAIA, *Informe de actividades realizadas por el Consejo Directivo (June 1961–July 1962),* 8.

51 Avidar to Israeli Foreign Ministry (July 27, 1962), ISA, 103/1. The best and most detailed discussion of the Jewish community's response and the repercussions of the affair can be found in Senkman, "El antisemitismo."

52 Movimiento Nacionalista Tacuara, *El caso Sirota y el problema judío en la Argentina* (Buenos Aires: MNT, 1962).

53 Avidar to Israeli Foreign Ministry (July 27, 1962), ISA, 103/1.

54 On US Jewish organizations' pressure on the State Department and the Argentine ambassador in Washington, Roberto Alemán, for an end to the wave of anti-Semitism see for example Slawson to Martin (June 28, 1962) and Sonnabend to Alemán (June 28, 1962), YIVO-NY, AJC files, box 2.

55 McClintock to US State Department (August 21, 1962), NARC-W, 835.413/8-2162, and (August 23, 1962), NARC-W, 735.00/8-2362. On the arrest of young members of Tacuara and the dispersal of their demonstrations see McClintock to US State Department (September 13, 1962), NARC-W, 735.00/9-1362; (November 26, 1962), NARC-W, 735.00/11-2662; and (November 29, 1962), NARC-W, 835.411/11-2962.

56 Weekly Reports by the US Embassy in Buenos Aires (November 3, 1962), NARC-W, 735.00(w)/11-362, and (December 1, 1962), NARC-W, 735.00(w)/12-162; McClintock to US State Department (December 22,

1962), NARC-W, 835.411/12-2262; Hoyt to US State Department (January 31, 1963), NARC-W, 735.00/1-3162; DAIA, *Informe de las actividades (August 1962–September 1963)*, 7–8; and *New York Times* (October 19 and 30, 1962).

57 Quoted in Cohn, *Not Free to Desist*, 548.

58 *La Luz* (October 5, 1962); and Monk to Slawson (July 2, 1962), YIVO-NY, AJC files, box 3.

59 Avidar to Israeli Foreign Ministry (July 27, 1962), ISA.

60 Kitron, "South American Jewry and Its Problems," 163. See also his article "Immigration from Argentina in the Months January–June 1963," [Hebrew] *Be-tefutzot Ha-gola* (Spring 1964): 13–17.

61 Two later peaks in immigration from Argentina were 1973 and 1977, in the context of the political turmoil then shaking the country: Perón's return from eighteen years in exile and his victory in the presidential elections of 1973, and the establishment of a brutal military dictatorship in March 1976, which ushered in the era of the "disappeared" (*desaparecidos*).

62 Sergio Della Pergola, "Demographic Trends of Latin American Jewry," in *The Jewish Presence in Latin America*, eds, Judith Laikin Elkin and Gilbert W. Merkx (Boston: Allen and Unwin, 1987), 94, 99.

5 Deconstructing Anti-Semitism in Argentina

David Sheinin

For the Argentine military *golpistas* who overthrew the teetering government of María Estela Martínez de Perón (Isabel) in March 1976, the nation was poised to fight the first battles of a Third World War.[1] The testimonials of Alicia Partnoy, Jacobo Timerman, and dozens of others show that many of those in a position of power during the dictatorship (the *Proceso*) – from guards at illicit detention centers to high level military officers – incorporated a vicious anti-Semitism into those fantasy-ridden battles. While Jews represented some 2 percent of Argentina's population during the dictatorship, they accounted for as many as 10 percent of those disappeared.[2] Jailers told Blanca Brecher, a prisoner in Olmos jail, that she was tortured more regularly than other prisoners because she was Jewish. Inez Vázquez indicated that during her incarceration, pregnant women were generally not tortured. An exception was made in the case of Esther Herzberg because she was Jewish.[3] Timerman's *Preso sin nombre, celda sin numero* (Prisoner Without a Name, Cell Without a Number) had a dramatic international impact when it appeared in 1980 and again when its English translation was published a year later. A distinguished journalist with connections and friendships among highly placed Argentine politicians and military officers, Timerman was taken by surprise when detained, tortured, and imprisoned. *Prisoner* underlined the taunts and violence inspired by anti-Jewish sentiment that Timerman faced behind bars. Anti-Semitism was a constant in Argentina's detention centers and at the core of why the Argentine military tortured and killed. One guard kicked Timerman every time he passed by; the prisoner learned eventually that this was because the guard "can't stand Jews."[4] Timerman's captors questioned him repeatedly and under torture on what the journalist supposedly knew about an Israeli plan to invade Patagonia. The so-called *"Plan Andina"* was paranoid mythmaking that, according to then US assistant secretary of state for human rights and humanitarian affairs Patricia Derian, reached as high as the junta itself. But Timerman's jailers believed it to be true. These and other tortures Timerman faced undermined his sense of identity as an Argentine. For his jail guards, Timerman's Jewishness made him a subversive.[5]

Prisoner's exposé of how central anti-Semitism was to the military's internal war was not Timerman's only dramatic revelation. He wrote that he was "stunned – amazed, almost unable to encompass" what he began to understand as the passivity of Argentina's Jewish leaders in the face of the dictatorship's deadly attacks on Jews.[6] This revelation shook the international community almost as much as the charges of anti-Semitism themselves. For many Jews and non-Jews, Timerman's riveting commentary was their first in-depth look inside a violent South American dictatorship. Timerman was featured on the front page of the *New York Times Magazine* and in dozens of newspaper articles in North America and Europe. Pressure from Jews in the United States and many others forced the junta to release Timerman from prison. His citizenship revoked, the journalist was allowed to move to Israel. So important was his ongoing criticism of the military regime that the Argentine government mounted an elaborate disinformation campaign in Argentina and the US to try to discredit Timerman's claims. Not surprisingly in light of their silence over human rights abuses, many prominent Argentine Jews refused to give credence to Timerman's book.[7]

Though published six years later, Alicia Partnoy's *The Little School* also holds an indictment of the links between anti-Semitism, Argentine military ideology, and the violence of state terror. Though less convinced than Timerman of anti-Semitism as a cornerstone of military repression, Partnoy nonetheless notes anti-Jewish feeling among prison guards and the complicity of many Argentine Jews in the military's actions. "So many rabbis," she wrote, "thank God for the coup that has saved them from 'chaos.'"[8] A range of odd and chilling anti-Semitic tacks characterized the Proceso. The military combined the contradictory accusations that Jews were working for an international "Jewish capitalism" as well as an international "Jewish Marxism." There were cases reported of efforts to carve stars of David or crosses onto the bodies of Jewish prisoners. Swastikas and anti-Semitic slogans were routinely painted in detention centers. Like Timerman, other Jews in detention were accused of disloyalty to Argentina as a result of their supposed Zionism.[9]

The ambivalence of high-ranking officials in the *Delegación de Asociaciones Israelitas Argentinas* (Delegation of Argentine Jewish Associations, DAIA) toward the vicious attacks on Jews by the dictatorship can be explained by decades of entrenched institutional anti-Semitism in Argentina; for DAIA, not much had changed after the coup. The government placed limitations on the immigration of Jews to Argentina in the 1930s and 1940s. Jews were routinely barred from public office and from working as teachers. Anti-Semitic nationalist paramilitary groups attacked Jews during Tragic Week violence in 1919 and again in the

1940s. In the early 1960s, in the aftermath of the abduction of Adolf Eichmann by Israeli operatives, there was a renewal of anti-Jewish violence in Argentina leading to the death of a Jewish student. In the 1970s, before the coup, both right-wing anti-communist gangs and left-wing guerrillas identified Jews as their enemies. What DAIA did not anticipate was that while before 1976 there were limits on the anti-Semitism practiced by government and other bodies, after the coup such limitations vanished.[10]

The response of many Argentine Jews at the time of the coup may have mirrored that of some German Jews to Hitler in the early 1930s. Though the junta's references to its role in saving "Western Christian civilization" was unnerving for Jews, many convinced themselves that, as good Argentines, they were to be included under the umbrella of the "civilized." Ironically, despite a persistent DAIA refusal to condemn military officials, Marcos Resnizky, the twenty-two-year-old son of DAIA president Nehemías Resnizky, was kidnapped by the army in part for being the son of a "Zionist" leader. The elder Resnizky was quickly able to speak with US Secretary of State Cyrus Vance and Interior Minister Albano Harguindeguy on behalf of his son. But it took four days to win Marcos's release, by which time he had been brutally tortured.[11]

This episode did not end DAIA's refusal to take on the junta over anti-Semitism. In fact, relations between DAIA and Harguindeguy grew closer. In March 1978, for example, the polish author Marek Halter wrote in *Le Monde* that "Jews in France were more frightened than those in Argentina."[12] A furious Harguindeguy insisted that Resnizky write a refutation. "Jewish life" according to Resnizky, in response to Halter, was "free in Argentina."[13] In contrast to DAIA's silence, one Jew spoke out dramatically against the dictatorship. The American conservative rabbi Marshall Meyer had reached Argentina in 1959 and remained until 1985. Loud and uncompromising, Meyer made many in the Argentine Jewish establishment nervous. His sermons at Bet El synagogue in Buenos Aires featured regular attacks on military violence and drew Jews and non-Jews.[14]

The military imagined a Jewish enemy in a variety of forms. A disproportionate number of supposed subversives were Jews. There was a fantasy among some that Israel, and Jews abroad more generally, represented part of an amorphous and dangerous threat to Argentine sovereignty. This menace also supposedly incorporated Amnesty International, the Soviet Union, and French socialists among others. In addition, and like Nazi ideologues forty years earlier, the Argentine military highlighted the writings of three Jews – Einstein, Marx, and Freud – as dangerous to the fabric of Argentine society. The military targeted psychologists and psychiatrists with particular ferocity in the aftermath of the coup, many of whom were identified as Jews and, as such, a threat.

After the coup, for example, the psychoanalyst Eduardo Pavlovsky, for example, only managed to escape through a consulting room window during a therapy session, as armed men burst through the door to detain him.[15]

To be sure, though much of the dictatorship's anti-Semitism was paranoia inspired in part by longstanding racist assumptions among some Argentines, such sentiments also reflected in part the particularly strong opposition to the Proceso among North American Jews – in contrast to the passivity of some Argentine Jewish community leaders. As early as September 1976, before a special session on human rights in Argentina in the US House of Representatives, Burton Levinson, president of the Latin American Affairs Department of the Anti-Defamation League (ADL) of B'nai B'rith, reported that anti-Semitism was a factor in illicit detentions.[16] Argentine leaders resented and were afraid of American Jews in part because the latter were unrelenting and effective opponents. In the international campaign to undermine the dictatorship and to expose its brutality, there was likely no one more tenacious, more active, or more prominent in the media and in US political circles than Rabbi Morton Rosenthal of ADL – and Argentine leaders knew it.

ADL excelled not only at exposing how the dictatorship targeted Jews, but also in linking those acts to larger questions of human rights violations. Moreover, Rosenthal wanted it known how effective ADL was. He often made no secret of precisely how he interacted with US political leaders and Argentine officials. The result suggested, with probable accuracy, that ADL had at the very least contributed to influencing the dictatorship on human rights, and perhaps had been responsible for junta decisions on releasing prisoners or on other questions. On March 17, 1982, for example, Rosenthal wrote to ADL regional offices to report that, "Rafael Rey and six other prisoners on whose behalf we have intervened are now free men. The seven are part of a group of sixty prisoners who have been under a form of parole called *libertad vigilada* (supervised liberty). Now that their parole status has been eliminated and they are entirely free, Rafael Rey can be reunited in Israel with his wife and six-year-old daughter, whom he has never seen." As on other occasions, Rosenthal's memorandum not only identified this victory, but reported on contact with the Argentine Embassy in Washington, instructed regional ADL offices on reporting the news, and provided an update on other developments including that Argentine authorities had given permission to air the television series "Holocaust."[17]

ADL's vocal pressure on the junta was only one of many such actions by Jewish organizations and individuals across North America and in other countries as well. In Toronto, for example, according to the non-Jewish activist and Argentine political refugee Paulina Maciulis, many Canadians supported the work of the groups she helped to organize – the

Emergency Committee for Argentine Political Prisoners and Refugees and the Group for the Defense of Civil Rights in Argentina. But Jewish organizations were the only ethnic groups that played a significant role in pressing the Canadian government to act against the Argentine junta. Spearheaded in large measure by the reform Holy Blossom synagogue, under the leadership of Rabbi Gunther Plaut, many Canadian Jews and Jewish organizations worked with the Argentine refugee community. This link between grassroots opposition to the Argentine dictatorship and Jewish communities occurred in dozens of cities in Canada and the US.

If the opposition overseas among Jews to the junta was explicit, organized, and determined, the Argentine military's approach to Jewish opponents or perceived opponents was more complicated. It had a paranoid, anarchic, and irrational quality that was reflected in the experiences of Jacobo Timerman and other Jews, and that was evident in how the authorities attacked their perceived enemies more generally. But it also had a very methodical element that is the focus of the remainder of this essay. An anti-Semitic and exaggerated concern about foreign Jewish influences, particularly on US politics, informed and represented an important aspect of the dictatorship's growing obsession with foreign human rights pressures after the coup in March 1976. The belief among high ranking Argentine military officers that Jews in the US and elsewhere somehow controlled US economic policy and US politics toward Argentina helped prompt an elaborate defense of the state of human rights in Argentina that sought to discredit foreign critics, including ADL. Jewish pressures from other countries were closely, often inseparably tied to the larger question of how to defend against external criticisms generally.[18]

During 1976 and 1977, there was a constant escalation in foreign pressures on the Argentine junta over reports of widespread human rights abuses. These attacks came principally from governments in Canada, the US, and Western Europe, but also from non-governmental human rights groups like Amnesty International and the Canadian-based Inter-Church Committee on Human Rights in Latin America. Argentina's military rulers made these attacks a priority. They labeled them communist-inspired and described their activities in terms that suggested a concerted, conspiratorial attack on the nation. Intelligence reports characterized the campaigns overseas in favor of human rights activist Adolfo Pérez Esquivel and Jacobo Timerman as psychological operations. Argentine authorities responded through an increasingly convoluted combination of justifications, denials, and lies. Even as the military built a public mythology suggesting their supposed active support for human rights domestically and internationally, the generals entrenched a political culture of deliberate dishonesty and concealment.[19]

In international fora, the junta adopted several tactics to show Argentina to be pro-human rights. Like the government of Augusto

Pinochet in Chile, for example, Argentine authorities trumpeted their supposed commitment to indigenous rights, including the return of communal lands and water rights. At international conferences, the Argentine government took a vigorous interest in the rights of women. In July 1980, for example, at a meeting in Denmark, as many pregnant women were being held and tortured, the education minister of Corrientes province, Elizabeth María Sigel de Semper, announced that "as a result of their own abilities and their determination, Argentine women have achieved a situation of equality with men in all areas . . ."[20] Where possible, the military sought to project an image of itself as progressive and proactive on the question of anti-Semitism. In 1982, while many Jews avoided the military draft like the plague, the Argentine high command trumpeted its standing order granting leave to Jewish recruits on the high holy days.

Most of the Argentine military's defense-of-human rights regime was targeted at rebutting foreign claims of human rights abuses in Argentina. After the March 1976 coup, the first problem that reached the international stage was the thousands of refugees from military violence who crowded the embassies and consulates of Buenos Aires and other Argentine cities. By the middle of 1976, there were hundreds of foreign inquiries over what humanitarian actions the military might take to alleviate the situations of the asylum seekers. As early as July, the Argentine government recognized that it would have to develop a command center to coordinate the official response to foreign accusations on human rights. The command center would be composed of representatives from a number of ministries and government departments, based on the inextricable links quickly developing between foreign and domestic policies, and charged with explaining to foreigners the "real Argentina."[21]

In June the US State Department issued the first of many strongly stated diplomatic representations touching on a specific case, that of Julio Tiffemberg, detained by the military in the city of La Plata. The vice rector of the University of Chicago, whose brother was a high ranking Treasury Department official, was behind the request for information. Argentine officials believed fervently that it was no accident that this first major US intervention on human rights focused on an Argentine Jew. According to the junta, "important members" of the US Jewish community had passed on their alarm to the State Department, accusing Argentine officials of having hurled anti-Semitic abuse at Tiffemberg during interrogation. One Argentine officer tied the influence of the US Jewish community to banking in the US. It would be essential, he noted, that on the next visit of Argentine Economy Minister José Martínez de Hoz to the US, there be no animosity from US Jews.[22] This was the first of a series of incidents that helped convince the Argentine generals that the US Jewish community was intent on destroying Argentine military rule.

The Argentine sense that US and other Jews were somehow setting policy in Washington can be tied to a more generalized misunderstanding of how the Carter administration formulated human rights policy, ascribing too much significance to factors that, more likely, had little impact on thinking in Washington. In 1978, for example, Argentine military leaders distinguished themselves from their Chilean counterparts in several spheres. They believed wrongly that human rights problems counted less for Argentina than for Chile in the minds of US policy makers. They attributed this difference to *de facto* President Jorge Rafael Videla's support of Washington's signing of the Panama Canal Treaties; to what they believed was a more measured and dignified Argentine diplomatic conduct in international circles; and to there having been no Argentine equivalent to the assassination of the diplomat Orlando Letelier in Washington.

Beginning in 1977, US policy toward Argentina changed to reflect the Carter administration's emphasis on human rights. Argentine authorities moved to characterize the US policy shift and equivalent pressures elsewhere as communist-influenced and set about fabricating an international image of Argentina as a defender of human rights.[23] Amnesty International quickly figured prominently among identified enemies of the Argentine dictatorship. In November 1976, representatives of Amnesty visited Argentina to investigate allegations of massive human rights abuses.[24] In press conferences and a report that followed, Amnesty confirmed many of the worst suspicions held in the international community, that the Argentine military had embarked on a brutal internal war. Argentine authorities fought back with outright denials, reference to Argentine tradition, and legalistic obfuscation. The regime's first line of defense was the same as it was in the face of charges of anti-Semitism. It cited Argentine constitutional protections of individual rights and guarantees against excesses and arbitrary powers of the state. It also noted the country's adherence to the UN's Universal Declaration of the Rights of Man and the equivalent Bogotá Declaration for the Organization of American States, as though the signatures in and of themselves constituted a defense of human rights.[25]

In 1978, as a result of human rights abuses in Argentina, section 620B of the America Foreign Assistance Act (Humphrey–Kennedy Amendment) ended US military training programs in Argentina and the sale of military equipment. The Argentine government linked Jews to the amendment and even blamed Jewish organizations for Jimmy Carter's pro-human rights stand in Argentina. In reference to a proposed visit to Buenos Aires in 1980 by Maxwell Greenberg, Abraham Foxman, and Morton Rosenthal of ADL, a defense ministry memorandum highlighted the "intimate relationship between B'nai B'rith and the Human Rights bureaucracy of the Carter Administration." In response to a stated objective of the visit

– that the mission was to learn more about the state of the Argentine Jewish community – Argentine officials believed that this would be impossible. ADL had closed minds, firm positions, and was unlikely to learn anything. Moreover, the government worried that the proposed visit would likely generate conflicts within the Argentine Jewish community because ADL had repeatedly criticized Argentine Jewish leaders for downplaying anti-Semitism and had accused the Argentine Jewish community of collaborating with the dictatorship. The interior ministry reasoned that while the visit should be approved, the Argentine government should establish contact in advance with both the local Jewish community and the Israeli embassy to avoid a new round of negative publicity on anti-Semitism.[26] As late as May 1981, Foreign Minister Oscar Camilión wrote to Interior Minister General Horacio Tomás Liendo that the power of the US Jewish community in the US congress was such that the government should release Jewish prisoners from detention, including Deborah Benshoam and Natalio Mehlul.[27]

For their own purposes, Argentine authorities recognized the crucial distinction between the constitutionally defined legal process and the extra-legal, *de facto* actions of military units. They simply denied the existence of repressive processes outside of what was constitutionally and legally mandated. In 1980, the UN Working Group on Disappeared Persons strongly criticized the record of the Argentine military. The Argentine government responded only in very general terms, insisting that societal violence was the result of left-wing revolutionaries over whom the government had only been able to assert control in 1978, two years after the coup. Without that victory, there could never have been any respect for human rights in Argentina. In the meantime, according to the government, such terrorist groups and their allies were directly responsible for a campaign of misinformation about supposed disappearances.[28]

One of the most anticipated dangers for the Argentine dictatorship was the 1979 visit of the Inter-American Human Rights Commission (CIDH), which had received multiple complaints of anti-Semitic persecution and was determined to shed light on Argentina's most famous case involving human rights and Jews, that of Jacobo Timerman. Unwilling to risk further isolation in the international community, the Argentine military approved the mission, but immediately set about creating a false image of human rights in Argentina and cracking down on groups that might leak the truth to commission members. Argentine leaders worried about the specifics of the CIDH itinerary requests – including meetings with Timerman and ex-president Isabel Perón – as well as the potential ambiguities and surprises that the visit might hold.[29]

The military's initial panicked response to the commission included a proposal for an immediate Argentine initiative for an inter-American convention to make torture an international crime. Police and military authorities would immediately be instructed on how to better interpret international norms on human rights violations. Most hypocritically, personnel in each branch of the service were ordered in early 1979 to assess the cases of all of those detained in their respective custodies. Even as the junta was protesting foreign characterizations of the regime as systematically ignoring the judicial system, this review of cases – which was to conclude no later than May 1979 – would entrust officers in charge of those in illegal detention with determining whether prisoners were "innocent," "guilty," or "doubtful." Remarkably, the Interior Ministry instructed that those found innocent were to be freed immediately; the government was conceding secretly and internally that innocent prisoners were being held. Guilty prisoners were to be hustled into what the government identified surreptitiously was a corrupt judicial system; once "found" guilty by their military captors, these prisoners would then have their detention legitimized through condemnation by the courts on which the military knew they could count.[30]

The CIDH saw only what the government wished them to see. "In loco" visits proceeded only with commission members respecting Argentine sovereignty – meaning that they would not be permitted to question what Argentine authorities offered as evidence of the state of human rights. The visitors interviewed whomever they wished in federal or provincial police custody. This was meant to reinforce the Argentine military position that extra-legal detentions, executions, and torture did not exist. No military facilities or detention centers were accessible.[31]

Despite the Argentine military's preparations, the CIDH visit was a human rights success. On the eve of the commission visit, the UN Subcommittee on the Prevention of Discrimination and the Protection of Minorities voted 18–1–4 to condemn Argentina for human rights abuses in a report to the UN Committee on Human Rights. Argentina was the lone vote against the motion. Meanwhile, the CIDH met with a broad range of human rights activists in Argentine cities and, while carefully kept from the worst Argentine atrocities, issued a scathing condemnation of the regime in early 1980. The Argentine government reacted as it had in the lead-up to the visit. Officials from a number of ministries denied what they could. The foreign ministry claimed that the CIDH conclusions were wrong, that they reflected a dangerous interference in Argentine affairs, and that they jeopardized the functioning of the Organization of American States.

While we know that the CIDH repeatedly pressured Argentine authorities on anti-Semitism and the Timerman case, it is hard to know what role the visit played in helping bring about Timerman's release. The visit coincided with a supreme court decision on a petition of habeas corpus that paved the way for the junta decision to apply a loss of citizenship order to Timerman, and allow for his deportation to Israel. It is also clear that concern over Jewish pressures in the Timerman case overlapped with a more generalized worry about foreign influences. In January 1979, the state security and internal intelligence agency Secretaría de Inteligencia del Estado (Secretary of State Intelligence, SIDE) determined that the Timerman case was the most pressing issue in US–Argentine relations in the area of human rights. While SIDE blamed the "Jewish community around the world" for the campaign to free Timerman, it found that international pressure went far beyond the Jewish community, organized simultaneously in the US and Western Europe. As in other human rights related episodes involving Jews and non-Jews, Argentines saw a conspiracy against their country. They also worried about international perceptions of Argentina – as though, somehow, without these annoying episodes of human rights related critiques, the world would view the generals in a positive light – and the dangers posed by individual antagonists. In the Timerman case, SIDE singled out the work of *New York Times* writer Juan de Onís as particularly damaging, noting that he had abandoned his journalistic objectivity toward Argentina in his reporting of the Timerman case.[32]

Once Timerman had been released, the Argentine government tracked his activities and assessed his effectiveness through his contacts with Jewish organizations. Argentine intelligence observed in 1981 that the volume of such pro-Timerman material was declining. In mid-1982, SIDE charted Timerman's waning influence and effectiveness. It pointed out as well that in Israel, he was being attacked for his connections to the so-called "Graiver terrorist group" and for his "false pro-Zionism." "Timerman," SIDE reasoned, "has the support of only one Jewish group in the United States, that uses him to attack the Reagan government from the perspective of his old terrorist ties." It noted also that while working to promote his book *Prisoner Without a Name, Cell Without a Number*, he regularly tried to show that Jews were being persecuted in Argentina. "In this latter area," SIDE observed, "he has not achieved the desired result. In general each of the Jewish organizations in the countries that he has visited have rejected his accusations. Because of this, Timerman and his campaign will continue to wane quickly."[33]

The Argentine military watched for signs that its international propaganda suggesting a pro-human rights regime in Argentina was having a positive impact. SIDE reported enthusiastically, for example, on a breakfast meeting of the National Committee of American Foreign Policy on November 3, 1981 at which Rabbi Robert Scheiner spoke on the topic "Argentina 81." Scheiner had met with *de facto* President Roberto Viola and reported at the breakfast meeting that within twenty-four hours of his meeting with Viola, the Argentine government had released a satisfactory declaration condemning all forms of religious intolerance. SIDE also reported that Scheiner had praised the freedom with which the

Argentine media published the statements of the Mothers of the Plaza de Mayo and had pointed out that priests, pastors, and rabbis were regularly able to visit political prisoners in Argentina. Scheiner discredited Timerman pointing out that there was no connection whatsoever between Argentina and Nazi Germany.

Argentine authorities approved of the links between American Jews, the Reagan administration, and a thaw in US–Argentine relations at the end of the Carter administration. In May 1981, Argentine Foreign Minister Camilión reminded Interior Minister Liendo that any action that might be taken on behalf of Jewish prisoners Benshoam, Mehlul, and Norberto Liwsky, among others, would go a long way toward improving US–Argentine relations.[34] Relations did improve quickly. The Reagan administration pressed for and won the repeal of Kennedy–Humphrey. It based a decision to improve ties with Argentina on the CIDH having found no official policy of anti-Semitism in Argentina during its visit. Though the administration conceded that a disproportionately high number of Jews had disappeared during the dictatorship, this was due to their high representation in terrorist groups. Moreover, in 1981 Reagan took Viola's comments at face value when, before the Senate and House Foreign Relations Committees, he stated that he was aware of anti-Semitism in Argentina and was taking action against it.

In reference to a major human rights prize Timerman received from Columbia University, SIDE established that US diplomat Henry Schlaudemann had specifically announced that this private initiative would have no impact on US–Argentine ties, which were "excellent in all regards." The Argentines cultivated allies among fierce anti-communists in the US and elsewhere. In an April 1982 letter to the Argentine government, Oswaldo Hernández-Campos, the National Coordinator of the Cuban-American Conservative Political Action Committee, denounced a February appearance by Alicia Partnoy at Georgia Tech University. He also lamented that the US press was controlled by "leftist elements." "We will do all we can," he went on, "to defend your point of view."[35]

With the fall of military rule in 1983, the elected government of President Raúl Alfonsín set about reversing Argentina's sinister reputation on human rights. But both Alfonsín's administration and that of his successor, Carlos Menem, had problems closing the book on the country's authoritarian past. Alfonsín presided over both the prosecution and imprisonment of top dictatorship generals, but also agreed to the controversial Final Point and Due Obedience laws that allowed many more military repressors to walk free. In international fora, Argentine diplomats followed a cautious line that stressed a strong public opposition to racial or ethnic discrimination of any kind, but that reflected a pragmatic tendency to avoid any confrontation with the US. Menem's inability or unwillingness to solve the mystery of the *Asociación Mutual Israelita*

Argentina (Israeli Argentine Mutual Association, AMIA) bombing of 1994 reminded many of Proceso-era anti-Semitism. In one particularly poignant political inheritance from the last dictatorship, the Argentine government quietly fought a Jewish family in the 1990s over a violent episode from the dictatorship period. Under military rule, the Tucumán businessman José Siderman had lost his property to the military government under a brutal and unlawful seizure. More than ten years later, the Siderman family filed a civil suit in the US District Court for the Central District of California against the Argentine government for damages. The Argentine government quietly settled for six million dollars in 1996, but not before fighting the Sidermans and trying to discredit their claim. In one particularly unsavory strategy, the Menem administration tried to show that Siderman had in fact sold his Gran Hotel Corona to someone else before the military seized it. The Siderman family victory in a California court came in spite of the efforts of Argentina's elected government, not because of those efforts – a phenomenon that was perpetuated, as is seen in the next chapter.[36]

Notes

1 Daniel Barberis et al., *Los derechos humanos en el 'otro país'* (Buenos Aires: Puntosur, 1987), 42.
2 Marguerite Feitlowitz, *A Lexicon of Terror: Argentina and the Legacies of Torture* (New York: Oxford University Press, 1998), 90.
3 Edy Kaufman, "Jewish Victims of Repression in Argentina Under Military Rule (1976–1983)," *Holocaust and Genocide Studies* 4 (Fall 1989): 483.
4 Jacobo Timerman, *Prisoner Without a Name, Cell Without a Name* (New York: Alfred A. Knopf, 1981), 55. See also Federico Rivanera Carles, *Las escuelas judías comunistas en Argentina* (Buenos Aires: Biblioteca de formación política, 1986) and Matilde Mellibovsky, *Circle of Love Over Death: Testimonies of the Mothers of the Plaza de Mayo* (Willimantic, CT: Curbstone Press, 1997).
5 Timerman, *Prisoner*, 73–4; Diana Taylor, *Disappearing Acts: Spectacles of Gender and Nationalism in Argentina's "Dirty War"* (Durham: Duke University Press, 1997), 61–2. See also Ricardo Feierstein, *Contraexilio y mestizaje: ser judío en la Argentina* (Buenos Aires: Editorial Milá, 1996).
6 Timerman, *Prisoner*, 78.
7 Genaro R. Carrió, *El caso Timerman: materials para el estudio de un "habeas corpus"* (Buenos Aires: EUDEBA, 1987), 137; Ramón J. A. Camps, *Caso Timerman: Punto Final* (Buenos Aires: Tribuna Abierta, 1982), 26–9; Feitlowitz, *Lexicon*, 97.
8 Alicia Partnoy, *The Little School: Tales of Disappearance and Survival in Argentina* (Pittsburgh: Cleis Press, 1986), 63.
9 Kaufman, "Jewish Victims," 486–7.
10 Leonardo Senkman, "El antisemitismo bajo dos experiencias democráticas: Argentina 1959/1966 y 1973/1976," in *El antisemitismo en la Argentina,*

compiled by Leonardo Senkman (Buenos Aires: Centro Editor de América Latina, 1989), 18–23, 37–42.

11 Feitlowitz, *Lexicon*, 101.

12 Quoted in Feitlowitz, *Lexicon*, 101.

13 *Ibid.*

14 Feitlowitz, *Lexicon*, 98; Ignacio Klich, "Política comunitaria durante las juntas militares argentines: La DAIA durante el proceso de reorganización nacional," in *El antisemitismo en la Argentina*, 278–9.

15 Mariano Ben Plotkin, *Freud in the Pampas: The Emergence and Development of a Psychoanalytic Culture in Argentina* (Stanford: Stanford University Press, 2001), 219.

16 Feitlowitz, *Lexicon*, 100.

17 Rosenthal to ADL Regional Offices (March 17, 1982); Rosa Mery Riveros to Comisión Encargada de Pedir por los presos políticos judíos, Collection of Paulina Maciulis, Toronto; "Argentina's Jews: Days of Uncertainty," *Boston Globe Magazine* (November 29, 1981).

18 J. L. García et al., *Fuerzas armadas argentinas: el camino necesario* (Buenos Aires: Galerna, 1987), 45–53; Ernesto López, *Seguridad nacional y sedición militar* (Buenos Aires: Editorial Legasa, 1987), 55–77; Horacio Verbitsky, *La última batalla de la tercera guerra mundial* (Buenos Aires: Legasa, 1987); "Buenos Aires is the capital of the Aryan World . . ." *Canada/Argentina Bulletin* 3 (January–February, 1981): 3.

19 Asociación Madres de la Plaza de Mayo, *Massera el genocida* (Buenos Aires: Editorial La Página, 1998), 59; Lois Wilson, *Turning the World Upside Down* (Toronto: Doubleday, 1989), 91–2; Bill Fairbairn, "The Inter-Church Committee on Human Rights in Latin America," in Christopher Lind and Joe Mihevc, *Coalitions for Justice* (Ottawa: Novalis, 1994), 169–73.

20 "Discurso pronunciado por la Señora Elizabeth María Sigel de Semper, Ministra de Educación y Cultura de la Provincia de Corrientes," Argentine Ministry of Defense Documents (hereafter MDA).

21 "Proponer Establecimiento 'Unidad de Trabajo' Sobre Derechos Humanos" (July 5, 1976), MDA.

22 Carlos Keller Sarmiento, "Informar acerca comunicación telefónica con Embajador en Estados Unidos" (June 4, 1976), MDA; "Silencing Jacobo Timerman," *Washington Post* (March 31, 1979); "Argentina Spurns Plea to Free Liberal Publisher," *Washington Post* (April 17, 1979).

23 Wolf Grabendorff, "De país aliado preferido? Las relaciones entre la Argentina y los Estados Unidos: 1976–1981," in *El poder militar en la Argentina, 1976–1981*, compiled by Peter Waldmann and Ernesto Garzón Valdéz (Buenos Aires: Editorial Galerna, 1983), 157–61; David Pion-Berlin, "The National Security Doctrine, Military Threat Perception, and the 'Dirty War' in Argentina," *Comparative Political Studies* 21 (October 1988): 382–407.

24 Juan José Prado, *Derechos humanos: conceptos introductorios para su estudio* (Buenos Aires: Oficina de Publicaciones del CBC, Universidad de Buenos Aires, 1997), 24–5.

25 *Ibid.*, 155–63; Interior Ministry Memorandum (March 21, 1977), 102 MDA.

26 Morton M. Rosenthal, "Headlines and Footnotes: Free Timerman!" *The*

National Jewish Monthly (April 1979): 1–3; Foxman to President Roberto Eduardo Viola (November 18, 1981), MDA; Joel Barromi, "Israeli Policies Toward Argentina and Argentinean Jewry during the Military Junta, 1977–1983," *Israel Affairs 5* (Autumn 1998): 27–44.

27   Camilión to Liendo (May 5, 1981), MDA.

28   "Reunión con Grupo de Trabajo sobre Personas Desaparecidas celebrada el 18/9/80" (September 19, 1980), MDA.

29   CIDH, *Informe, 1976* (doc. OEA, Ser.L/V/II 40 doc. 5 del 11 de febrero 1977); Alberto R. Jordán, *El proceso, 1976–1983* (Buenos Aires: Emecé, 1993), 167.

30   Memorandum (1979) Ministry of the Interior, MDA.

31   "Aspectos Básicos para la Visita de la Comisión Interamericana para los Derechos Humanos" (August 1979) Ministry of the Interior, MDA; Elizabeth Jelin, "The Politics of Memory: The Human Rights Movement and the Construction of Democracy in Argentina," *Latin American Perspectives* 21 (1994): 38–58.

32   Poder Judicial de la Nación, Suprema Corte (September 7, 1979); Enrique López, Ministerio de Relaciones Exteriores (October 2, 1979); SIDE doc. 205 (January 16, 1979), MDA.

33   Centro Nacional de Inteligencia, Secretaria General, "Informe sobre la campaña que utiliza los derechos humanos (período del 21 dic al 30 abr 82)," MDA.

34   Camilión to Liendo (May 5, 1981), MDA.

35   Hernández-Campos, Memorandum (April 9, 1982), MDA.

36   Efraim Zadoff, *A Century of Argentinean Jewry: In Search of a New Model of National Identity* (Jerusalem: Institute of the World Jewish Congress, 2000), 18–19; Diego Melamed, *Los judíos y el menemismo* (Buenos Aires: Editorial Sudamericana, 2000), 151–77; Elena de la Cruz, "Presentan una demanda contra gobierno argentino," *La Opinión* (September 3, 1996); "For First Time, US Court to Weigh Claim of Rights Abuses in Foreign Land," *New York Times* (September 2, 1996); "ACLU SO California Announces Settlement in Landmark Human Rights Case for 85-year-old Tortured in Argentina's 'Dirty War,'" *ACLU Media Advisory* (September 13, 1996).

6 After the AMIA Bombing

A Critical Analysis of Two Parallel Discourses

Beatriz Gurevich

International terrorism is a category of transnational political disorder.[1] A political disorder is like "a wasting disease," said Niccolo Machiavelli. "To start with it is easy to cure but difficult to diagnose; after a time, unless it has been diagnosed and treated at the outset, it becomes easy to diagnose but difficult to cure."[2] Thus was the situation in Argentina when the second terrorist act during the presidency of Carlos Menem (1989-99) obliterated the building of the *Asociación Mutual Israelita Argentina* (Israeli Argentine Mutual Aid Association, AMIA), on July 18, 1994.[3]

This chapter documents the nature of the terrorist attacks in Buenos Aires and the role of corruption in the obstruction of justice. It also examines from a comparative perspective the demands made by the *Delegación de Asociaciones Israelitas Argentinas* (Delegation of Argentine Jewish Associations, DAIA) and *Memoria Activa* (Active Memory, MA) to the successive Argentine governments for justice. DAIA is the official political representative of the Jewish collective entity. Active Memory is a grass-roots movement created by victims' families that in July 1998 began demanding justice and denouncing the intentional deviations in the investigation of the AMIA bombing – every Monday at 9:45 a.m. in front of the Supreme Court of Justice of the Nation in Plaza Lavalle.

Argentina as a Target of Islamic Fundamentalist Terrorism

Islamic fundamentalist terrorism ceased to be a foreign phenomenon for Argentina on March 17, 1992, when Hezbollah, an armed branch of Islamic Jihad, claimed responsibility for the bombing of the Israeli Embassy in Buenos Aires.[4] The majority of Argentine civil society perceived and explained this attack as a transnational effect of the Middle East conflict, and as a result of Argentina's foreign policy during the Gulf War. On the basis of this conjecture many interpreted the bombing of the Israeli Embassy in Buenos Aires as retaliation for the killings by the Israeli Defense Forces of Abbas El Mousawi, secretary general of the pro-Iranian Lebanese guerrilla Hezbollah (Party of God), along with his wife and son. Indeed, in February 1992, at Mousawi's funeral, Hezbollah's spiritual leader, Sheikh Fadlallah, vowed revenge.[5]

"Demanding Justice"
Mirta Kuperminc was born in Argentina in 1955, and obtained her Masters degree in fine arts at the National School of Fine Arts in Argentina. She occupies an important position both in Argentine artistic life and in the local Jewish community. Active Memory selected her to create a monument honoring the victims of the AMIA bombing. The monument, "Demanding Justice," is located in front of the Supreme Court in Plaza Lavalle in Buenos Aires.

Not paying attention to what local and international experts and journalists pointed out, the Argentine Supreme Court of Justice in charge of the investigation of the act against the embassy overlooked the fact that Hezbollah had claimed responsibility for the bombing and constructed several capricious hypotheses.[6]

By 1996 the thesis subscribed to by the court was that the obliteration of the Israeli Embassy was a product of an "internal explosion." This thesis was sustained on the basis of an Argentine Academy of Engineers' report issued four years after the bombing. The report pointed out that the devastation was caused by the explosion of an arms cache in the basement of the building. In another odd twist, two of the Supreme Court judges, Adolfo Vázquez and Carlos Fayt, began investigating why some Israeli diplomats were poised to leave Argentina the night of the attack. The judges also suspected that Jewish extremists might well have carried out the act in order to thwart the peace process. The court also paid little attention to multiple accusations against the federal police for not investigating why the embassy's police guard was off duty and why the neighborhood police patrol was mysteriously unaccounted for at the time of the bombing.[7] There were other incriminating elements connected to the terrorist attacks to the Israeli Embassy largely overlooked by the investigation.[8]

Similar misleading mechanisms functioned in the case of the obliteration of the AMIA building. Immediately after the event, the CIA office in Buenos Aires asserted that Syrian authorities might have been behind this terrorist act, together with Iran. But soon enough US agencies began to divert attention from Syria, focusing exclusively on Iran. According to some analysts, this was due to the American and Israeli perception that Syria could be co-opted for the peace process. On the other hand, following the Syrian lead could have been embarrassing to the Menem administration, since revealing the details of Menem's previous dealings with Hazefal Assad and his regime would not have been flattering and might even have been incriminating.[9] Thus, not following the Syrian lead all the way was congenial to all parties concerned with the investigation, except to the victims' families. Due to the accusations against the misleading course of both attacks' investigations, the Argentine Congress created in July 1996 the *Comisión Bicameral de Seguimiento de la Investigación de los Atentados contra la Embajada de Israel y la AMIA* (Bicameral Commission for the Continuation of the Investigation of the Attacks Against the Israeli Embassy and AMIA; hereafter Bicameral Commission).[10]

After more than a year of work the report of the Bicameral Commission argued that, "the work of the Supreme Court of Justice of the Nation in its first stage was not what had been expected by any Argentine," and added that the Supreme Court's failure "left open the possibility for the second terrorist act in 1994." Although Hezbollah had already claimed responsibility soon after the 1992 bombing of the embassy, the court issued a formal statement holding Hezbollah responsible for the act in May 1999. This report was issued by the secretary of the court, Esteban Canevari, and it did not shed any light on a possible "local connection".[11]

The Local Connection

Taking into consideration that Jewish entities constitute a priori privileged targets for the armed branches of the Islamic Jihad, the inclusion of

Argentina in the map of Islamic terrorism might seem solely related to the visibility, importance, and demographic dimension of Argentina's Jewish community. However, both terrorist attacks examined here almost certainly have to do with an important local political factor of attraction.

When Menem took office in 1989, the leadership of the Argentine Jewish community and the Jewish Agency in Israel were concerned about the possibility of an upsurge in anti-Semitism/anti-Zionism, based on Menem's ties to Libya's president Muhamar Kahdafi, to Syrian authorities (Menem is of Syrian descent), and to members of the rebel army group, the *carapintadas*. These preoccupations disappeared quickly once Menem's international policy became clear. According to political scientist Carlos Escudé, Argentina's foreign policy under Menem underwent a "dramatic change." Argentina abandoned the Non-Aligned Movement, and aligned itself with the US; it changed its voting profile in international forums; and it adopted a clear pro-Western policy. Following these leads, the Condor II missile project was scrapped and the Tlatelolco Treaty for the prohibition of nuclear weapons in Latin America was ratified. Menem fulfilled an agreement with Egypt, sending the Condor II. [12] He did not, however, honor a commitment to deliver nuclear technology to Libya and other Arab countries. [13] At the same time, Menem distanced himself from leaders of the carapintadas. [14]

In his first press conference after the AMIA bombing, Menem pointed to the carapintadas as the local factor responsible for the terrorist act. Hours later, Minister of Defense Erman González rejected this possibility. [15] In August 1994, after denying his original statement, Menem denounced Iran and confirmed the existence of strong evidence that implicated Iranian agents – evidence that dovetailed with DAIA's findings that Iran bore sole responsibility. The Secretaria de Inteligencia del Estado (Secretary of State Intelligence; SIDE), the Mossad, and the CIA supported this supposition, although at first the CIA office in Buenos Aires asserted that Syrian authorities might also have been behind the terrorist act. According to Joe Goldman and Jorge Lanata, authors of *Columnas de Humo*, the Argentine government changed its accusations from Syria to Iran because this thesis was consistent with US interests in the Middle East. [16]

Actions and Reactions in Light of the Cover-Up

La denuncia, AMIA/DAIA's official report published in 1997, maintained that the bombings represented a part of the Middle East conflict, recommended investigating Monzer al Kassar, and diplomatically shied away from suggesting a Syrian connection. [17] *La denuncia* also indirectly recommended the need to investigate some local leads. [18]

By contrast, a 1999 report prepared by congressional deputies from *Acción por la República*, a political party headed by Domingo Cavallo, suggested that vacillating finger-pointing at Syria and Iraq showed "ignorance of the geopolitical alliances in the Middle East . . . [and that] The clear objective was to divert public attention away from any suspicion that [the Menem administration] was involved in the attacks." The report also implied a cover-up tied to concealing Menem's illegal campaign financing and his unfulfilled campaign promises to Arab countries as a key trigger for the bombings.[19]

Data gathered by the Bicameral Commission (1996–2000) confirms the euphemistic denunciations made in the 1999 report *La denuncia* while providing information on local Buenos Aires connections in the attacks. Judge Juan José Galeano and prosecutor Eamon Mullen went still further when they made it known that some local collaborators were police officers and members of the carapintadas. At the Campo de Mayo military base outside Buenos Aires, Galeano found evidence that army personnel had helped prepare the attack, providing explosives and intelligence.[20] However, neither Galeano nor DAIA seemed to be interested in following up on the "local connection," that is, the structure that provided the logistical support for the terrorists. This was in spite of the fact that evidence had surfaced showing that members of the Buenos Aires provincial police might have also participated in the attacks. In both federal and provincial police, corruption is endemic, and even some high officials are linked to drug trafficking and other criminal activities. Four of the twenty suspects brought to trial for participating in the AMIA bombing are former police officers, among them, Captain Juan José Ribelli, a high official of the provincial police.[21] With the approval of DAIA and AMIA, and some of the victims' relatives, the people who have been brought to trial are only a small part of the investigation. Active Memory opposed the institution of the oral trial for the AMIA case, fearing that it would become another failure and that it would result in the investigation's closure.[22]

1997: A Turning Point

One important effect of the AMIA attack was to shift the Jewish community to the center of mainstream Argentine politics. Just days after the bombing, on July 21, AMIA/DAIA invited all Argentines to a public demonstration outside congress. Some 155,000 Jews and non-Jews gathered to repudiate terrorism and impunity. Menem however was absent. His advisers and the leadership of DAIA had recommended that he stay away in order to avoid expressions of hostility. In light of the second attack, the failure of the court's investigation of the embassy attack was re-dimensioned. During the gathering, Rubén Beraja, who had become president of DAIA in 1991, spoke forcefully and addressed a broad and growing concern among Argentines that without a serious and professional investigation of the attacks, Argentina would likely remain a potential target for Islamic terrorism. He emphasized the need for quick and efficient results and added that this time there would be no tolerance for a second failure in the investigation.

Two years after the destruction of the AMIA building, in 1996, it became evident that DAIA and AMIA's leadership had softened their initial claims. However, while Jewish leadership seemed to avoid any confrontation with government authorities, Active Memory radicalized its position denouncing the increasing number of irregularities in the investigation being coordinated by Judge Juan José Galeano.

The public performance that took place at the third anniversary of the AMIA building's destruction reflected the growing dissatisfaction and even anger of important segments of Jews. On this occasion and in behalf of Active Memory, Laura Ginsberg spoke scathingly against the Argentine government and denounced the failed investigation of the bombings. At the same gathering Minister of the Interior Carlos Corach, himself a Jew, was heckled. Beraja was forced to pocket his prepared speech and improvise a tough condemnation of Iran. Thousands in the audience repudiated his words by turning their backs to the podium.[23] Until 1997, the proximity of DAIA and AMIA's leadership to the government both in discourse and action seemed to be accepted by the Jewish actors as an adequate means of pursuing the investigation. The exception to this were those people who had inside information that Beraja's conduct might have been related to the compromises derived from his bank position and to the fact that in Argentina banks are very dependent on political factors. The growing perception about Beraja's dual relationship with President Menem and Minister of Interior Carlos Corach led to increasing public expressions of disapproval, as seen in the meeting of July 18, 1997.[24] Although he had been publicly repudiated, Beraja declared on radio only three months after the commemoration ceremony that he was "pleasantly surprised by the intensity of the work and the direction the investigation had taken."[25]

With the publishing of AMIA/DAIA's report *La denuncia* the authors meant to offset Argentine Jewish dissatisfaction with both organizations' weak response to the inadequate judicial proceedings in the wake of the bombings. But the report had no such impact because although it provides some important data, by the time it was published Argentine Jews were well aware that DAIA had overlooked the compelling denunciations made by prestigious local and international actors, among them Active Memory and Rabbi Avi Weiss, Senior Rabbi of the Hebrew Institute of Riverdale and National President of the Coalition for Jewish Concerns, who had spoken at a Hearing before the Committee on International Relations of the US House of Representatives in September 1995.[26] In 1997, many suspected that the leadership of DAIA/AMIA knew and silently accepted the government's efforts to stonewall the investigation. Such perceptions produced many conflicts among the victims' families and inside the Jewish collective entity. Thus, the gathering in commemoration of the third anniversary of the attack, on July 18, was a turning point. Previous to the gathering, victims' families had endorsed the speech that Laura Ginsberg would read in the name of the Active Memory. After the commemoration, however, in light of the government's reaction, DAIA/AMIA's leadership tried to "discipline" the members of Active Memory by stating that speeches like Ginsberg's weakened the possibility of a thorough investigation.

Days after the third anniversary, through Corach, the government invited Beraja and the president of AMIA, Oscar Hansman, to go to the Casa Rosada, the presidential office building, and apologize publicly for Ginsberg's speech. Beraja and Hansman accepted the "invitation," went to the meeting with Corach, and gave testimony to the press stating their disagreement with the speech. This laid the groundwork for a deep conflict between AMIA/DAIA, which had praised Judge Galeano's work, and Active Memory, which had been systematically denouncing the investigation's irregularities at the Monday morning gatherings in front of the Supreme Court. As a result of the pressure coming from the leadership of DAIA and AMIA and in order to preserve what is known as "community unity," some of the victims' families opted to leave Active Memory and created a new group with the name *Familiares y Amigos de las Víctimas* (Families and Friends of the Victims, FFOV), which showed its identification with the Jewish organizations.[27]

Active Memory persevered in its criticism. In July 1999, the organization accused the Argentine government before the Inter-American Commission of Human Rights (CIDH) of the Organization of American States for its non-investigation of the attacks. Validating Active Memory's charges against Galeano's investigation, the CIDH appointed jurist Claudio Grossman, president of the commission, as observer of the oral trial.[28]

Local and International Networks and Legal Practices

In framing new strategic alliances, Menem's administration considered it important to build transnational political networks with international organizations and agencies that could become significant political interlocutors for lobbying activities. With this aim the government strengthened its links with the leadership of Argentina's main Jewish organizations, especially DAIA, in the hope that the latter might function as a bridge with international Jewish organizations, especially in the US. At the same time, DAIA had been undergoing a deep transformation since Beraja's advent to the presidency in 1991. Under Beraja's strong and decisive leadership, DAIA expanded its role in civil society through increased participation in various initiatives with the aim of promoting greater tolerance toward ethnic and religious differences. For example, DAIA encouraged the government to create the *Instituto Nacional contra la Discriminación* (National Institute Against Discrimination, INADI) and is a member of the agency.[29] But the bombing of AMIA altered in a deep and contradictory manner the dynamic that ruled the relationship between the Jewish organizations and the Menem administration.

In 1995, during a conference on terrorism held in AMIA's educational center, the US State Department's Counter Terrorism Coordinator, Philip Wilcox, went one step further suggesting what many Argentines already understood, that transnational crimes could not be solved at the local level. DAIA urged the government to adjust to global standards in matters of security.[30] As early as August 1994, before the hearing of the Human Rights Sub-Committee of the US House of Representatives, Beraja in the name of DAIA had asked the US Congress for help in investigating the AMIA attack. He highlighted the "transcendent threat of international terrorism" and signaled the importance of legislative measures in Argentina in combating terrorism. He also asked for sanctions against countries that sponsored terrorism and praised Menem's security measures on behalf of Jewish organizations. In an effort to stress the anti-Semitism at the root of the AMIA bombing and the menace of international terrorism, Beraja emphasized the importance of cooperation between Argentina's SIDE and the security agencies of other countries. He also pointed out that the UN Security Council Resolution had not mentioned that the terrorist act had "wounded the core of Jewish life in Argentina."[31]

Here and in other contexts, DAIA's discourse was consistent with the ideological orientation underlying transformational processes in Argentina. Menem, of Peronist origin, came to deny his ideological origins and embarked on an overwhelming program of state reform in the best neo-liberal way. Following this lead, Argentina aligned with the US on Iran and international terrorism, and with Israeli interests in the Middle East. In 1994, DAIA began to stress the importance of tighter controls over the "triple border" area of Puerto Iguazú (Argentina), Foz de Iguazú (Brazil), and Ciudad del Este (Paraguay), where foreign security services had found "dormant" Islamic terrorist cells and where terrorists could easily move back and forth across frontiers.[32] Corach corroborated this information. In September 1995, the chief of intelligence services for the Paraguayan federal police recognized that Ciudad del Este was a Hezbollah sanctuary and that the "triple border" was the main drug trafficking and money-laundering center for the region.[33]

To encourage Southern Cone governments to fight international terrorism, Beraja attended a hearing of the US House Foreign Affairs Committee on September 25, 1995. At the hearing, Philip Wilcox stressed the determination of the Argentine government to solve the Buenos Aires bombings. Beraja and Wilcox attributed poor investigation results until that point to poor coordination among Argentine security and intelligence networks and to the lack of cooperation on the part of the provincial police. Beraja told members of congress that the terrorists responsible for the second blast had to have secured support from "diplomatic personnel or individuals linked with the Iranian Embassy in Buenos Aires." One of the "cells of activists identified with Islamic fundamentalism that had been established in Argentina" probably played an important role in the attack. Provincial police "involved in the illegal dealing of cars" were "accessories," and Ciudad del Este "constituted a center of support of fundamentalist terrorism in Latin America." For Beraja all of this constituted a network about which SIDE had important evidence.[34]

At the same meeting, Warren Eisenberg, deputy director of the Center for Public Policy of B'nai B'rith, joined Beraja in praising Judge Galeano's work as coordinator of the investigation. Following the Gallic system of law, Galeano was empowered to gather information and to prosecute. But Rabbi Weiss spoke out against Beraja's position, and went much further. He denounced the Argentine government as "stonewalling the investigation and [argued] that a cover-up operation was taking place." Weiss had collected evidence that, "Menem employed many people with extreme right-wing or neo-Nazi views or criminals with murderous pasts in the state intelligence service, people with notorious backgrounds like Pascual Oscar Guerrieri, a repressor during the last military dictatorship (1976–83), [who had been] appointed by Menem as an adviser to SIDE . . . One cannot expect individuals with this kind of view," Weiss went on, "to carry out a serious investigation into either bombing . . . " Weiss also pointed out the complicity of the *Dirección Nacional de Migraciones* (National Bureau of Migration, DNM). In January 1990, the "Syrian terrorist Monzer Al Kassar – linked to *Achille Lauro*'s hijacking – had been permitted to enter Argentina by [Aurelio Carlos] Martines [alias ZAZA], a former member of the *Escuela de Mecánica de la Armada* (Naval Mechanics School, ESMA), and the director of immigration." Thus, Monzer al Kassar is possibly a crucial yet never-fully-investigated link between Syria, Menem's unfulfilled promises to Hafez al Assad, the terrorist attacks, money laundering, and perhaps other arms-trafficking-related scandals of the Menem administration. Al Kassar was even granted Argentine citizenship during Menem's tenure, allegedly upon the initiative of the president himself. Years later, multiple facts corroborated the denunciations made by Weiss during the hearing. Weiss also complained that there had been no meaningful investigation of the order to embassy and AMIA police guards to abandon their posts before each attack. He denounced Beraja's defense of Galeano and Menem: "It was clear from the very beginning of the AMIA investigation that the police had one preferred lead – Iran, and that they were not going to give serious consideration to other leads that would embarrass the Menem government."[35]

The words, "Esta es la casa" (This is the house), refer to the AMIA building
Clorindo Testa was born in Naples, Italy, in 1923, and graduated in architecture from the University of Buenos Aires in 1948. Among the many buildings whose design he has been a part of is the Argentine Hebrew Society (1994-95). His sculptures include "La Casa," constructed out of some debris of the AMIA building that was not carted away.

Active Memory's criticisms – backed by the Center for Legal and Social Studies (CELS), the Center for International Justice and Law (CEJIL), and its legal representatives, Alberto Zuppi and Pablo Jacoby – are similar to those of Weiss. Active Memory had sued the Menem administration through the CIDH of the OAS for having violated the right to justice of the AMIA victims and their relatives, and accused the Argentine government of ignoring an important warning from a Brazilian agent in Italy,

Wilson Dos Santos. In 1993, Dos Santos alerted the Argentine Consulate in Milan to the possibility of a second terrorist act in Argentina. In the first days of 1994, Dos Santos warned the Argentine Consulate in Milan a second time about the possibility of an attack. At the time, Dos Santos also visited the Brazilian and Israeli diplomatic missions. The Argentine Consul, Norma Fassano, admitted that she was warned in July 1994 by Dos Santos. Fassano passed the warning along to the Argentine Foreign Ministry on July 19, a day after the bombing, adding that Dos Santos had disappeared.[36] In March 1994, Robert Gelbard, Assistant Secretary for International Narcotics matters of the US State Department, expressed concern that the permeability of Argentine borders could facilitate possible attacks by fundamentalist groups.[37] The Argentine government paid little attention to these successive alerts.[38]

Active Memory further charged that by failing to properly investigate the attacks, the Argentine government had lost and destroyed evidence. Rubble from the explosion, for example, had not been saved. Extracted with power drills immediately after the attack, the ruins of the AMIA building were tossed into dump trucks along with destroyed car parts and human remains, later used as landfill along the coast of the Rio de la Plata. Police and judicial authorities ignored many clues. Witnesses to the AMIA bombing were summoned to give statements only some days after the act. The police claimed that the witnesses had been difficult to locate; however, Active Memory had been able to find addresses for each of the bombing witnesses immediately and without difficulty. Active Memory's most damning accusation was that SIDE tampered with the investigation while DNM simply refused to cooperate. Judge Galeano inexplicably "lost" crucial evidence in the case. Police officers arrested during the investigation were supposed to have been held incommunicado, unable to communicate outside of the prison. They were not. Although the government designated funds as a reward for information leading to the arrest and prosecution of anyone associated with the bombing, the information was never made public.

On September 7, 1999, CIDH accepted Active Memory's presentation and urged the Argentine government to answer the charges. Active Memory has been gathering strength since its formation in 1994, and especially after the rupture with DAIA/AMIA in 1997. It has now become an important moral force and an outspoken critic of the poor investigation of the terrorist acts. Hundreds of intellectuals, artists, journalists, and human rights activists have denounced the irregularities of the judicial investigation and the responsibility of the Argentine state in the organization's weekly gatherings in front of the Supreme Court. In 2001, on the eve of the trial against the twenty persons accused in the AMIA bombing, Raul Kollmann, perhaps the journalist most familiar with the investigation of the bombing of AMIA, reflected that "the real problem is that the

Argentine government was never interested in solving the case. At times, only fifteen to twenty people were assigned to the case, while after the Oklahoma City bombing 5,000 law enforcement officials were deployed right away. The US sent over 1,500 agents to Africa after the bombing of the embassies in Tanzania and Kenya. Those agents interrogated 10,000 witnesses in four days. In Argentina, witnesses are still waiting to be called. And it took over three years to put together a 100-person team of investigators that never functioned properly."[39]

As time passed with no results from the investigation, confrontations and controversies inside the Jewish community grew. The groups that represent the victims' families added to the argument over the pace of the investigation, and over what style of relationship Jewish organizations should have with the government. Two camps emerged. The AMIA/DAIA camp supported a close relationship with the successive governments and approves up to the present time the way in which Judge Galeano coordinated the investigation. Together with AMIA/DAIA, the FFOV is one of the three complainants in the joint accusation before the judiciary. After having praised Judge Galeano's work for almost ten years, the FFOV is now calling, in 2004, for the impeachment of the judge for allegedly participating in paying off Telleldín. The Active Memory camp has criticized successive Argentine governments since July 1997 for their responsibility in stonewalling the investigation and made precise accusations that certain people are responsible for the cover-up. In 1999, Active Memory brought a legal case against Galeano and his investigation. The organization decided not to participate with AMIA, DAIA, and FFOV in their joint accusation presented to the judiciary. The judges of the oral trial authorized an independent accusation, given that Active Memory's accusations point in a direction different from those of DAIA/AMIA and FFOV. The reports of the Bicameral Commission and Acción por la República are congruent with Active Memory's point of view.

Why Did the Investigation Fail?

In an interview published by the *Miami Herald* on April 17, 1997, Carlos Escudé, a member of the Academic Committee of Proyecto Testimonial, argued that Beraja, as president of a Buenos Aires bank, was too dependent on government goodwill to be a trustworthy activist for DAIA: "If I were a shareholder of his bank, [said Escudé] I would applaud, but it is a definite conflict of interest."[40] After the failure of *Banco Mayo* in 1998, it became known that Beraja's bank had received special aid from the *Banco Central de la República Argentina* (BCRA), when the sequence of bank failures began. At present, Beraja is in prison and is being prosecuted by the *Sala* I of the *Cámara Federal,* a federal court, on charges of having co-authored the crimes of fraud through unfaithful administration and jeopardy of public administration.[41] With the intention of defending himself, Beraja presented a legal charge against the former president of BCRA, Pedro Pou, accusing him of anti-Semitism. In fact, Pou's intolerance toward religious and ethnic diversity was evident, but the BCRA decision to close Beraja's bank seemed to have had nothing to do with Pou's ideology. Even after leaving his position in DAIA, Beraja continued with his traditional practice of intermingling personal with institutional affairs at every opportunity. In 1998 Beraja chose Marta Nercellas, DAIA's lawyer in the case of the AMIA bombing, as his personal lawyer, to defend him from the accusations of illegal practices that permeated the financial operations in the bank and of leading it to failure.[42]

Since the bombing, all the promises of a thorough investigation made by the successive Argentine governments were broken. Carlos Menem (1989–98) and Fernando De la Rúa (1999–2001) seemed to have been stonewalling the investigation. When Fernando De la Rúa reached the presidency in December 1999, he promised a swift resolution of the AMIA affair, but the policy of concealment continued. The chief of the Unit of Investigation of the Attacks in the Ministry of Justice, Nilda Garré, fostered the investigation diligently after 2000. However, she was forced to resign in 2001 after DAIA complained about her belief in the importance of the information provided by an anonymous witness (named "C") who was a repentant chief of Iranian intelligence. DAIA argued that Garré had damaged the investigation by revealing that the witness charged that members of Menem's government, even the president himself, received $10 million to protect Iran from being investigated. Instead, AMIA's authorities invited Garré to a conversation with the aim of listening to her observations on the topic. What Garré said in 2001 was no news; it was already published in 2000. Generally, Garré's opinions disturbed Jorge De la Rúa, minister of justice and brother of the president. She publicly maintained that police logbooks had been altered and electronic address books and planners of various suspects erased as part of an official cover-up. In an interview, Garré pointed out that, "Not only has there been no support for getting to the bottom of this case, you can also say [referring to an article by journalist Larry Rother] that some government organs have actively sabotaged the investigation." She added "State intelligence and the federal police are clearly involved . . . but there is also evidence pointing to the involvement of agencies ranging from Immigration to the Foreign Ministry."[43] Active Memory took seriously Garré's opinions and hoped that she would open classified documents considered important for the investigation by Active Memory's lawyers, Pablo Jacoby and Zuppi. During Eduardo Duhalde's (2002–3) presidency SIDE issued a report pointing out that Hezbollah was responsible for the attacks against the

Israeli Embassy and AMIA, and it made no progress on the "local connection." In April 2003, Nestor Kirchner was elected president of Argentina. Since he took office in May, he has stated that the investigation of both terrorist acts would be treated as a "state problem." Although it is impossible to predict the future results of the investigation, the substantive difference between Kirchner's administration and the previous ones is that his government concretely shows that the investigation of the AMIA bombing is a matter of state and not the problem of an ethnic and religious group living in Argentina. Following these leads, on June 5, 2003, Kirchner promulgated a decree opening files of SIDE that might have some relation to the terrorist acts and authorized intelligence agents to give testimony in the oral trial. Duhalde had rejected a request to open the files and presented a report of dubious importance.

A retrospective view of the ten years that have passed since the bombing show that DAIA failed to represent the legitimate interests of its constituency and AMIA silently went along with DAIA's policy. After Beraja had to leave office in 1998, Rogelio Cichowolsky, widely regarded as Beraja's right-hand man, was elected president of DAIA. A sizable bloc of community organizations represented under the group's umbrella organization contested the election and have effectively seceded from DAIA. After the vote was taken, several major organizations said they would not take their seats on DAIA's executive council. The Hebraica Association, DAIA's largest constituent group, called Cichowolsky's election "irregular" and issued a statement supporting its own president, Gilbert Lewi, who quit the executive council in protest over the vote. Cichowolsky was elected under a system in which all organizations, regardless of size, have one vote. As a result, Hebraica's 50,000 members have the same weight as a 50-member group in the provinces. After José Hercman succeeded Cichowolsky it was clear that the organization would continue with the same orientation and practices. Hercman was one of DAIA's vice-presidents since the time of the AMIA attack and one of Beraja's most trusted collaborators. At the present time, the confrontations inside DAIA's executive committee are the tip of the iceberg that reflect the individual and collective Jewish actors' concrete demands and disagreements with DAIA/AMIA's continuation of the investigation coordinated by Judge Galeano, and the discrepancies about the work of Martha Nercellas, the lawyer representing DAIA.

On May 12, 2004, Gilbert Lewi, former president of Hebraica, became president of DAIA. As soon as he took office, Lewi asked DAIA's executive committee to make a public self-criticism and to ask for the resignation of Martha Nercellas, the legal representative of DAIA in the oral trial. Lewi pointed out that there is a conflict of interest in representing DAIA and at the same time representing Beraja, who was prosecuted and put into prison for fraud and illegal activities. Beraja is perceived by most Jewish actors as having obtained personal benefits for overlooking the stonewalling of the investigation and the cover-up of those truly responsible during Menem's government.[44] For the same reason, most people disagree with Nercellas when she argues that Beraja's imprisonment is a matter of anti-Semitism.[45]

Conclusions and Questions

The rational terrorist thinks through his goals and options, adopting a cost-benefit analysis. He weighs the defensive characteristics of a target against his own ability to attack, and in the case of transnational operations he evaluates the possibility of local tactical support and greater impunity. Terrorists chose Argentina twice in relatively close succession. Hezbollah claimed responsibility for the embassy bombing. Both attacks took place during Menem's presidency. All of this suggests that Menem's unfulfilled pre-electoral promises to Arab countries might have contributed significantly to Argentina having been targeted. At the same time, what facilitated the second bombing was what Jean Cartier-Bresson calls "corruption networks" that are "structured in a clandestine manner by mobilizing multiple 'resources,' such as financial interests, obedience to hierarchy, solidarity, family, and friends."[46] Such networks, when tied to officials within the Menem administration, to members of the security and intelligence agencies, and to the absence of judicial independence, facilitated impunity.

Concomitantly, neither the Menem nor the De la Rúa and Duhalde administrations were interested in suffering the destabilizing effects of an effective investigation that fully uncovered and exposed the inefficiency and the involvement of security forces, rogue military, and intelligence agencies in the attacks. Although Menem may have had more to hide than De la Rúa (especially in relation to his promises to Syria, previous to the pro-Western shift in Argentina's foreign policy), the negative attitude of the De la Rúa administration towards Nilda Garré's investigative zeal clearly demonstrates that his administration also obstructed justice, although perhaps to a lesser extent than Menem's. In the case of Duhalde, the accusation that some members of the Buenos Aires province police were complicit with and indirectly involved in the bombing might explain why he rejected investigating the so called "local connection" of the attack.

While the 1992 and 1994 bombings remain unsolved in the sense that no material executor of the attacks has been brought to justice, it is known:

1   that the bombings were an offshoot of the global phenomenon of

Islamic fundamentalist terrorism and its suicidal instrument for mass murder, and directly linked to Hezbollah and Iran;

2   that they were partly motivated by Menem's broken pre-election promises to Arab countries, and by the geopolitical gambits of the early months of his administration, especially *vis-à-vis* Hazef al-Assad, who also wielded direct influence on Hezbollah;

3   that local elements were involved in the logistics of the attacks;

4   that an important segment of these local elements was officially linked to a state apparatus that does not fully respond to legitimate chains of command, as proven not only by the involvement of rogue police and military elements, but also by SIDE's boycott of CIA activities when it leaked to the press the photograph of the latter's chief operative in Argentina during the De la Rúa administration;

5   that corrupt practices such as placing the Syrian national Ibrahim al Ibrahim as special advisor to the Argentine customs office, or granting an Argentine passport to the Syrian arms merchant and terrorist-suspect Monzer al-Kassar, facilitated all sorts of illegal trafficking, probably including those that were logistically necessary to carry out the attacks;

6   that neither the Menem, De la Rúa, or Duhalde administrations were willing to investigate fully and risk some measure of destabilization of their governments for the sake of solving the cases, and moreover, that they concurred in obstructing justice.

AMIA/DAIA defended Judge Galeano's work and stressed security matters with the aim of preventing future attacks, as did the Argentine government. But legislation is still faulty and politicians seem at a loss when it comes to defining clear aims in the defense and intelligence areas. There is very little congressional control of intelligence activities and congress has no control whatsoever over the agencies' budgets, in the opinion of Eduardo Estévez, a congressional aide to the Radical Party bloc and an expert in security and intelligence.

Active Memory advocated against impunity maintaining that security is impossible without a thorough and effective investigation. In 1999, backed by CELS, CEJIL, Alberto Zuppi, and Pablo Jacoby, Active Memory presented its case before CIDH of the OAS. It charged that constitutional principles had been violated by the Argentine state and by irregularities in Galeano's investigation. Active Memory accused the Argentine government of not conducting a serious investigation of the attacks.

The two main groups that followed up on the investigation coordinated by Judge Galeano were DAIA/AMIA/FFOV, and Active Memory. In addition, the *Agrupación por el Esclarecimiento de la Masacre Impune de la AMIA* (Group for the Clarification of the Unpunished Massacre at AMIA,

APEMIA), a small but strong group of victims' families, was created in 2002 by Laura Ginsberg.

It would be incorrect to assert that if DAIA/AMIA had brought stronger pressure to bear on the government and on the Bicameral Commission, the investigation would have been more successful, because the lack of political will to investigate the bombings is related to conflicts of interest and to corruption among political actors of the Menem administration, members of the intelligence and security agencies as well as members of the federal police and the police of the province of Buenos Aires. Nevertheless, what is clear is that over the years the leadership of DAIA/AMIA did not denounce the government cover-up and overlooked Active Memory and APEMIA's accusation against the government, although it was based on empirical evidence. Regarding these two groups, any pressure from them was unlikely to cause anything more than some embarrassment to the national administration, that is, until Kirchner took office. When Kirchner became president, he and Minister of Foreign Affairs Rafael Bielsa began to pay more attention to the demands of Active Memory and APEMIA.

When in September 2001 (thirteen days *after* the attack on the Twin Towers and the Pentagon) an oral trial of some twenty subjects accused of providing logistical support for the terrorists finally began, the OAS commission validated Active Memory's charges by appointing Claudio Grossman, president of the commission, as observer of the trial.[47]

For Argentine Jews, the failure in the investigation of both attacks caused a crisis of representation. With the start of open court hearings three years ago, prosecutors and attorneys say that the evidence that has emerged so far is merely the tip of the iceberg. Intelligence agents confessed that with the approval of Judge Galeano, $400,000 was paid to convince Carlos Telledín, one of the accused, to testify against the implicated police officers. As a result, Galeano was removed from the case in November. The attorneys representing AMIA and DAIA are demanding life sentences for Telleldín and three of the four former police officials. FFOV is also calling for life sentences for Telledín and the police officers; and after almost ten years of following DAIA/AMIA's leads in the matter of demands, FFOV is asking for the impeachment of Galeano. The harmony between DAIA and FFOV has lapsed. Active Memory also wants a life sentence for Telleldín, but not for the four former police.

For years Active Memory denounced Judge Galeano for stonewalling the investigation and in 1999, presented a formal accusation against him before the judiciary. The prosecution admits that the investigation was sabotaged from the start by intelligence agents and federal and Buenos Aires province police officers, who created false leads, bribed witnesses, and allowed key evidence to be lost or removed, such as sixty-six cassette tapes containing telephone conversations among the accused.[48] This was one of the accusations presented by Active Memory before the Inter-American Court on Human Rights of the OAS. One of the most important testimonies in the oral trial came from Abolghasem Mesbahi, known at the start as "Witness C" – a former Iranian intelligence agent in Europe who has received protection from the German government. He said Iran's former deputy intelligence minister, Said Emami, had told him that Menem sent an envoy to the government in Tehran to demand $10 million to cover up Iran's alleged role in the attack. According to investigators, Mesbahi's description of the purported envoy could fit Jorge Lelli, a close Menem associate who served as cultural attaché in the Argentine Embassy in Iran. But that is difficult to verify, since Lelli died in a car accident in Argentina just two months after "Witness C" testified for the first time, and Emami died in prison after purportedly confiding in Mesbahi. Emami's death was reported as a suicide.[49]

The AMIA case is a paradigmatic example of the faults of the Argentine judiciary and of the networks of corruption that permeated the political sphere, including the government. Important questions still remain.

Would the investigation of the attacks have had more success if the leadership of the Jewish organizations had seriously demanded a thorough investigation, as Active Memory did, instead of praising Judge Galeano and acquiescing to the official policy? Why were DAIA's authorities so opposed to Active Memory's claims?

Ten years after the bombing, Jewish community buildings in Buenos Aires are still walled off with reinforced concrete. Can the barriers that now surround Jewish buildings in Buenos Aires guarantee security when justice fails and impunity remains an unsolved problem? All these questions pose a basic dilemma related to the decision of preserving the continuity of the historical system of centralized organization, in which DAIA is considered the sole political representative of the community, or instead to accept the fact that even the national authorities no longer perceive DAIA as the authorized voice of the whole Argentine Jewry.

Notes

1 The term "terrorism" was given no specific meaning in UN General Assembly resolution 3314 of 1974.

2 Niccolo Machiavelli, *The Prince* (1961), 39.

3 On the local connection, see Claudio A. Lifschitz, *AMIA, porque se hizo fallar la investigación* (Buenos Aires: Departamento Editorial, 2000), 149–55, and Archivo de la Cámara de Diputados de la Nación (hereafter ACDN) (expediente 1656-D-002000), 1–5.

The Asociación Mutual Israelita Argentina, the second Jewish institution created in Argentina, is a development of the *jevrah kedusha* founded by Ashkenazim immigrants in 1894. The first Jewish institution was the temple *Congregación Israelita de la República Argentina* (CIRA) founded in 1862 with the name of *Congregación Israelita de Buenos Aires*. For the Argentine people, the building of Pasteur 333 symbolized the Jewish community of the country. The AMIA building hosted the *Delegación de Asociaciones Israelitas Argentinas* (Delegation of Argentine Jewish Organizations, DAIA), *Instituto Científico Judío* (Jewish Scientific Institute, IWO), *Vaad Hajinuj* (Central Board for Jewish Education), and *Vaad Hakehilot* (Federation of Argentine Jewish Communities). On the Argentine Jewish community see Haim Avni, *Iahadut Argentina: Mamadá Hajevratí udmutá Hairgunit* (Jerusalem 1972), 33–102. The bomb that razed AMIA's building killed eighty-five persons, left more than a hundred wounded, and destroyed adjacent buildings around the block. Many of the victims were AMIA officials and users of the different social services provided by the institution; others were temporary workers remodeling the building and passers-by on their way to jobs or schools.

4   Hezbollah, established following the 1982 Peace for the Galilee War in Lebanon, is an umbrella organization of various radical Shi'ite groups and organizations that adhere to a Khomeinistic ideology. As a result, Iranian influence increased in Lebanon. The organization is led by clerics, who see in the adoption of the Iranian doctrine a solution to the Lebanese political malaise. This doctrine includes the use of terror as a means of attaining political objectives. The "radicals" especially regard the export of revolution as one of the main goals of Iranian foreign policy. In the same ideological context, the struggle against all alien ideological and cultural influences, primarily against Western predominance over Islamic nations, has led Iran to adopt Jihad against "heretics" everywhere. This has been directed mainly against the US and its allies. Expert Eli Karmon notes that prior to 1992, Iran, and even Hezbollah, did not attack any Israeli or Jewish target abroad and preferred instead to encourage Hezbollah to strike Israeli military objectives in Libya. But after the Madrid Peace Conference of October 1991, a spate of deadly attacks was launched against Israel as well as Jewish targets throughout the world. According to Karmon, the two attacks in Argentina against Jewish targets, in 1992 and 1994, were terrorist attacks perpetrated in the name of Jihad. (Eli Karmon, "Iran's Policy on Terrorism in the 1990s," paper presented at the International Conference on Recent Trends in Research on Terror and the Fight against Terror [Department of Political Science, Haifa University, May 10, 1998]).
On the informal peace conversations between Israel and Syria that began in 1992 see Itamar Rabinovich, *El Umbral de la Paz. Las conversaciones sirio-israelíes* (Buenos Aires: Universidad de Tel Aviv/Eudeba, 2000), 60–61. These conversations took place between 1992 and 1995. This explains in part Israel's low profile in its claims to the Argentine government in behalf of a serious investigation of the embassy bombing in Buenos Aires and its acceptance of the hypothesis that responsibility for the terrorist act was really Iran's and not Syria's.

5   On the killing of Abbas el Mousawi and claims for revenge see *The Jerusalem Report* <www.jrep.com/Mideast/Article-0.html>.

6   On the judicial opinion about the responsibility for the bombing of the embassy see ACDN, exp. 1856-D-00/2000 <www.ardiputados.

gov.ar/2000/1856> and *Microsemanario* 7 (1997), first section <www.fcen. uba.ar/prensa/micro/1997/ms275a.htm>.

7   In 1997, the Argentine Minister of Foreign Affairs, Guido Di Tella, admitted that the investigation of the Supreme Court was "lamentable" (Juan Salinas, *AMIA, el atentado* [Buenos Aires: Planeta, 1997], 57). Up to the year 2000, no one had been brought to justice for that act of terrorism. On the measures adopted by SIDE see Lifschitz, *AMIA, porque se hizo fallar la investigación*, 10–11. Lifschitz worked with Judge Juan José Galeano in the judicial investigation, until he (Lifschitz) began denouncing its irregularities. For more on the irregularities in the Supreme Court's work see <www.fcen.uba. ar/prensa/micro/1997/ms290a.htm>.

8   ACDN, exp. 1856-D-00/2000 and exp. 1852 <www.ardiputados. gov.ar/2000>. <www.google.com.ar/search?q=cache:3qJ85tViJ4C:www1. hcdn. gov.ar/dependencias/ cjpolitico/ despachos/Boggiano>. See also Report of the Bicameral Commission for the Continuation of the Investigation of the Terrorist Acts Against the Israeli Embassy and the AMIA Building (hereafter Bicameral Commission) <www.seprin.com/informes/info_bicall.htm>.

9   About the promises made by Menem to the Syrians see Joe Goldman and Jorge Lanata, *Cortinas de Humo* (Buenos Aires: Planeta, 1994). On the likely responsibility of Syria see also ACDN, expediente 1656-D-00-2000, Proyecto de Resolución, "La causa Embajada y la pista Siria: el atentado a la Embajada de Israel y Monzer Al Kassar." According to this document, in 1992 the CIA presented a report to the US House of Representatives informing it that Iran and Syria had signed an agreement of nuclear cooperation and co-sponsored terrorist attacks. In a series of articles published in the newspaper *Diario Río Negro* on January 11, 12, and 13, 2000, Norberto Bermúdez and Carlos Torrengo developed the same hypothesis on the basis of legislative sources. See "Lo que no se investigó sobre los atentados" (Parts I, II and III); "Los acuerdos y compromisos secretos de Menem y los árabes;" "El dominicano Nemen Nader habla desde Madrid: 'Menem recibió 40 millones de los países árabes en 1988;'" "Munir Menem: entre Damasco y la Rosada." See also *La denuncia* (Buenos Aires, Planeta, 1997), 41–3.

10 Report of the Bicameral Commission, 1996 <www.seprin.com /informes/info_bicall.htm>.

11 On the investigations of the embassy and AMIA bombings see the *dictatum* of the Bicameral Commission, 1996.

12 On Menem's foreign policy see Carlos Escudé, *Foreign Policy in Menem's Argentina* (Gainesville: University Press of Florida, 1997), 4.

13 On the broken promises of Menem to Kadhafi see the prologue by Juan Salinas, "La larga de Yabrán" and the chapter "Mercosur" in Christian E. Sanz, *La mafia, la ley y el poder: la relación entre Alfredo Yabrán y el poder en el marco de la ley de privatización correo* (Buenos Aires: Ediciones Dunken, 1996) <www.seprin.com/informes/yabran.htm>. Salinas was chief researcher in the investigation of the terrorist attack against AMIA during the presidency of Alberto Crupnicoff. See Julio Rajneri, "'Río Negro' va más lejos con la pista Siria. ¿Pudo llegar tan lejos la venganza, como para provocar los atentados antijudíos en Buenos Aires?" *Diario Río Negro* <www.seprin.com/informes/amia.htm>; Bermúdez Norberto, *La pista Siria*

(Montevideo: Urraca, 1993); Eduardo de Miguel and Gabriel Pasquini, *Blanca y radiante* (Buenos Aires: Planeta, 1995); Martín Granovsky, *Misión cumplida* (Buenos Aires: Planeta, 1992); Roman Lejtman, *Narcogate* (Buenos Aires: Sudamericana, 1993); Daniel Santoro, *El hacedor* (Buenos Aires: Planeta, 1994); and Hernán López Echagüe, *La frontera* (Buenos Aires: Planeta, 1997).

See J. Salinas, "Larga historia de Yabrán," 164–6. In relation to Menem's state commitments see ACDN, exp. 1656-D-00/2000 <www.ardiputados. gov.ar/2000/1656-1.htm>. According to official sources, Syria and Libya seem to have given forty million dollars to Menem for his pre-electoral political campaign in 1988. See Norberto Bermúdez and Carlos Torrengo, "Lo que no se investigó sobre los atentados" part 1 <www.seprin. com/informes/amia.htm>. The Argentine Senate and the Chamber of Deputies sanctioned "with the force of law" the obligation to investigate the terrorist attacks on the embassy and AMIA (ACDN, exp.1856-D-00/2000 and exp.1652-D-00/2000 <www.ardiputados.gov.ar/2000/1656-1.htm>. These documents refer to many of the accusations made by Active Memory and by *Diario Río Negro* and others, as well as Juan Salinas' investigations referenced in *AMIA, el atentado*.

14 "*Carapintadas*," meaning "painted faces" colored black with bitumen, is the name of a group of military extreme right nationalists that led two uprisings against the democratic government of former president Raúl Alfonsín in 1987 and 1988 and a third uprising against the president Carlos Menem in 1990. The leader of the group is the charismatic ex-colonel Mohamed Ali Seineldin, under arrest since the 1990 uprising. Seineldin is well known for his strong anti-Semitic feelings. The carapintadas reacted against the trials and imprisonment of the top military officers involved in the Falklands War.

15 Soon after the terrorist act, in his first press conference, Menem said: "Son los mismos del 3 de diciembre [of 1990, the date of the only military rebellion during Menem's government], resabios del nazismo y de los sectores fundamentalistas [the carapintadas] que salieron derrotados en el país." At first, Menem held the carapintadas responsible, and pointed out the imprisoned head of the rebellion, Mohamed Ali Seineildin, as one of the instigators of the attack on AMIA (J. Salinas, *AMIA, el atentado*, 41).

16 For more information on the Syrian lead see Goldman and Lanata, *Cortinas de Humo*. On the likely responsibility of Syria see also ACDN, expediente 1656-D-00-2000. See note 9.

17 On the gathering organized by AMIA and DAIA on July 21, 1994, see <http://www.atentado-amia.com.ar/avance/1999/avance03.html>.

18 AMIA/DAIA official report, *La denuncia* (Buenos Aires: Planeta, 1997), 41–3.

19 See the *Second Report* (1999) of the Bicameral Commission, which was created in 1996. See also the reports compiled by Acción por la República. Both groups investigated Al Kassar's participation in the bombing. Kassar and Ibrahim Al Ibrahim, chief of the Argentine customhouse, closely linked with Menem, are being investigated in relation to their participation in the AMIA bombing. On Kassar see "Argentine Terror," *For The Record (FTR)-5* (recorded broadcast) <www.spitfirelist.com/ftr-old.htm>. Kassar, a

weapons dealer and drug smuggler, was a primary operative functioning on behalf of George Bush, Oliver North, and others in the Iran-Contra scandal ("Terrorism in Latin America/AMIA Bombing in Argentina," Hearing before the Committee on International Relations, one hundred fourth congress, September 28, 1995 [Washington, D.C.: US Government Printing Office, 1996]). On the responsibility of Syria see "Proyecto de Resolución" (ACDN, exp.1656-D-00/2000) <www.ardiputados.gov.ar/2000/1653-3.htm>. On Al Kassar see Mark Aarons and John Loftus, *Unholy Trinity. The Vatican, the Nazis, and Soviet Intelligence* (New York: St. Martin's Press, 1992), xix; and *La denuncia*, 42–3.

20 Bicameral Commission, 1997.
21 The most conspicuous is Juan José Ribelli, a high-ranking officer of the provincial police. On the police and army officers sent to jail by Galeano see Sergio Kiernan, "Unfinished business. The bombing six years later" (American Jewish Committee, New York, 1999) <http://www.ajc.org/InTheMedia/Publications.asp?did=146>, and the American Jewish Committee's "Annual Report on AMIA Bombing: Trial Exposes Executive, Judicial Corruption" of November 29, 2001.
22 On Active Memory's opinion about the oral trial and about the investigation coordinated by Judge Galeano see *AVIZORA,_Periodismo para pensar* <http://www.avizora.com/atajo/informes/caso_amia_0001.htm>, <www.asambleas-argentinas.org/breve.php3?id_breve=248>, and <www.memoriaactiva.com/novedades_abajo.htm>.
23 Sergio Kiernan, *Una leve esperanza: el atentado a la AMIA, cinco años después*, American Jewish Committee <www.atentado-amia.com.ar/avance/2000/texto02e.html>.
24 A paradigmatic example of the personal relation developed by Beraja with political actors linked to the Menem administration is the case of the son of Minister of Interior Carlos Corach, who was hired into a high position at Beraja's bank in 1996; he was one of the few who would recover his total investment after the bank's failure in 1998, section: Banco Mayo, 368 Cierre <www.archiv.com.ar>.
25 On Rubén Beraja's opinion of the investigation of both terrorist acts see <http://old.clarin.com/diario/1997/07/14/t-01101d.htm>; Gabriel Levinas y Cecilia Moguilansky, "La Simulación," <http://www.elportenio.com/la_simulacion.htm>; and *Clarín Digital*, "AMIA: buscan frenar la interna" (July 26, 1997) <http://old.clarin.com.ar/diario/1997/07/26/t-00901d.htm>.
26 Testimony of Philip Wilcox (US State Department's Counter Terrorism Coordinator) in a Hearing before the Committee on International Relations, on International Terrorism in Latin America, US House of Representatives, 104th Congress, September 28, 1995 (Washington, D.C.: US Government Printing Office, 1996), 20–1.
27 The cliché "unidad comunitaria" (community unity) has been especially used by members of the Argentine Jewish establishment of the "central organiz-ations" – AMIA, DAIA, and OSA (Argentine Zionist Organization) for many years. These organizations were in their full splendor until the mid-1970s. This cliché was frequently used during the period of state terrorism (*Proceso*

de Reorganización Nacional, 1976–83) with the aim of silencing the public critical expressions towards the leadership of DAIA. When the dictatorship came to an end, important segments of the Jewish constituency criticized DAIA for having overlooked what was happening with the Jewish *desaparecidos* (missing people), and for not denouncing the strong anti-Semitism that cut across the Armed Forces. In the years of the Proceso, Rabbi Marshall Meyer created the *Movimiento Judío por los Derechos Humanos* (Jewish Movement for Human Rights) with the aim of attending to the demands of Jewish families that perceived that DAIA was not doing all that was necessary to help them. After the AMIA bombing the cliché was used for the purpose of controlling the critics of DAIA's leadership. The rationale underlying the control of free speech is that the best strategy is to have solely one voice to represent the community. Facts have proven that in critical situations more voices arise spontaneously and the results, in the decade of the 1970s as well as in the present, have been to the benefit of the community, in multiple senses.

28 On Active Memory's presentation before the Inter-American Commission of Human Rights (hereafter CIDH) of the OAS see <www.memoriaactiva. com/index.htm>. On the condition of observer during the oral trial of the AMIA case of the president of the committee, Claudio Grossman, see *Clarín* (September 24, 2001), section: Politics (Argentina) <www.pagina12. com.ar/2000/00-10/00-10-13/pag18.htm>. Argentina is a signatory country of the Costa Rica Pact, which established a supranational court for legal cases involving human rights. The complete version of the presentation before the CIDH on Costa Rica is at Active Memory's website <www.memoriaactiva.com/index.htm>.

29 DAIA expanded its role in civil society through increased participation in the creation of the *Instituto Nacional Contra la Discriminación* (National Institute Against Discrimination, INADI) and other initiatives that contributed to the strengthening of democracy. Beraja's role as one of the founders of INADI is a paradigmatic example of his vision of the role of the state in promoting tolerance and education against all forms of discrimination. Traditionally, DAIA had limited its political activity to confronting anti-Semitism. Its expanded policies were consistent with the process of cultural democratization that had begun during Raúl Alfonsín's presidency, in 1983, and that continued under Menem's.

30 Testimony of Philip Wilcox (US State Department's Counter Terrorism Coordinator) in a Hearing before the Committee on International Relations, on International Terrorism in Latin America, US House of Representatives, 104th Congress, September 28, 1995 (Washington, D.C.: US Government Printing Office, 1996), 20–1.

31 *Ibid.*

32 All major intelligence services agree that mafias based in the Arab immigrant enclaves of Ciudad del Este (Paraguay), and Foz de Iguaçu (Brazil), run criminal industries such as money laundering and smuggling of contraband and people. These mafias finance a network of terrorists belonging to Hezbollah, Hamas and other groups, thanks to porous borders, corrupt officials, and the availability of illicit documents and weapons. These cities together with

Puerto Iguazú, in the Argentine province of Misiones, are in the so called "Triple Border."

33 On security in the "Triple Border" see *La Nación* (September 22, 1997) <www.lanacion.com.ar/97/12/22/o01.htm> and <www.mrecic.gov.ar/politica/tratados/paragua2.htm>. On terrorism and trafficking in the triple border see <www.meib.org/articles/2001_12.htm>.

34 Testimony of Rubén Beraja (president of DAIA) in a Hearing before the Committee on International Relations, on International Terrorism in Latin America, US House of Representatives, 104th Congress, September 28, 1995 (Washington, D.C.: US Government Printing Office, 1996), 19.

35 *Ibid.*, 20–2.

36 Dos Santos had frequently been to the Triple Border between Argentina, Brazil, and Paraguay, which is well known for its Lebanese population and sleeper Hezbollah cells. The Iranian prostitute mentioned by Dos Santos is Nasrim Mokhtari, who has a police record with eight prostitution-related arrests (see "Iranian woman charged in Argentine blast probe," *Agence France-Presse* (December 4, 1998); "Argentina charges Iranian woman in Israeli Embassy bombing," *Dow Jones International News* (December 4, 1998); "Argentina detains Iranian woman," *Chicago Tribune* (December 5, 1998); "Argentine police arrest Iranian woman over Israel Embassy attack," *Deutsche Presse-Agentur* (December 5, 1998); "Argentina holds Iranian in Embassy bombing," *The Jerusalem Post* (December 6, 1998); "Argentina releases Iranian woman linked to Jewish bombings," *Dow Jones International News* (December 22, 1998). In April 1992 Dos Santos and Mokhtari began a relationship in a Buenos Aires café in an embassy neighborhood. He learned that she picked up clients at a bar near the National Congress. A legislator had helped her obtain an Argentine passport. She hung out at an Iranian butcher shop near the doomed AMIA building. There she introduced Dos Santos to two Arab friends, who would later accompany them on visits to the Iranian Embassy, chauffeured by one of them, who was a cabdriver, free of charge. Dos Santos testified that he later helped them move merchandise into Argentina across the border. They met with Arabs and returned from Ciudad del Este with a heavy metal suitcase that Dos Santos brought into Argentina with the help of Nora González, the then-chief of the Argentine customs station (according to testimony, González, also known as Fat Nora, helped Arab smugglers move people and goods across the border, and died in a car accident soon after the AMIA blast in 1994). In December 1992, Dos Santos accompanied Mokhtari to Italy at her expense. They went on to Zurich, where to Dos Santos' surprise they met with the men from the butcher shop in Buenos Aires. That night Mokhtari showed him a suitcase full of money and confessed that she and her friends had taken part in the bombing of the Israeli Embassy. She was helping them prepare one last "job" in Buenos Aires scheduled for mid-1994, after which she would quit. The target was a building undergoing renovation. Dos Santos said he was a courier and interpreter for her and her friends in Italy, Switzerland, and Germany. Then he got scared and returned to Brazil. But he did not go to the authorities until the following year, an omission that raises suspicions. Investigators believe Dos Santos may be concealing his role as an accomplice,

or may be an operative working for Brazilian or American intelligence (he has a long history of entries into the United States, including one with a visa obtained in London, unusual for a Brazilian of modest means applying in a third country). In November 1994, in Argentina, he gave his ten-hour deposition to federal police about Mokhtari and her friends. A few days later, however, with a terrified look, he retracted his account in front of Judge Galeano, who charged him with perjury. He spent about a week in jail, was conditionally released, and fled to Brazil. Investigators corroborated key details of his original version. According to the FBI report, for example, the butcher shop he said he visited with Mokhtari was the sometime workplace of an Iranian immigrant who has been identified as a spy. Details such as Mokhtari's cabdriver match prior evidence of Iranian cells operating under the guise of taxi drivers, students, and meat-related businesses in Buenos Aires. Investigators believe that this network, along with Hezbollah terrorists and Argentine accomplices who provided the van used in the bombing, was coordinated by the former cultural attaché of the Iranian Embassy. Among clues pointing to the attaché is his cellular phone, which was detected a few blocks away from the AMIA building at a key moment before the bombing (see Sebastian Rotella, "Deadly blasts and an itinerant's tale: hazy figure may hold the key to anti-Semitic bombings in Argentina," *Los Angeles Times* (April 17, 1999); "Key witness to Buenos Aires bombing located in Brazil," *Associated Press Newswires* (November 18, 1998); "Key witness arrested in bombing of Jewish Community Center," *Agence France-Presse* (November 19, 1998); "Argentina bomb witness to testify," *AP Online* (November 22, 1998); "Iranian held in '92 Argentina blast," *AP Online* (December 4, 1998); "Swiss extradite Jewish Center bombing suspect to Argentina," *The Jerusalem Post* (December 24, 2000). The attaché, Mohsen Rabbani, was barred from Argentina after testimony by an Iranian defector (protected witness "C") identified him as his country's espionage chief in the region (see "Argentine court denies passport to Iranian bombing suspect," *Agence France-Presse* (January 14, 1999).

37 On Robert Gelbard's statements see the article by Karina Donángelo and Pablo Rodríguez Leirado in *Al Margen* <www.almargen.com.ar/sitio/seccion/politica/index%281%29.html>.

38 On the behavior of the Argentine Minister of Foreign Affairs see <www.pagina12.com.ar/2001/01-01/01-01-06/pag12.htm>.

39 On the accusation presented by Active Memory before the CIDH see <www.memoriaactiva.com/oea_abajo.htm>. On Raúl Kollman's opinion see Raúl Kollmann, "El escrito del juez admite errores y maniobras en la investigación," *Pagina 12* (March 5, 2000).

40 See Katherin Ellison, "Argentina to Investigate Nazi Loot Complaints of Inaction Prompt Decision by Government," *Miami Herald* (April 17, 1997), section: Front, edition: final, 16A.

41 The charges made by Judge Adolfo Bagnasco against Beraja are "coautor de los delitos de defraudación por administración infiel y fraude en perjuicio de la administración pública" <www.elportenio.com/beraja.htm> caché archive.

42 On Pou's destitution see *Clarín*, section: Economy (May 27, 1999). On

Beraja's legal situation, see <http://ar.geocities.com/veaylea2000/verbitsky> and <www.news.bbc.co.uk/hi/spanish/latin_america/ newsid_1297000/1297206.stm>. In a letter to the newspaper *Pagina 12*, Pou argued that the central bank had helped prop up Beraja's bank more generously than it had assisted any other bank, with $350 million in aid. The two reports made public in 2001 by the *Comisión Especial Investigador a sobre Hechos Ilícitos Vinculados con el Lavado de Dinero de la H. Cámara de Diputados* (Special Committee of Investigation on Illegal Acts Linked to Money Laundering of the House of Deputies of the National Congress; CEIHIVLD) revealed the type and magnitude of illegal practices that permeated the financial operations coordinated by Beraja. Through a parliamentary indictment, CEIHIVLD accused Pou of failing to fulfill his duties as a public functionary, for tolerating dubious operations of money laundering, and for fiscal evasion in favor of certain banks, one of which was administrated by Beraja. Finally, Pou was obliged to resign from his position on the BCRA by a decree signed by President De la Rúa after considering the *dictatum* of the CEIHIVLD.

43 See interview by Larry Rother, *Iran Press Service* (July 21, 2002) <www.iran-pressservice.com/articles_2002/jul_2002/iran_argentine_jewish_centre_227 02r.htm> and <www.convention-france.com/2_0588.htm>.

44 On Beraja's prosecution see <http://ar.geocities.com/veaylea2000/verbitsky> and <www.news.bbc.co.uk/hi/spanish/latin_america/newsid_1297000/129 7206.stm>.

45 On different opinions about what happened with the investigation of the AMIA bombing and the attitude of government officials and the establishment of AMIA/DAIA see *Nueva Sion* <http://www.nuevasion.com.ar/sitio/nuevasion/MostrarNoticia.asp?edicion=33&seccion=22&noticia=1 125>.

46 Jean Cartier-Bresson, "Corruption Networks, Transaction Security, and Illegal Social Exchange," *Political Studies* 44 (1997), 469–70.

47 For the text of Active Memory's presentation before the Inter-American Commission of Human Rights see <http://www.memoriaactiva.com/oea.htm>. The accusation was formally presented by Memoria Activa's lawyer, Alberto Zuppi, who had represented the Italian Embassy during the Otto Priebke extradition case. Chilean jurist Claudio M. Grossman is Dean of American University's Washington College of Law, as well as President of the Committee (*Clarín*, September 24, 2001).

48 About the "lost" 66 cassettes of taped conversations with suspects in the case against the police, being handled by the Third Federal Oral Tribunal, coordinated by Judge Galeano see <http://sundial.ccs. yorku.ca/cgi-bin/wa?A2 =ind0303&L=lacyork&F=&S=&P=1169>.

49 On the circumstances of the death of Emami and Lelli see <http://www.ins. onlinedemocracy.ca/print.php?sid=2252> and <http://www.old.clarin.com/diario/2003/11/06/p-00801.htm>.

Part III

Identity and Hybridity

Identity and Memories of Cuban Jews

7

Robert M. Levine

T he quandary to be faced when researching the Jewish community in Cuba is that statistics, perceptions, and memories differ widely, as revealed in my research over the past two decades, in which I have interviewed dozens of persons and conducted research in such archives as the YIVO Institute for Jewish Research, the American Jewish Committee, and the Library of Congress.

The first quandary, which influences perceptions about the nature of Jewish communities, is that the Cuban Jewish community in the US, mostly in South Florida, often demands what seems to be a proprietary right to guarantee that studies written about its history be celebratory, and not raise questions. In the forty-some years of exile in Florida, many Cuban Jews have become as wealthy, or wealthier than before, and there remains a lack of clear understanding about the role of academic scholarship within a community long self-segregated and not easily accessible to outsiders. In other words, published historical analyses that do not celebrate, or that refer to internal conflict during historical moments within the Jewish community are disparaged. These *"Jubans,"* in the unpleasant-sounding term used outside as well as inside the Cuban Jewish community, show displeasure when they want to, and although they do not intimidate, they make inquiry all the more difficult.

In addition, in terms of assembling and counting data, it is difficult to determine something as basic as the size and characteristics of the Cuban Jewish community. Data accepted by almost all researchers come from estimates provided by institutional sources – heads of Jewish charities, religious organizations, welfare agencies, schools, and the like. We read that of the thousands of Jews who emigrated to Cuba between 1898 and 1939, refugees from Nazi-dominated Europe numbered 2,000; that the Cuban Jewish community in 1958 on the eve of Fidel Castro's revolution numbered 14,000 or 15,000; and that almost all of them departed into exile during the first years of the new regime.[1] The trouble is that these figures are highly inaccurate. How deep the flaw depends on how they were generated and, even more seriously, on what definitions they were based.

The source of the inaccuracies is that counts of Jews not only in foreign lands, but also in the US were, and continue to be, based on institutional affiliation. For Cuba, this fact, owing to the social history of Cuban Jewry, was unusually problematic. Only Jews who then belonged to synagogues, or registered for subsidies from Jewish welfare agencies, or who applied for visas to emigrate, or, under Castro, signed up to receive Passover shipments of matzos and cooking oil, were counted. This presents no major difficulty for researchers examining the institutions themselves, especially synagogues and Jewish schools. But it presents a major dilemma when applied to broader themes in social history, especially because institutional counters looked askance at Jews who chose to be unaffiliated or, worse in the eyes of communal leadership, married Roman Catholics or became entirely secular.

We think we know how many Sephardic Jews of the eastern Mediterranean landed in Cuba and made the island their home. Yet even these figures are approximate, because in spite of the stereotype that family-oriented Sephardic Jews remained religiously observant and closely organized, interviews with elderly Cuban Jews reveal that many Sephardic men, who outnumbered women in immigration to Cuba succumbed to human nature and married outside their faiths. Ashkenazi immigrants from Eastern Europe brought with them a higher ratio of men to women as well. They also tended to be less religiously observant – and, among the socialist and labor Zionists – hostile to organized Judaism and religious observance. Counting the number of Ashkenazi Jews who arrived in Cuba – and the number who departed – remains very elusive.

Most Jewish arrivals in Cuba, especially the Ashkenazim, considered the island little more than a steppingstone to the US. From 1924 on, nativist legislation enacted by the US Congress based entry to most applicants from Eastern Europe. Thousands of Jews who came to "Hotel Cuba," as they cynically referred to the island, subsequently entered the US in spite of the barriers. Since this meant marrying a mail-order US bride – supplied by professional Jewish brokers – or traveling to Mexico and subsequently crossing the border into the US, or obtaining forged country-of-origin papers, which were rare because of their high cost but possible, we likely will never know the totals.[2] My research shows, however, that this out-migration may have totaled *half* the entire Jewish population of Cuba in any year between 1924 and 1940. "Official" histories ignore these out-migrants entirely.

Another issue, not exactly a quandary, was the fact that historical studies of Cuba traditionally examine its life as a function of Havana, its capital city, and not through the vantage point of the provinces, to which many Jews, especially Sephardim, emigrated. In 1887, Havana's population stood at only 250,000, some of these refugees from the years of warfare in the countryside. Two decades later Havana had grown to 300,000, swollen by the arrival of a large number of Spanish immigrants, who, by the early 1900s, made up a quarter of the city's total population. Another quarter were blacks and mestizos, mostly internal migrants, as well as small numbers of Chinese, Sephardic Jews from Turkey and Morocco, and Arab Muslims and Christians from the Ottoman Empire. Popular culture began to extend to urban residents: sports periodicals, theatrical and musical performances, public recreation, and artisanship. The weakening of the power of the former slave-holding aristocracy and the departure of the peninsular upper class opened opportunities for upwardly mobile Cubans, many of whom forged business alliances with US bankers and businessmen. US culture, especially films and baseball, became the rage. Bull fighting had exited with the Spanish; now baseball and horse racing became wildly popular among a wide variety of social classes. Cuban music excelled at versatility, jumping from the countryside to city clubs and dance halls.

The Sephardic Jewish arrivals in Cuba came as part of a greater emigration from the declining Ottoman Empire, and were joined by members of many diverse ethnic and religious groups from the same parts of the Middle East. There were Marronite Christians, Armenians, Muslims, Orthodox Christians, Chaldeans, and others. Of the Jews who came to Cuba as part of this migration, most came from Turkey. The influx started in 1902, centered around the expansion of Cuba's sugar industry, which lasted until it peaked in 1920. In 1918, an estimated 90 percent of the Jews living in Cuba had come from the Ottoman Empire. Following the Greek occupation of Thrace, Macedonia, and Anatolia between 1919 and 1922, conditions there worsened, and Jews had to flee from poverty and hunger. Many left during this period for the New World. Other Jews, who were not so destitute in Turkey, took steps to emigrate to Cuba, where they had family members who had emigrated ahead of them. The Sephardim, as Margalit Bejarano explains, "created chains of emigration from their home towns to specific areas" in Cuba.[3] The earlier settlement of a relative in a neighborhood in Havana, or in a town elsewhere on the island, often determined where an immigrant family would settle.

Sephardic Jewish immigrants spoke Ladino, the centuries-old derivative of fifteenth-century Spanish mixed with Hebrew, and written phonetically in the Hebrew alphabet. Because Ladino was closer to Cuban Spanish, they had an easier time of adjustment to Cuban life than their Jewish compatriots, the Eastern European, and Yiddish-speaking Ashkenazi. Both groups settled in Old Havana, near the port, on streets ironically named Jesús, María, and *Inquisidor* (Inquisitor), as Bejarano notes. They ultimately engaged in commerce, although at first they lacked the capital to open retail stores, and many had to start out as street peddlers, selling trinkets and other wares manufactured by family members in sweat shops. The Jewish peddlers, as well as Arab peddlers, often sold on credit, making it possible for poor families to make purchases, since Spanish shopkeepers enjoyed a monopoly of the retail trade, and therefore made it almost impossible for working-class Cubans to purchase consumer goods. Selling on credit enraged the shopkeepers, but paved the way for immigrants to enter manufacturing and eventually to prosper and to enter the upper economic class, if not the highest social class, from which they would always be excluded.

An interesting difference between the Sephardic and Ashkenasic Jewish arrivals to Cuba was that the East European Jews desired fervently to gain entry to the US, which, by the early 1920s, began to shut its doors to new immigrant groups considered undesirable. Sephardic groups, however, in many cases preferred to stay in Cuba; they felt comfortable with the local culture, which was family-oriented and which was rooted in extended families. They liked the climate, and they adjusted easily to the language. In 1919, the Hebrew Immigrant Aid Service (HIAS), the international Jewish relief agency founded in 1881, helped two hundred Turkish Jews to immigrate to Cuba. Further, several Jews from Turkey who had emigrated previously to the US, left voluntarily and came to Cuba. They did not speak English, they did not like the cold, and they found peddling in Cuba an easy enterprise rather than working at factory jobs in port cities along the east coast of the US.

During the mid-to-late 1930s, refugees from Nazi-occupied Europe dominated in-migration to Cuba, and may be counted fairly accurately because the paths to entry were limited to the few European passenger ships whose ports of call included Cuba. We know that the number of refugee arrivals between 1935 and 1939 was around two thousand in all. Less known is that within a year after the tragic turning back of the *S.S. St. Louis* in June 1939, despite the strenuous and ultimately heroic efforts of its captain, Nazi party member Gerhard Schroeder, to find a haven for its Jewish passengers, secret negotiations between international Jewish welfare agencies and Cuban immigration officials led to the arrival of twenty-five hundred to three thousand additional Jews, mostly Polish Ashkenazim involved in the diamond business stranded in overrun Belgium. The reopening of Cuban ports to these Jewish refugees had nothing to do with compassion or humanitarianism. Instead, Cuban officials accepted opportunities for enormous bribes, and at higher levels, the Cuban government reckoned that having a diamond industry would benefit the island's economy.[4]

Another conventional usage by historians that deserves to be challenged is the term "Jewish community." This implies communal unity and convergence of interests. Instead, closer examination of communal dynamics in Cuba – as well as throughout the hemisphere during most of the twentieth century – reveals that there never was a unified Jewish community. Rather, the "Jewish" population remained divided into competing, and sometimes mutually hostile, groups: atheistic labor Zionists versus observant Jews, Ladino-speaking Sephardic Jews versus Yiddish-speaking Ashkenazi Jews. For example, the Ashkenazim called the Sephardim "lazy" and "backwards," and the Sephardim mocked the Eastern European Jews for their materialism and for allowing women to work. German-speaking Jewish refugees disparaged both major groups as lacking culture and education. English-speaking American Jews, constantly present in Cuba since 1898, kept their distance from other Jews, importing Reform rabbis from the US who neither spoke Spanish nor attempted to learn it.

Since Turkish Jews tended to settle in neighborhoods or communities in which earlier arrivals from the same towns and cities in Turkey had come, enmities carried over from the Old World to the New. Jews from smaller European countries or language groups – Hungary, Greece, Bulgaria, Latvia, and Yugoslavia – found themselves socially ostracized from other Jews. Before World War II, marriages between Sephardic and Ashkenazi Jews were condemned by both communities, much as if they were unions with non-Jews. Such barriers tended to fall in small towns and cities earlier than in Havana, where self-segregation was bolstered by communal institutions. The first Jewish institution to list as its founders both Ashkenazi and Sephardic Jews was Havana's *Patronato*, established in the mid-1950s, but only the wealthiest and most influential Jews could aspire to membership. Two years after the Patronato opened, in fact, wealthy Mediterranean Jews began construction of a Sephardic community center patterned after the Patronato. For the large majority of Cuba's Jews, then, internal communal segregation remained intact through Castro's rise to power in January 1959.

After the 1959 Revolution

Jewish institutional sources claim that twelve thousand Jews resided in Cuba in 1959, although somewhat mysteriously this figure has risen to fourteen thousand and even fifteen thousand in recent years. Of this total, moreover, it is said that more than 90 percent abandoned the Castro regime and sought exile. Given that most Cuban Jews who settled in South Florida expressed the same political views as members of the emergent Cuban-American elite, and energetically opposed Castro, who confiscated their businesses and drove them from their homes, few challenged these figures. After all, to assert that virtually the entire Jewish population of Cuba left made the point they sought to make: that Cuban Jewish exiles hated Castro as much as anyone else. In reality, for decades they had been considered outsiders, excluded from most of the professions and from the patronage jobs taken for granted by Cubans from the elite. During the 1950s they reveled in their rising prosperity although they remained excluded from the Big Five clubs and the other gathering places of Cuban high society. In oral history interviews, however, subjects rarely felt comfortable to explain their feelings about having been ostracized, not only from club membership, but also from government patronage jobs and other forms of graft and payoffs lubricating the Cuban way of life. Once in Miami, as exiles in the US, many former Cuban Jews spoke with a single voice, faintly praising Fulgencio Batista, castigating Castro, and negating inferences that anti-Semitism ever played a significant role in pre-1959 Cuban life.

In Miami, they reacted to the indifference of local synagogues and communal organizations, and, during the 1960s and 1970s, formed independent parallel communal associations – the Cuban-Hebrew Congregation and Temple Moses for Sephardic Jews, rather than seeking to affiliate with "Anglo" Jewish communal organizations. As the decades passed, the Cuban-American Jews remained within the Cuban exile enclave, voting overwhelmingly Republican in contrast to Jewish voting patterns everywhere else in the US, retaining their use of Spanish, and becoming involved in such groups as the Cuban Jewish Auxiliary of the Greater Jewish Federation.

If then one counts the thousands of individuals born to Jewish parents or raised consciously as Jews in Cuba as "Jews," despite their choice of secular, intermarried, or atheistic paths, especially after 1959, one sees a very different picture from the one currently given. In Cuba, heads of Jewish organizations worked hard to dismiss Jews they considered embarrassments. In the 1920s, Jewish leaders understandably cringed when anti-religious Zionists held parties on Yom Kippur and when Yiddish-speaking Jews dominated early efforts to establish a communist party on the island. Less understandable perhaps was the cold shoulder given by institutional Jewish associations to the new German-speaking refugees coming from Nazi Europe during the mid-1930s, in part because the German Jews considered themselves culturally superior to the East European and Mediterranean Jews already on the island, and in part because Jewish leaders, facing continued poverty among many of the island's Jewish population, argued that relief aid to the German-speaking Jews – necessary because the Cuban authorities refused to permit the new arrivals to earn any money from working – should come from Jewish agencies in the US and abroad. Ironically, Cuban Jewish leaders considered themselves to be on good terms with Batista, who essentially ran the government between 1934 and 1944, but they did not press him very hard on the issue of refugee relief.

Wartime brought many changes for the Jewish community on the island. By 1944, many if not most of the German-speaking refugees had been allowed to depart for the US, and the remainder of Cuba's Jewish population began to fare better economically as US investments in Cuba brought economic improvement. By the late 1950s, a disproportionately high percentage of Cuban Jews favored Castro as an alternative to Batista, and in the first months of the revolution, held several high positions in Castro's government, including at the cabinet level. This embarrassed Cuban Jews who left the island. In reaction, Cuban Jewish leaders, led by Sender Kaplan, the son of an Ashkenazi rabbi and for two decades the head of the Organization of Cuban Jewish Associations, insisted that most Cuban Jews had chosen exile. But if one counts as Jews those born or raised as Jews before out-marrying, or those who chose secular, non-observant lives, the count of Cuban Jews who left after 1959 falls to 50 percent or less. I do not argue that this taints the struggle of Cuban Jews to rebuild their lives in exile. Rather, I simply challenge the flawed ways of counting, and point out the reasons why holding to a narrow definition excludes thousands of men and women whose stories as supporters of Castro's revolution also deserve to be recorded and heard as a historically significant variant of Jewish history.

The practice of Jewish organizations to count only those identified and affiliated as Jews is followed everywhere, except Israel, where Jews are lumped together to counter growing numbers of Arabs. In the US as well as in Latin America, such institutional counts privilege the Orthodox, highly affiliated because of the institutionalized basis of Orthodox religious practice. Few Orthodox Jews, by definition, lead secular lives to the point that they stand outside institutional boundaries, whereas liberal Jews, or those who simply consider themselves Jews because of their heritage, or because – unless they change their names – are fated to continue to be considered Jews by others, have a much greater chance of being excluded from "official" censuses carried out by Jewish institutions.

The Nature of Memory

In preliminary research for a new videotaped documentary on the Batista years between 1952 and 1959, I have found that respondents offer interpretations of these years heavily based on their own personal experiences. Cubans who fled Castro, including Cuban Jews, overwhelmingly emphasize the serenity of the period. For them, it was a time of prosperity, live and let live, tranquility, and warm memories. When questioned about the repressive nature of the police, they say that they were unaware of such things, that they were not "involved." When asked if they had to pay the police for "protection" for their businesses, they shrug and say that the payments were not excessive, that they were "part of doing business."

They remember the presence of foreign tourists, but express unawareness of sordid nightclub acts, or that Cuban doctors performed abortions for thousands of US women annually. When asked about mounting opposition to Batista as the 1950s progressed, they say that they were not aware of it; some remember supporting Batista, whom they remember as "decent," "patriotic," and "friendly."

Those who fled Batista during the 1950s, or who remained in Cuba through the Castro period, remember very differently. They tell stories of police brutality, of massive corruption in government, of the need to bribe officials for virtually anything, and of student violence against the regime. They remember the presence of US gangsters, nightclub acts featuring naked women and live sex acts, and the turning away of blacks by hotels and resorts "because the managers said that their American clients would not feel comfortable" if blacks were admitted. Some remember that Batista himself was denied membership in the Big Five clubs because he was of mixed racial origin, and was not "cultured." They remember the period as a dictatorship, harsh to its enemies, and intimidating to everyone else.

That many Cuban Jews remember the Batista years warmly should not come as a surprise. Memory is selective, and likely becomes more selective with the passage of time. But even the US-born children of these Cuban Jewish exiles feel for the most part the same way. They have internalized their parents' views, even if filtered through the lens of [partial] assimilation.

The acceptance of the Cuban-Jewish exile community's assertion that nearly all of Cuba's Jews emigrated after 1959 obscures the fact that since 1990 there has been a revival of Jewish life on the island, a function of the Castro regime's loosening of pressures against religious observation. Cuban exiles said that few Jews under the age of seventy-five still lived in Cuba, but in reality a small core of committed and observant Jews maintained their institutions, aided by foreign Jewish organizations, especially in Canada, Mexico, and Venezuela. The only aid before the late 1990s from the US came from a tiny group headed by Cuban Jew Eddy Levy, whose Miami-based group made regular visits to Cuba transporting medicines, clothing, and ritual items. For his efforts, the blind Mr. Levy was branded a communist sympathizer by his hardline Jewish compatriots in South Florida.

On the island, a new generation of Cuban Jews, most of them families with one partner having been raised as a non-Jew, and in many cases (using US terminology) inter-racial, has revived Jewish religious practice. This has occurred not only in Havana, but also in Santiago de Cuba, Camagüey, Matanzas, and elsewhere. Old Havana's Patronato has emerged as the center of Jewish life. Its physical renovation was funded by a grant from the Harry and Jeanette Weinberg Foundation of

Baltimore, with smaller donations from a number of Jewish Cubans in Miami discreetly sending assistance through the Greater Miami Jewish Federation. Most Cuban-Jewish exiles in the US, however, do not consider the revival to be significant. In 2001, for example, a Cuban-Jewish exile in Miami, magazine publisher Betty Heisler-Samuels, published a semifictional autobiographical memoir, *The Last Minyan in Havana.*[5] She was referring to her family's experience leaving Cuba forty-one years earlier, in 1960, sidestepping the new revival that has become especially energetic after 1999.

These comments are not meant to disparage the hardships experienced by Cuba's Jews, some of whom were forced to abandon their homes for the second time in their lives. Some managed to transfer significant assets, but others came with very little. Jews were among "the first to leave Cuba," Rachel Lapidot of the Miami Jewish Federation told a reporter, "because they had the experience of (escaping) Europe."[6] For some, this probably was true, although many non-Jews fled at the same time, including many close to the corrupt and venal Batista government. This raises a final question. Given that Miami's Cuban Jewish community has for years elected to follow the same hard-line exile politics as the larger non-Jewish enclave, how might that political decision be explained in light of traditional Jewish support for progressive causes elsewhere in the US?

Notes

1 See for example Dan Freedman, "Jewish Cuban-Americans," *San Antonio Express News* (April 22, 2001): 6A.

2 In the mid-1980s, Mark D. Szuchman and I produced an original documentary "Hotel Cuba." Mexico was the jumping-off place of choice, although a few entered by way of Jamaica or the then British Bahamas.

3 Margalit Bejarano, "From All Their Habitations: Sephardic Jews in Cuba," *Judaism* 201 (Winter 2002): 96–108.

4 This post-1939 emigration is either overlooked or downplayed in the historical literature. See Judith L. Elkin, *Jews of the Latin American Republics* (Chapel Hill: University of North Carolina Press, 1980; rev. edn. Holmes and Meier, 1998).

5 Betty Heisler-Samuels, *The Last Minyan in Havana* (Chutzpah Publishers, 2001), cited by Freedman, "Jewish Cuban-Americans," 6A.

6 Rachel Lapidot, quoted by Freedman, "Jewish Cuban-Americans," 6A.

8 While Waiting for the Ferry to Cuba

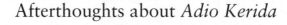

Afterthoughts about *Adio Kerida*

Ruth Behar

In some ways you might say that my entire life was a kind of preparation for making my documentary, *Adio Kerida* (Goodbye Dear Love). After all, the film is about Cuban Jews and I am a Cuban Jew. Or rather, I'm a Cuban-American Jew or a Jewish Cuban-American. Or, as they say in Miami, I'm a "Juban." I was born a Jew in Cuba and came to the United States as a child. I grew up in New York, where I spoke Spanish at home and learned to speak English in school, and have spent a large part of my life explaining how it is that I am both Cuban and Jewish, since this combination of identities has continually baffled people in the US, though less so in recent years, thanks to the discovery, at last, of multiculturalism.

Certainly one of my most basic motivations in making *Adio Kerida* was to find my own identity reflected in other Jewish Cubans. I wanted to make visible the way a variety of people negotiate the mix of being Jewish and Cuban. But the story quickly grew more complex than that. In the process of conceiving *Adio Kerida*, I made a strategic political choice. I decided to focus on Cuba's Sephardic Jews, rather than looking at the whole Cuban Jewish community, which includes Ashkenazi as well as Sephardic Jews. In other words, rather than looking at Jewishness as a single, monolithic category, I chose to call attention to the diversity of the Jewish experience, and to challenge the Ashkenazi-centered view of what it means to be a Jew.

Sephardic Jews view themselves as Hispanic people who are connected to both the Arab and African worlds because of their history of cultural and emotional interpenetration with those worlds. They descend from the Jewish populations expelled by the Spanish Inquisition in the fifteenth century. After the expulsion, they settled in the countries of the Ottoman Empire and northern Africa, which welcomed them and made it possible for them to live as Jews among Muslims. "Sepharad" means Spain in

Hebrew. Sephardic Jews are notable for having clung with a passion to their nostalgia for Spain and their love for the Spanish language, despite having been forced to leave Spain because of their ethnic and religious identity. They are misunderstood and often discriminated against in terms of the novels of Philip Roth and the movies of Woody Allen. Beyond the Jewish world, Sephardic Jews are virtually unknown as a community and they are almost invisible in the contemporary world of literature and the arts. The Cuban Sephardic community, both on and off the island, offers so rare a mix of cultural traditions – Spanish, Turkish, African, Jewish, Cuban, and American – that it remains a mystery and has not yet been portrayed in any depth in literature, art, or film.

My own autobiography motivated me to want to learn more about the Sephardic Jews. Although both my parents were born in Cuba, they brought to their marriage quite distinctly different Jewish traditions. To be less diplomatic about it, let's just say they argued a lot when I was growing up. It took me years to understand that their disagreements were rooted in the cultural split between my mother, the daughter of Ashkenazi immigrants from Poland and Byelorussia, and my father, the son of Sephardic immigrants from Turkey. In my mother's family, my father was known as "*el turco*," and this was not a term of endearment. Instead, it was a way of referring to my father's hot temper, unforgiving soul, and patriarchal dominance. The Ashkenazi side, which thought of themselves as more rational, tolerant, and modern, viewed those character flaws as elements of a primitive Turkish character. I learned this early in life, because whenever my mother got angry with me she'd say I was just like my father. And my mother's family, in which I largely grew up, always reminded me that with my dark, curly hair, my less than good temper, and my own inability to forgive, I too was more like my relatives on the other side, more like the turcos.

In retrospect, I realize that I was fortunate to have known more than one way of being Jewish. It allowed me to understand from an early age that Jews were a diasporic people and had always had to find ways to creatively mesh their Jewish identity with the culture of the people they lived among. On a more critical note, I learned early on that, for reasons that eluded me, the Ashkenazi Jews had gained the upper hand in defining what it meant to be a Jew. When I was growing up, on the first night of Passover we always held our first Seder at the home of my maternal grandparents and ate gefilte fish, matzo ball soup, and boiled chicken. On the second night, always *the second night*, we went to the home of my paternal grandparents and we ate haroset made with raisins and dates, egg lemon soup, stuffed tomatoes, and a holiday almond cake dripping with honey; this cuisine, my mother always reminded me, was very delicious but very bad for our figures, and indeed my father's mother was quite fat. Finally, at the end of the eight days of Passover, as if trying to resolve the contradiction of our doubled Jewishness through gastronomic means, my father would insist on taking my mother, my brother, and me to El Rincon Criollo on Junction Boulevard in Queens for Cuban black beans and palmilla steak with onions.

In short, the Sephardim were mysterious to me, even though as a "half-fie" and an ill-tempered soul I was a part of them. I didn't really know who these people, "my people," were. It all came down to the basic fact that being my father's daughter and being Sephardic were inseparable things for me. Inheriting my Sephardic identity from my father was a vexed issue because for many years he and I were locked in a contest of wills. In our life together, my father had usually either been absolutely furious with me or not speaking to me at all. As a teenager I'd upset him by going to college against his will and as a grown woman I'd upset him by writing stories about him and my mother that he thought shamed and dishonored them. When I began to travel regularly to Cuba in the 1990s, I further upset him by returning to the country from which he had fled at great risk in the early 1960s, and he viewed my desire to reconnect with Cuba as yet another manifestation of my ingratitude and disrespect.

So naturally, given this history of heartbreak between my Sephardic father and me, I knew I had to make *Adio Kerida* and I had to make it for my father. Although I couldn't convince my father to go to Cuba with me, I would go and make this film for him. I would dedicate it to him, even if I had to do it against his will. I would show him what kind of people we are, we the Sephardic Jews, with our strong tempers and our inability to forgive. For despite the years of conflict with my father, I had never given up my Behar last name, the name I inherited from my father, the Béjar that is still the name of a town in northwestern Spain. And as I embarked on the making of *Adio Kerida*, it is this name that I would find all over Cuba, both among the living Sephardic Jews I met and the many Sephardic Jews who have departed to the next world and whose tombs abound in the cemeteries of the island.

Once I realized that *Adio Kerida* would be for my father, I hoped that he would appear in the film. But he vehemently refused. So I began filming in Cuba, until I could convince him to cooperate (in other words, while waiting). One way or another, I was going to get him to be in my film, and this informed the other key strategic political choice I made. I decided that I would include in my film both Sephardic Jews who remain on the island and Sephardic Jews from Cuba who now reside in the US. This meant that my film would create a bridge that doesn't yet exist in reality. The Sephardic Jewish community of Cuba is divided by the politics of revolution and exile, and many members of the community who live in the States are unwilling to return to Cuba or even be in touch with fellow Sephardic Jews on the island. In my film, these Cuban Sephardic Jews would be shown side by side, embracing their common Sephardic and Cuban heritage.

Adio Kerida was the culmination, for me, of a long process of reconnecting with Cuba and of forging ties with the literary, artistic, and intellectual communities of both the island and the Cuban-Americans left in the US. I have traveled back and forth to Cuba since 1991, going three times a year for brief but intense visits.

I first returned to Cuba in 1979 as a graduate student, in hopes of gaining permission to carry out my dissertation fieldwork in anthropology on the island. This was during the famous moment of the thaw in US–Cuban relations led by then President Jimmy Carter, when it appeared that normalization of relations would soon take place. After much internal debate, Cuba both released political prisoners and agreed to the family reunification program, which allowed over a hundred thousand Cuban-Americans who left the island in the 1960s to return to visit their families between 1978 and 1979. But then, in 1980, came the Mariel exodus, which took everyone by surprise, leading to the dramatic departure of one hundred and twenty thousand Cubans to the US. Blame for the mass exodus was placed on the *gusanos*, the so-called worms of the revolution. The returning immigrants came to be viewed as a contaminating force, who returned to Cuba to flaunt the wealth they had obtained as immigrants in the capitalist US. Relations between the US and Cuba returned to their previous freeze and Cuban-Americans were again viewed as suspect by the official island sectors. My desire as a Cuban-American to return to the island to do research was no longer looked upon with favor. Unable to return, I embarked on a long detour as an anthropologist, doing research in Spain and then Mexico, before finding myself in Cuba again in the 1990s.

In 1979 it had been impossible to leave the city of Havana without official government permission. Foreign visitors, especially from the United States, were carefully watched. As a Cuban-American I was especially suspect and was appointed my own personal spy. At the time I was too innocent to realize that the friendly young man, who always sat next to me on the bus and wanted to know everything about me, was monitoring my activities. When I returned in 1991, I discovered quite another Cuba, a country whose survival now depended upon tourists, including those who came from the great enemy to the north, maintaining its embargo against the naughty communist island, and making it illegal, in fact, for people from the US to visit as tourists. This was a Cuba whose survival now also depended upon offering a new kind of welcome, including to those Cuban-Americans who were not the confident, idealistic Marxists who returned to Cuba with the Antonio Maceo Brigades of the 1970s. By the 1990s the island was extending its welcome even to those wishy-washy Cuban-Americans of the left, uncertain liberals who hadn't yet made up their minds about Cuba.

It was a painful era, when Cuba sought to maintain its revolutionary goals while making the transition from being dependent on the former Soviet Union to becoming an independent player in the new global economy. The country was badly in need of hard currency, mired by all accounts in an economic and moral crisis. On a Cuban television cooking show, women were shown how to make breaded grapefruit-rind "steaks" for their families to curb hunger pangs. Contradictions between socialist ideology and everyday social life grew ever more dissonant. By the mid-1990s the US dollar had become a legal currency in Cuba. Essential items like soap, detergent, and cooking oil could only be obtained with dollars, yet Cuban salaries continued to be paid in Cuban *pesos*. The informal economy expanded as more and more Cubans went hustling for dollars, and tourism – including sex tourism – became a major sector for economic growth.

At the same time, after three decades of suppressing religious observance, the government ceased to penalize any Cubans, including party members, who openly practiced religion. Increasing numbers of Cubans began to return to Catholicism, Protestantism, Judaism, and Santeria, among other religions, in search of spiritual solace. With the return of God to Cuba, the island became safe again for people from the US to visit. They began to come in record numbers, bolstered by the fact that the embargo permits them to travel to Cuba legally if they are traveling as part of a humanitarian mission to deliver religious assistance.

Not only was religion legally an open door for people from the US to cross the border into Cuba, but so too was the larger category of cultural exchange. The charm that Cuba holds for so many US visitors has precisely to do with the fact that Cuba represents a form of utopian dreaming carried out in opposition to US political interests. By the late 1990s numerous people from the US were traveling to Cuba in search of the unique independence of Cuban music, art, and literature. Ry Cooder's "Buena Vista Social Club" musical CD, followed by Wim Wender's documentary about Cooder's heroic discovery of the lost ancient Cuban mariners, brought new attention, and nostalgia, to bear on Cuba and suggested to US citizens that their embargo was depriving them of the richness of Cuban culture.

The US market is now flooded with CDs of Cuban music (you can hear them in any Starbucks or Borders), new films about Cuba, novels and memoirs about Cuba, ethnographies of Cuban Santeria, photography books about Cuba, and architectural studies of the island. A Cuban revolution is happening in the United States and it has created an insatiable desire for all things Cuban.

My own return journey to Cuba, which began over a decade ago and is still in progress, unfolded in the midst of all these 1990s developments. As the years passed, and I traveled back and forth to Cuba from Michigan for more than thirty visits, I began to recognize that my return journey, even though it was profoundly personal and spiritual and began long before what I call "the Cuba boom," could not be seen as any more or less exalted than the Cuba journeys of Cooder, or the sex tourists, or the gallery curators, or Pastors for Peace, or Jewish Solidarity, not to mention the journeys of all the other Cuban-Americans who were embarking on their own personal and spiritual quests. I found myself unable to think of Cuba as a field site and in my first emotional reencounters with the island I turned to poetry, one of my youthful passions. But the anthropologist in me wanted to know whether my experiences had a social foundation, and so I became involved in creating a collective tapestry of voices and visions of Cubans of the island and Cubans of the diaspora who were of my generation, likewise seeking a common culture and memory.

During these years of visits to Cuba I attended Jewish services at the synagogues in Havana and also took trips to the provinces to get to know the synagogues and Jewish communities in Cienfuegos, Camaguey, and Santiago de Cuba. But I wasn't in any way trying to study the Jews of Cuba. I myself was still uncertain about what my Jewishness meant to me. I'd spent years of my life studying Catholic cultures in Spain and Mexico and keeping my Jewish identity well hidden so as not to raise any eyebrows, especially since I was so readily accepted in the communities I studied because I am a native Spanish speaker. Although I took pleasure in meeting Jews in Cuba and found it moving to attend services at the Patronato synagogue in Havana, which is just down the street from where I lived as a child, I rarely snapped any pictures or carried out interviews.

I wanted simply to be a Jew in Cuba and not have to explain my identity to anyone. I found that the combination of Cuban pluralistic tolerance and revolutionary secularism made it easy to be a Jew in Cuba. I could openly say I was Jewish to any and every Cuban. This was immensely liberating after my years of *conversa*-like hiding of my Jewishness in Spain and Mexico. In turn, I felt comfortable among the Jews of the island because they were often as uncertain about their Jewishness as I was about mine. Not that Judaism was foreign to me. After all, I went to Hebrew School and can read liturgical Hebrew, and my family observed the major Jewish holidays. But over the years I'd lost touch with my Jewish identity. I was no longer sure what kind of Jew I wanted to be. I found it reassuring to be among Jews in Cuba who didn't quite know what to say or do at Jewish services, to be among Jews who were learning how to be Jews. If there was hope for them, there was hope for me. Later, as my son Gabriel's bar mitzvah approached and I decided to learn how to chant Torah along with him, I took pleasure in seeing that the Jews in Cuba, whom I'd gotten to know over the years, were becoming more confident and knowledgeable about their Jewishness too.

The four synagogues in Havana – Chevet Ahim, Adath Israel, El Patronato, and el Centro Hebreo Sefaradí – had never been shut down (although the fifth, the US synagogue, had been allowed to fall into ruins). Yet Jewish services were largely attended by older people during the 1960s, 1970s, and 1980s. The Jewish community, once at least fifteen thousand strong, had been decimated by the Cuban revolution, which undertook to nationalize the many small businesses owned by Jewish Cubans, the majority of whom left in the early 1960s and resettled in Miami and New York. With only a few thousand Jews left on the island, a number that eventually declined to around a thousand, it was difficult to maintain a strong Jewish community. In addition, the Cuban revolution frowned upon religious observance of any kind. Jews weren't singled out for persecution because of their ethnicity or faith, but they chose like other Cubans to pull away from religion and to suppress any sense of their own ethnic difference in order to fully integrate themselves into the revolutionary process, which was firmly rooted in nationalism and unity.

But by the 1990s, in the new atmosphere of religious tolerance, Jewish families and Jewish young people began to flock to the synagogues once more. Most of these Jews were of mixed heritage and many were discovering their Jewishness for the first time. Motivations for coming out as Jews were diverse. Some were attracted by the possibility of exploring their spirituality because it had previously been taboo. Others were glad for the Sabbath meals that were offered after the services. Yet others, learning that the Israeli government would cover the voyage and resettlement of Jewish Cubans who wanted to leave the island, treated the synagogues as travel agencies that could yield a ticket out of Cuba and to a new life in Israel.

Throughout the revolutionary period, Jewish life had been sustained on the island with the assistance of Jewish organizations in Canada and Latin America, which sent matzo and wine on Passover and provided other modest but essential help. But it wasn't until the 1990s that major support began to arrive through the American Joint Distribution Committee and B'nai B'rith. Helping the Jews of Cuba to survive as Jews became a priority of these Jewish American organizations, which set up "missions" to assist the Jews of Cuba through donations of food, medicine, clothes, and books, as well as through Jewish education, which is most desperately needed in a country where there is not even a single rabbi.

These missions had a very strong impact indeed. By the end of the century, Jewish synagogue life in Cuba was beginning more closely to resemble standard Jewish practice in the US. The Patronato synagogue, which I'd seen in the early 1990s with a leaking roof that let in the doves, had been restored to its former grandeur and updated with computers and a video screening room. Although the Jewish community appeared to be shrinking as a result of elderly deaths and recent immigration to Israel, more and more Jewish American visitors continued to arrive on the island on good will "missions" to save the last of the Jews who survived communism. Jewish American visitors became so ubiquitous that it seemed as if every Jew in Cuba had at least ten Jewish Americans who wanted to help him or her continue being a Jew in Cuba.

The Jews of Cuba, by the end of the century, had become an exotic tribe. To outsiders they had come to seem as rare as the !Kung of the Kalahari Desert, and as over-studied, over-observed, over-photographed, over-anthropologized, and elusive.

In the midst of this largely Ashkenazi-American "discovery" of Jews on the island, I entered the scene with a video camera wanting to make *Adio Kerida*. But where was I to place myself as a Cuban-American Jew of mixed Ashkenazi-Sephardic heritage? It was December of 1999, the century was ending, and I felt an immense urgency to begin telling the story I knew about the Jews of Cuba. I thought of following in the footsteps of filmmaker Dennis O'Rourke and making a kind of Jewish-Cuban version of "Cannibal Tours," focusing my camera on the Jewish American tourists who came on missions to see the Jews of Cuba. I knew I was, to an extent, complicit in their exoticizing gaze, for in the end I too would be returning to the United States. And yet, though I wanted to incorporate a strong touch of irony in my film, it wasn't a tonality I wanted to sustain for the entire piece. There were too many other sentiments, experiences, and forms of knowing I wanted to examine. So I opted instead to show how my own shifting identity, as a returning Cuban Jew, a cultural anthropologist, and a tourist in my native country, opened a window onto a range of diasporic identities.

With minimal funds and little previous filmmaking experience (I'd studied photography and made a short 16mm film in graduate school), I jumped into the project of *Adio Kerida*, assisted by Gisela Fosado and Umi Vaughan, graduate students in anthropology at the University of Michigan, who were embarking on their own ethnographic research projects in Cuba, in itself yet another phenomenon of the "Cuba boom." (For Anglo-American ethnography had departed the island after the embargo, with the sole exception of Oscar Lewis's trilogy, which brought him much suffering. A new generation of young anthropologists is now doing ethnography in Cuba.)

I didn't have a script, and I had only a rough idea of who would be the main protagonists of the story. One thing I knew from the start: the documentary would be called *Adio Kerida*, which is the title of a popular Sephardic song of nineteenth-century origin. *Adio Kerida* was one of the few Sephardic songs I knew by heart and could actually sing. It was among the few remnants of Sephardic culture that had been passed on to me. And the song spoke of unforgiveness, the quality that my Ashkenazi family had seen as a strongly Sephardic characteristic. It is, indeed, the bitter lament of a lover who utters an angry goodbye after a beloved's rejection.

I was drawn to the song because I felt it could reference many layers of goodbyes, from the bitter goodbyes of Sephardic Jews, who were forced to leave their beloved Spain in 1492, to the more recent goodbyes of Sephardic Jews who had left Cuba in the 1960s, and yet more poignantly, to the immediate goodbyes of those Sephardic Jews who were leaving the island for Israel even as I hurried to interview them. I also felt the song could reference the desire for return that is so often the other side of exilic departure, and speak to my own desire to find a way to return to Cuba, in contrast to my father's definitive goodbye.

With the lyrics to the *Adio Kerida* song in my head, I went in search of Jewish spaces, the synagogues and Jewish cemeteries where Jews had left traces of their presence on the island. One of the most important epiphanies took place early in the process of filming. As José Levy Tur, the director of the Centro Hebreo Sefaradí, was showing us the nine Torahs brought to Cuba from Turkey by the Sephardic Jews, I could hear live Afro-Cuban music and singing from some place close by. Interrupting the interview, I asked José Levy where the music was coming from and he casually told me it was coming from next door, from the space that had once been the main sanctuary of the synagogue. As he explained, the Jewish community was now so small that their religious services had been moved to what had once been the women's meeting room, the room we were in. But what had been the majestic main sanctuary was located next door. Moving to the back of the room, we discovered a peephole through which we could look to the other side and see the musicians, who turned out to be Síntesis, a well known Afro-Cuban musical group. We then went outside and entered through the main door of the synagogue to the old sanctuary, which was now used as a rehearsal space by Síntesis. They were rehearsing the song "Obbatala," the name of a Santeria deity, and I was struck by the way an Afro-Cuban working of spirit now inhabited what had once been a Jewish religious space.

This mutuality, the play of disparate identities, spiritualities, and histories within shared spaces, became central to the film. The reality of Jewish-Cuban and Afro-Cuban religiosity existing side-by-side was brought home to me in the relationship between José Levy and his daughter Danayda, who is Afro-Cuban and has been brought up by him as a Jew. Not long after, while observing the children in the Sunday Hebrew school at the Patronato synagogue, I met an Afro-Cuban boy, Miguelito, whose mother told me he liked to drum Afro-Cuban rhythms on the buckets he uses to take his bath. As soon as I saw him drumming passionately on the buckets, a Jewish star dangling from his neck, I knew that Miguelito had to be in my film. What I couldn't have predicted is that on my last filming trip in the summer of 2001, he would announce on camera his upcoming departure to Israel with his family.

The broken star in the Guanabacoa cemetery, near Havana, Cuba

Danayda and Levy, Havana, Cuba

Another different, painful goodbye story had already been told to me by Alberto Behar, whose name, curiously, is the same as my father's.

Alberto's revolutionary father, who rejected religion throughout his adult life, asked his son on his deathbed to bury him in the Jewish cemetery outside Havana. Confronted with the need to say the mourner's Kaddish, Alberto discovered he didn't know what a Kaddish was. He refused simply to repeat the words senselessly and was haunted for years by his inability to bid his father a proper goodbye. Only by learning to chant Torah was Alberto finally able to bring peace to his heart. Telling this story was for Alberto such a transformative experience that he subsequently pulled together all of his savings and had a tombstone built for his father in the Jewish cemetery.

Miguel practicing drums, Havana, Cuba

With these key stories in place, I began to look for other cultural fusions closer to home, in Miami. There, I was immediately attracted to Alberto and Elza Habif, sellers of Turkish good luck charms, whose mirrored store is full of protective eyes. SAMY, a flamboyant gay hairdresser who keeps both a Jewish *hamsa* and a pair of scissors from the Vatican in his salon and whose grandfather, Samuel Cohen, "was like a rabbi," offered some very necessary humor and bold honesty, while belly-dancer Myriam Eli, who merges flamenco, Afro-Cuban, and Turkish traditions in her dance, raised key questions about the "boxes" into which multiple identities have to fit in the United States.

For the closing fragments of the film's mosaic of Cuban Sephardic identity in the US diaspora, I came even closer to home, within my own extended family. My uncle Enrique, a nouveau street peddler, sells clothes from his truck on Miami streets in the tradition of my grandfather and other Sephardic street peddlers from Turkey. My aunt Fanny conserves a nightgown that belonged to her grandmother in Turkey and traveled with her mother, my grandmother, from Turkey to Cuba to the United States. And my cousin Isaquito uproariously remembers what it was like to grow up in a Havana tenement on Calle Oficios, where the Sephardic Jews, the turcos, lived upstairs looking out on the sea, above the prostitutes below, and where sometimes even the nicest of Sephardic Jewish boys succumbed to the temptation of visiting the ladies they delicately referred to in Turkish as *oruspu*.

Finally it came time to go to New York to see if my father would agree to be in my film. Although my father said he would only allow us to film him for fifteen minutes, he had clearly been preparing himself for his interview. He'd hunted down the lyrics to the "Adio Kerida" song and rehearsed his singing with my mother. When Gisela Fosado turned on the camera, he was clearly moved to be able to sing the song for us, and held his hand to his heart, trembling with emotion. Afterwards, he surprised me by walking around the house, giving a kind of tour and pointing out the significance of different objects he'd brought home from his journeys over the years, including a Sephardic cookbook from Istanbul. And I was overjoyed when he agreed to allow us to film him in the Rincon Criollo Restaurant. This was the one setting in which I had dreamed of capturing him, because this is his "little Cuba" and he is always in a good mood there.

It was only later, in the last stages of the editing process, that I realized we needed to balance out the Cuban part of my father's scene with the Sephardic part. I also wanted to connect the Cuban cemetery clips, where the Behar name hauntingly surfaces in so many of the tombstones, with cemetery clips in the US. With a bit of fear, I asked my father if we could film him in the Jewish cemetery in New Jersey where both his parents are buried and where he and my mother wish to be buried when their time comes. He willingly agreed and I went with Marc Drake, my other key camera person and editor, to be filmed with my parents there. It was, naturally, an eerie moment for me, one which reinforces the theme of goodbye, because my parents already know that their final resting place will not be in Cuba but in the US.

From the beginning, I expected to include my brother Mori in the film. He is such a strong counterpoint to me and is one of the few people who can always make me laugh. When asked to think about being Sephardic, the first association that comes to him is that all the women were very fat. This he then connects jokingly to his dedication to playing the bass, "the big old lady." He hates to travel and can't understand what this anthropology thing is all about. And yet he participates in my film by improvising beautiful piano music, most memorably around the "Adio Kerida" song, joining me in my journey through the medium he most adores.

In an early version of *Adio Kerida*, the movie ended with my brother and then cut to the ocean splashing wildly over the malecón of Havana.

But when I showed this version to colleagues and students in Ann Arbor in the spring of 2001, I was told that I ought to add a concluding scene in Michigan. I decided to create a scene that would revolve around a poem I'd written called "Prayer," about fears I've experienced often, of getting lost and not finding my way home.

Ruth Behar talking with her father, New York City at the South Street Seaport

I thought this scene was finished when the Spanish-language version of *Adio Kerida* premiered in the Havana Film Festival in December of 2001. But as I watched it several times in Cuba, I realized it wasn't yet complete. I came back to a snowy January in Michigan and realized that this snow and the desolation it evoked for me needed to be added to that last section. I also realized that the story of my own "intermarriage" to my husband David needed to be told, even if briefly, at the end, so that viewers could see that I too, like the Jews still on the island, had married out, was that kind of Jew who'd crossed the border.

After working on it for over two years, I tell myself that *Adio Kerida* is done. It has been enthusiastically received by the Jewish-Cuban community in Havana and Miami, and most crucially of all, my father likes it. My mother's eating of the mango on camera (my father calls it her "Mango 101") is now part of the folklore of the Jewish-Cuban community, as is my father's line about how he'll return to Cuba when the ferry from Key West is operating again.

Ruth Behar with the Torah in the Centro Sefaradi, Havana, Cuba

It's unusual to see a film that is so thoroughly Cuban and Latino, and yet focuses on Jewish identity. As a film that is mostly spoken in Spanish, it has a broad appeal for Latinos. The film has been shown already in two important Latino film festivals, in San Antonio and San Diego, and there is continuing interest in the film among Latino viewers. It hasn't been picked up quite so readily yet by Jewish film festivals (though it was shown in the Detroit Jewish film festival and will be shown in the Boston Jewish film festival), and I can only speculate as to whether this has to do with the Sephardic theme (always of lesser interest to Ashkenazi Jewish Americans, who run the festivals, than films about Israel, the Holocaust, and the ultra-Orthodox Lubavitch), or my touch of irony about Jewish American visits to Cuba, or the inclusion of Afro-Cubans and other Jews of mixed heritage in a film about Jews.

Or perhaps, my film is Jewish without being quite Jewish enough. It ends on a decidedly Cuban note, with the trio of Cuban musicians on the famous Habana malecón improvising a song about the split persona of Ruti/Ruth saying goodbye to Cuba, but returning every year to visit the island she left behind before she was old enough to remember it. Maybe this desire for Cuba is something only Jewish-Cubans can fully understand. The *kerida*, after all, is Cuba, but "beloved" is spelled in Ladino with a "k" rather than the correct Spanish *querida*, to emphasize that the beloved Cuba is always a fiction, always an imaginary homeland. And I expect that will still be true even if the ferry from Key West to Cuba ever starts operating again.

Note: This chapter is reprinted with kind permission from the author from an article that appeared in the *Michigan Quarterly Review* (Fall, 2002).

Caribbean Hybridity and the Jews of Martinique

For Michael M. Horowitz

William F. S. Miles

Little by little we assimilate [in the French West Indies] the prejudices . . . that come to us from Europe. But we don't accept everything . . . Antisemitism, for example, does not exist because there are no Jews, or so few.

> Frantz Fanon, *Peau Noire, Masques Blancs* (Black Skin, White Masks) (Paris: Editions du Seuil, 1952), 155

On account of the Holocaust, the Jews now allow themselves to do anything.

> French West Indian representative to the French National Assembly, in a private aside, March 2002

An Incomplete Créolité

More than any of the other French islands in the Caribbean, Martinique celebrates her diversity, her hybridity, her *métissage* – in short, her *créolité*. Once content to proclaim her identity *vis-à-vis* metropolitan France through her African heritage (qua *négritude*), modern Martinique fully assumes the full panoply of ethnic components of her past. In addition to the descendants of slaves, this reimagined community, to paraphrase Benedict Anderson, now consciously incorporates East Indian, Amerindian, Caucasian, and "Syrian" elements of her population. All these have blended together to create a multicolored Martinique pastiche. This créolité is Martinique's greatest claim to specificity within the greater French Republic.[1]

Yet one community remains excluded from this idealized collective sense of self: the Jews. Although there has been a Jewish presence, albeit not continuous, in Martinique since its establishment as a French colony in the seventeenth century, Jews are not included in the evolving

139

Martinican sense of self. Both sides are responsible. Martinicans, however multicultural in terms of race and ethnicity, remain singularly Christian, and especially Catholic, in terms of religious identity. From the Jewish side, the reticence stems less from conception of God than sense of place: even after three centuries, the Jews do not see themselves as rooted on the island. They are there, but self-marginalized; sociological maroons, would-be escapees from a surrounding society that, with some reason, they distrust. Until Martinique assumes the Jewish community within her sense of multicultural identity, and until Jews themselves overcome their reluctance to psychologically assume their geographical reality, the much-heralded créolité of Martinique will remain incomplete.

From the Ancien Régime to the Founding of the ACIM

The Original Martinican Jews[2]

Jews were among the earliest settlers of Martinique. Less than twenty years after Belain d'Esnambuc took possession of the island for France, Dutch Jews fleeing from Brazil, especially Recife, after the conquest by the Portuguese in 1654, took refuge on the northeast peninsula of Martinique, an area that is still known as Little Brazil.[3] Although they are credited with introducing the technology for the crystallization and whitening of sugar cane – including water and wind mills and irrigation canals – these "ex-*marranos*" suffered official persecution.[4] In 1659, under pressure from the Jesuits, they were prohibited from trading, and in 1683, Louis XIV ordered their expulsion from the island. They were fewer than eighty in number. Some fled to Barbados; others became "*conversos*," Christians by compulsion.

In the meantime, though, the Jews in seventeenth-century Martinique flourished economically after the ban on commerce was modified, and in fact Jews *not* trading on Shabbat were subject to a fine. Their wealth could be measured in ownership of slaves: one hundred. They were also relatively free to practice their faith:

"The Jews who are settled here use Saturday to conduct their ceremonies, oblige their Negroes and indentured servants to respect their Sabbath and to work on Sunday. [They] appear in public . . . from Holy Thursday to Easter Sunday, contrary to what is permitted in those communities in Europe where they are tolerated."[5] In the French Caribbean as in Europe, the Jews were disliked for their economic prowess, perceived as exercising a stranglehold on others: "I believe it necessary for the king to send a decree regarding the Jews. They have land, their own homes, Christian slaves, and a great quantity of Christian salesmen. They conduct almost all of the trade, and they are rapidly multiplying, so that trade is practically all in their hands."[6]

Prominent among these first Martinican Jews were Jacob Gabaye of Saint-Pierre, Martinique's first capital, whose property housed a rudimentary synagogue and a Jewish cemetery; Jacob Louis of Rivière Salée; Abraham Bueno of Marigot; Isaac Le Tob of Carbet; and especially Benjamin da Costa, agricultural pioneer of cocoa, indigo, and sugar cane. Da Costa chocolate and fruit jams, a delicacy learned from the indigenous Carib Indians who were later exterminated, were sold in Amsterdam, Bordeaux, and Bayonne. Da Costa's introduction of sugar processing in 1655 would forever change the landscape of the island.

It galled the island's Jesuit conscience that the Jews were not ghettoized: "They mix with Christians with impunity, drink and eat with them and, under the pretext of trade and business, deceive unsuspecting people and corrupt the innocence of Christian women and girls . . . Their children play with Christian children with no qualms whatsoever."[7] Finally, the infamous Code Noir of 1685, otherwise known as the document regularizing the practice of slavery in the French Empire, formalized Louis XIV's expulsion order of the Jews: "We instruct all of our officers to chase out of our islands all the Jews who have taken up residence there, along with all other declared enemies of the Christian name . . . under penalty of arrest and confiscation of property."[8]

Local enforcement of the French Caribbean *judenrein* policy, however, was somewhat lax. In 1695, the French chancellery took the governor of Martinique, the Count de Blénac, to task for allowing six Jewish families to remain there, reminding him that, "it is not permitted for any trader, or any one else practicing the Jewish religion, to settle in the French islands and colonies of America."[9] Presumably, de Blénac heeded the royal anti-Semitic call to order.

Nevertheless, as of 1727 Jews managed to trickle back to Martinique, among them the twenty-two-year-old Abraham, son of Anthoine, of the prominent Gradis family of Bordeaux, who came in 1728. Abraham, representing a company that provisioned the navy, especially with rum, worked closely with his brother David, and the firm later carried the Gradis name. Abraham, a bachelor with no known children, died at the age of thirty-two, leaving behind a notarized last will and testament that bequeathed his property to his two unmarried sisters Judith and Rebecca. French authorities nevertheless invalidated the will and claimed the inheritance for the royal treasury on the grounds that Gradis, as a Jew, had no legal status on the island.[10]

The Gradis family nevertheless prospered along with the island's sugar industry. Their plantation was situated in Basse-Pointe, on the island's northern shore; the Depaz family plantation (Lopes Depaz got his start as a salesman for the Gradises) was built near Saint-Pierre.[11] Apparently to regularize their status, in 1764 the "community of merchants of the Hebraic nation residing on [the] island" beseeched the king to authorize their residence, their construction of sugar mills, and their manufacture of other products. Whether officially or tacitly, royal approval seems to have been granted. As island sugar dissolved into Creole coffee, so did Old Regime Jewish families gradually dissolve into the surrounding West Indian society. Some, such as the Depaz, assimilated into the white French Catholic aristocracy, known as *békés*.[12] Others, such as the Bueno (becoming Lebon) and the Lévy, seem to have passed their names on to a black and brown population otherwise oblivious to the Semitic origin of their (probably slave-owning) ancestors.[13] With the holocaustal eruption of Mount Pelée that destroyed Saint-Pierre in 1902, few traces of Martinique's pre-modern Jewish presence remained, with the rare exception of the rum distilling Meyer family.[14] It was left to the collaborationist Vichy regime to revive the specter of anti-Semitism on an island that was home to so few Jews.

World War II

From 1940 to 1943 Martinique was ruled by Admiral Georges Robert, Vichy-appointed head of the French Antilles. Admiral Robert, seconded by Governor Henri Bresolles and then from early 1941 Governor Yves Nicol, obligingly applied the anti-Semitic legislation promulgated in metropolitan France to the colony.[15] Among the closest confidants of Robert was the Count of Cerezy, described by the British Espionage Service for Martinique as "very anti-Semitic." The count reputedly ordered the repatriation of would-be Jewish refugees to Martinique from North Africa and metropolitan France.[16] Among the Jewish intellectuals who passed through Martinique during this period was Claude Lévi-Strauss. The celebrated anthropologist is said to have been denigrated by the local regime as a "judeo-[free] mason in the pay of the Americans."[17] Among the "clandestine passengers" ordered into administrative internment at the military camp in Balata for being "individuals dangerous for the national defense and public security," were a certain Abraham Weisz and one Lévi.[18]

Anti-Semitic laws of Vichy France were reproduced in the *Journal Officiel de la Martinique* (*JOM*). As a result of the "law regarding the status of Jews" published in the *JOM* of October 26, 1940, numerous Martinicans were questioned. The archives contain the declarations of 236 such declarations of civil servants – teachers, judges, welfare workers (including nuns), and others – attesting to their "non-belonging to the Jewish race."[19] In a file entitled "suspicious agents" a cablegram from the governor's office dated December 10, 1940, refers to the "discreet investigation" of two civil servants suspected of being Jewish: Professor Salanski and Jean Kehrig. The files also contain the detailed declarations of Catholic ancestry, upbringing, and marriage of the suspiciously named (to Vichy) Guthmann.[20]

Two documents, carefully catalogued by the colonial Vichy authorities, attest to the presence of Jews on the island. A list from August 1, 1941, signed by the gendarme Captain Delpech, contains the names of 22 Jewish adults, including four women and one gentile woman with a Jewish husband whose child is counted as a Jew. (It was compulsory for Jews to so declare themselves.)[21] For these 23 adults the list enumerates fourteen spouses, five of whom are non-Jews, and twenty-seven children, three of whom are counted as non-Jews.[22] Of the 22 named Jewish adults, fourteen are listed as having French nationality, three Romanian, two Algerian, one Belgian, one Turkish, and one "Palestinian." Of the 55 persons thus listed as Jewish by the French authorities, thirteen (principally the families of the Algerians Joseph Michkal and Abba Simon Abadi, relocated in Palestine) were absent. Three months later, with the departure of the Stainer family, Madame Raymonde Hayman, wife of the non-Jewish court counsel, and the engineer Henri Halphen, the resident Jewish population had dropped to thirty-six.[23] Ten of these remaining Jewish heads of household worked as merchants, mostly in fabrics. They also included two photographers (widow Germaine Gold, 36 and Daniel Stern, 23), a doctor (Paul Stern, 31), a bank employee (Louis Sussfeld, 34), a long-haul cargo captain (Raymond Sazias, 39), a builder (Jacques Kalfon, 44), a merchant (Fortuné Danon, 48), and a soldier (Arnold Lato, 25, previously serving in French Guiana).[24] Martinique's sole teacher known to be Jewish, Ilija (Elijiah) Salanski (30), had been forced out of his profession.[25] Sarah Lazareff, wife of the prominent West Indian founder of the Clément rum distillery is also listed.[26] Although there was no deportation, only three of these Jews remained in Martinique after the war and left behind any known descendants. The three exceptions are Lazareff, Kalfon, and Danon (the first two of whom had non-Jewish spouses), all of whose children are thoroughly creolized.[27]

In the inner city neighborhood of Terres-Sainville (Fort-de-France), next to St. Antoine's Church and the headquarters of the Martinican Communist Party, there is a plaque that reads in French: "The French Republic renders homage to the memory of the victims of racist and anti-Semitic Persecutions committed under the de facto authority called 'Government of the French State' (1940–1944) Let us never forget."

Wreaths are laid at the monument annually on July 16 by representatives of the French government, the municipality of Fort-de-France, and the Jewish community to mark the roundup of Jews at Vel d'Hiv in Paris. A similar ceremony is also held at the better known, older and more centrally located war memorial, the *Monument aux Morts*, on the waterfront, for the annual French ceremony in April marking the "memory of the victims and heroes of the deportation."

Martinique veterans in commemoration of victims of French anti-Semitism

Wreath laying in Martinique for victims of French anti-Semitism

Rebirth of a Jewish Presence

The 1970s saw the rebirth of a Jewish presence in Martinique, a ripple effect of the Algerian war of liberation that ended in 1962. Considered French citizens by the Crémieux Law of 1870, with independence Algerian Jews felt constrained to leave their country. A few of those whose resettlement in France left them feeling restless or unfulfilled imagined the West Indies as a French land of opportunity more akin to their Mediterranean memories than the lifestyle others had recreated in the southern seaport of Marseilles; sheer climate also was a draw. Young adventurers, they found a niche for themselves as door-to-door salesmen specializing in bedding such as sheets and mattresses, novel electrical appliances including televisions, jewelry, and furniture. Overlapping with an extension of banking and credit services to rural families not previously benefiting from such facilities, these young Jewish traders served as middlemen of the new consumer economy.

While not considering themselves religious, this new wave of Jews did strive to preserve basic traditions of Jewish life. Religious services for the high holidays were held in individuals' homes, until space constraints necessitated the renting of hotel space. A Tiberias-based kosher butcher would travel across the Atlantic to perform ritual slaughtering.

In 1976 the *Association Cultuelle (sic) Israélite de la Martinique* (Hebrew Worship Center of Martinique, ACIM) was officially formed and registered with the prefecture. Until 1979 a building in Terres-Sainville was used as a synagogue, replaced by one in Plateau Fofo in Schoelcher. For high holidays and sacramental occasions, such as weddings, bar mitzvahs, and burials, a rabbi would be brought in from Caracas. Kosher meat was also imported from Venezuela. Even *Mimouna*, the specifically Sephardic festivity marking the end of Passover, came to be celebrated in Martinique.

In February 1996 a major step in the apparent anchoring of the community was taken with the inauguration of a new synagogue, *Kenaf Aaretz*, meaning wing or ends of the earth, in Anse Gouraud, Schoelcher. High-level representatives from the national and local governments, the cathedral, the armed forces, and civil society, including members of the local Palestinian community, attended. Traveling from Paris for the occasion, Jean Kahn, president of the *Consistoire Central des Institutions Juives de France*, and Joseph Sitruk, the Grand Rabbi of France, presided over the ceremony. The Kenaf Aaertz Community Center runs religious school classes, maintains a *mikva*, or ritual bath, sells kosher meats and wines, publishes a monthly newsletter, and employs a full-time rabbi. Independent of the center, located in the capital city, are two kosher restaurants, one of which also functions as a bakery and sells *challa*, the braided bread used for sacramental meals. Foodstuffs marked kosher are

available in the regular supermarkets. While awaiting municipal permission for a separate Jewish section, the cemetery in the heights of Terreville
in Schoelcher has a mausoleum entombing the handful of Jews deceased
and buried on the island.[28]

Israel Independence Day at Martinique synagogue

Purim play in Martinique

Demographic and Institutional Profile
of Martinican Jewry

There are approximately 450 Jews in Martinique today, representing 190 households.[29] Approximately 280 of the adults are official members of the ACIM. The vast majority are Sephardim from North Africa, particularly Algeria: pillars of the community come from families named Chicheportiche, Illouz, Marciano, Nakache, Taëb, Zaoui, and Zerbib.[30] Commerce, especially the sale of aluminum products such as security windows and doors, is the main occupation. Comfortable though not extremely affluent – purchase of second homes would be such an indication – more well-to-do members from time to time feel compelled to combine resources and purchase an airline ticket to repatriate the co-religionist who has fallen on hard times.

Even as the overall population of Martinique has increased by well over fifty thousand over the last two decades to its current size of about 388,000, the overall number of Jews resident on the island has remained stable. This reflects the highly mobile character of the Jews of Martinique.

"*Mais qui est juif?*" "Who is a Jew?" As throughout the Jewish world, this is a major preoccupation of the Jewish community in Martinique. Twenty-eight percent of the community is mixed, that is, either in or the product of a relationship between a Jewish and non-Jewish partner.[31] While this situation is common throughout the diaspora, it takes on an especially "spicy" character with the creolization of sexual mores in the Antilles.

There is no religious test for joining the ACIM or participating in its activities – just a simple membership fee is required. Thus, one can be an official member of the "Israelite" community and live as a Jew – even eat as a Jew, for there is a daily midday kosher meal for three dozen school-age children and weekly communal dinners for adults – even if according to Orthodox Jewish law, or *halacha*, one is not actually Jewish. Such ambiguity can persist for many years. When eventually confronted with a sacramental obstacle – refusal to perform a circumcision, bar mitzvah, or marriage – the ambiguity at times comes to an unpleasant head.

Cultural differences account for the gap in Martinique that distances the minoritarian French Ashkenazi Jews of East European origin from the French Sephardim hailing from North Africa. The former have been better assimilated through secular education and culture and therefore navigate non-Jewish society more comfortably. Attempts to impart more open and diverse approaches to Jewish learning and culture, for example, by opening a local chapter of B'nai B'rith, have foundered in the face of general incomprehension and reticence tinged with mistrust.

Intermarriage also accounts for some of the intra-Semitic tension. Most Ashkenazi adults on Martinique, especially those who are not members of the ACIM, are believed to be in mixed marriages, and traditionally there has been little outreach to incorporate them within Jewish community life. Only in 2002, for the first time, did the ACIM commemorate Holocaust Memorial Day (*Yom HaShoah*) within its programming. While not the result of deliberate snubbing, for some Jews of European descent the lack of Holocaust awareness among Sephardim reflected a lack of communal sensitivity, a tendency to regard the Shoah as a principally Ashkenazi preoccupation.[32]

Christine Clément, a Jewish psychotherapist practicing on the island, has identified Repressed Shoah Syndrome among a handful of troubled youth in Martinique. Second generation immigrants who are the offspring of survivors of the Holocaust suffer from the silence, and internalized pain, transmitted across the generations. Of mixed Jewish-West Indian marriages – "as a means of truly finishing, or attempting to finish, with their Jewishness" – they have no formal or affective connection with the Jewish community.[33] Though affecting relatively few children, the uncommunicated violence of the Holocaust would thus be part of the general problem of troubled youth currently plaguing Martinican society.

Formal unions between Jews, usually male, and West Indians, usually female, sometimes take a positive Jewish and creole direction. Coming from an intrinsically more spiritual background than that prevailing in the more secular Metropole, French West Indian converts to Judaism are said to embrace their conversion more fervently than is the case in France proper. For Martinican brides, conversion to Judaism becomes more than an act of matrimonial convenience. Whether formalized by Jewish weddings or not, over the last three decades Jewish-West Indian unions have progressively added "more color" to the Jewish community in Martinique.

If the question "Who is a Jew?" is a problem linking Martinique to the Jewish world at large, the question "Who is a Martinican Jew?" is more particular. It is also, given the ambivalent nature of Martinican identity writ large, more complex.

While the handful of French West Indians who have converted to Judaism are obviously Martinican, what about the Jewish families who have lived for several decades on the island? Jews who were born in North Africa, moved to France, and eventually settled in Martinique are unlikely to think of themselves as Martinican. But consider this testimony of a recently arrived Sephardic woman who began to teach at a Hebrew school. "It was the first day of class and the kids were speaking in a strange way. I was so new I didn't even know that it was Creole, or what Creole was. When I tried to make sense out of it all, and to put some sense into the kids, they were rebellious: "*On est juif martiniquais ici, Madame – on n'est pas juif français!*" ("We are Martinican Jews here, Miss – we are not French Jews.")[34]

And yet, and yet . . . Not even the békés, the Creole-speaking white descendants of the original French settlers from the seventeenth and eighteenth centuries, are universally considered to be Martinican by islanders "of color." Moreover, "being Martinican" also popularly means, except for a small number of independentists, "being (overseas) French." For the native Antillean, the "French(wo)man-one-is-not" is the (white) Metropolitan; but for the Martinican-born Jews, she is the (Sephardic) minority within greater France. Is the black West Indian Christian just as "French" as the Middle Eastern Jewish immigrant?

Inasmuch as Martinique is part of France, the ACIM comes under the formal jurisdiction of the orthodox and highly conservative Consistoire de Paris. All matters relating to conversion and recognition of religious status are therefore ultimately decided five thousand miles away. A rival messianic movement, the *Lubavitch*, has nevertheless made inroads in the Antilles and elsewhere in the overseas French departments and territories. Based in London, their *Ufaratsta* organization publishes a weekly newsletter *l'Hebdomadaire Juif des Iles* (Jews of the Islands), which it also mails to the synagogues in Guadeloupe, Tahiti, Réunion, and New Caledonia.

Images of Jews in Martinican Society

There is a great gulf between the Martinican intelligentsia and the general populace with regards to the image of the Jew. Ordinary islanders tend to lump all residents of Middle Eastern origin together, distinguishing naught between, say, Muslims of Palestinian origin and Jews from North Africa: all are *Syriens*. Not even wearing a Jewish skullcap, a *yarmulke*, which several members of the community now do in public, projects religious identification. One Jewish merchant relates how, in a conversation about events in Israel/Palestine with his Antillean physician, the latter assumed that his *kippa*-wearing patient was a pro-Palestinian Arab.

In the early-to-mid-1970s, the activities of some unsavory characters within the Jewish community tarnished its overall image. Some unscrupulous salesmen took advantage of a naïve and unsuspecting clientele in a countryside not yet serviced by electricity to sell overpriced appliances. The infamous Algerian Jewish Zemmour brothers – notorious throughout the French and North African underworlds for their racketeering and mafiaesque exploits – had a brief but unforgettable spell in Martinique. It must be remembered that, even as late as the 1970s, for adventurous Frenchmen the Antilles symbolized a kind of

Wild West, a tropical frontier without the same constraints and regimentation encountered in the Metropole. Some Sephardic strongmen have carried over their dubious reputations, including their revolvers, to this day. While most Shabbats are observed in synagogue, some shysters have spent them in prison.

Yet in the countryside, and for most religiously schooled Martinicans, *juif* still evokes foremost the Jew of the New Testament, the Jew who lived in an ancient land called Palestine. Even Aimé Césaire, Martinique's intellectual par excellence, rhetorically asked in an interview with this writer: "Jesus Christ was Palestinian, wasn't he? . . . What difference is there between a Palestinian and a Jew?"

Césaire was in fact the first Martinican to situate the image of the Jew within the construction of modern French West Indian identity. In his celebrated epic poem "Return to My Native Land" (1947), a literary fundament of négritude, Césaire evocatively invokes the Jew as (white) victim of racism:

> the famine-man, the insult-man, the torture-man . . .
> one can at any moment seize, beat up or kill – yes really kill him –
> without having to account to anybody,
> without having to excuse oneself to anyone.
> a jew-man,
> a pogrom-man
> a little tyke,
> a bum[35]

In his 1956 speech in honor of the eighteenth-century abolitionist Father Grégoire, Césaire noted that Grégoire's prior preoccupation was with the welfare of the Jews in France: "It is as if he naturally went from the ghetto [of the Jew] to the cabin of the slave."[36]

Four decades after its original publication, the above-cited passage was on prominent display in an international touring UNESCO exhibit on Césaire; in 1998, the exhibit came to Martinique itself. The exhibit's catalogue was more explicit in explaining the significance of the Jewish reference: "The Negro is also the Jew, the foreigner, the Amerindien, the illiterate, the untouchable, he who is different, the neighbor; in brief, he who, by his very existence, is threatened, excluded, marginalized, forgotten, sacrificed."[37]

"It is not that I am especially for the Israelis," says the man who wrote sympathetically for the Shoah Jew, "but it's necessary to put the matter justly. What motivates them is not racism but nationalism – it's not the same thing . . . The roots are historic, not racial . . . The Israelis have the impression that the state that was such a challenge to build – and it is young, after all – is itself at stake. Israel's essential motivation is its will to exist. It is anguished to see its future threatened."[38]

Aimé Césaire literally planted the most visible sign of a "Jewish" presence in the heart of Fort-de-France's Terres Sainville ghetto. In the square named for Father Grégoire, Césaire planted what became an enormous canopy tree: Enterolobium Cyclocarpium for the erudite; "Ears of Jew, Ears of Black" in the vernacular.[39]

Frantz Fanon, although less well-read in Martinique than outside, examines the Jewish question alongside that of the French West Indian at some length in *Black Skin, White Masks*:

"It was my philosophy professor, a native of the Antilles, who recalled the fact to me one day: 'Whenever you hear anyone abuse the Jews, pay attention, because he is talking about you . . .' I was answerable in my body and in my heart for what was done to my brother . . . [A]n anti-Semite is inevitably anti-Negro." And: "When I turn on my radio, when I hear that Negroes have been lynched in America, I say that we have been lied to: Hitler is not dead. When I turn on my radio, when I learn that Jews have been insulted, mistreated, persecuted [*pogromisés*], I say that we have been lied to: Hitler is not dead."[40]

A more recent treatment of Jews in the Antillean imagination is found in the literary and social science journal *Portulan*, whose second issue in 1998 is entitled "Jewish Memory, Negro Memory. Two Types of Destiny." *Portulan* editor-in-chief Professor Roger Toumson of the Université des Antilles-Guyane explains in the foreword the issue's aim to highlight the "paradox of the formation and persistent relevance of the judeo-negro paradign of [oppression and] emancipation."[41] Of the twenty-six contributors, eight are either Guadeloupean or Martinican.[42] Chapter themes include: the struggle for the freedom of Blacks and Jews during the Enlightenment (Joseph Jurt); Zionism and Pan-Africanism (Abdoulaye Barro); and Négritude et Judéité (Maurice Dorès).

Outside of intellectual circles, little attention is generally paid to Jewish issues and even less to the local Jewish community.[43] For those who are so conscious, the community is accurately perceived as extremely discreet, if not closed, and politically right-wing, that is, pro-Likud and pro-Ariel Sharon. There is no volition within the community to publicize its own views on the Arab–Israeli conflict: it regards the French, and therefore Martinican, media as hopelessly pro-Palestinian and anti-Israeli.[44]

An essay in the weekly mass circulation magazine of *France-Antilles* reflects the historicist view of Jews *vis-à-vis* Martinique. The article, a primer on contemporary "ethnic mixing" and créolité, invokes the seventeenth-century migration of Dutch Jews from Brazil and their role in introducing the sugar plant and the technology for its refining. "It is the era of sugar cane, born in India, worked by the Arabs and spread by the Jewish people during their long exodus." Descendents of Europeans, Africans, East Indians, Chinese ("when Confucius meets Descartes"), and Syrians are all featured.[45] That there are still, or again, Jews in Martinique, strongly organized around a community center and an impressive house of worship, is completely ignored.

An unusual interpretation of Jewish history and identity for Martinique was expressed in a free concert-cum-colloquium convened by the Rastafarian movement "One Love" on May 21, 2002. The event, held to mark the first anniversary of France's official recognition of slavery as a crime against humanity and to promote the campaign for reparations, featured a speech by One Love's Martinican leader Sékou Manga. Much of Manga's speech invoked ancient and modern Israel and argued not only for the relevance of Jews for French West Indians, but also for the very identity between the two, for Africans are the true heirs of the Old Testament covenant between the Hebrews and J(ehov)a.

Starting with the notion of the "deportation" of Africans into West Indian slavery, Manga invoked the deportation of the Jews during World War II, the precedent it created in international law as "crime against humanity," and the founding of the modern State of Israel as a positive model of reparations. "We need to follow the same logic . . . and demand the same rights and reparations."

Manga reminded the audience that Jews were deported not from Palestine but from Europe – indeed, long before the deportations under the Nazis in the twentieth century, the Romans under Titus deported them in the first century. "Do we not also have the right to regain our land, after only five hundred years?" he rhetorically asked the audience, precipitating applause.

Manga then invoked the all-important sign of the covenant: circumcision. For Manga, Martinique's African ancestors, even without an acquaintance with the Old Testament, bore this covenantal symbol. "Who is this people – who are these kingdoms – with whom the alliance through circumcision was made?" Manga insisted, quoting from Genesis.

Invoking both Herodotus and Arthur Koestler, Manga claimed that the ancestors of the current European Jews in Israel, the Scythians/Khazars, were not themselves circumcised. "History says that the people which today claims to be the inheritors of circumcision were not in fact so." Circumcision is purely African – as were the Hebrews.

"If today Israel leads the United States, and has it do her bidding, it is quite simply because this country pretends to constitute the children of Abraham" (loud applause). "If those who are not really the children of Abraham have such power when they pretend to be, what will be the power of those [the Africans] who really are?"

Martinique's ancestors, Manga went on, came from Canaan, not the Canaan wrongly believed to encompass latter day Israel and Palestine, but the "true" Canaan of eastern, central, and western Africa. The Congress of Berlin, which in 1885 partitioned the continent into European colonial zones, therefore actually divided Canaan; and France was a major colonizer of Canaan. "Is it by chance that France is the first country to recognize the crime against humanity? What is the divine Providence in this history?"

How the hundreds of casual concertgoers will assimilate the One Love message and its French West Indian deconstruction of Jewish history is difficult to assess. Even the slightest rastafarianization of Martinican society will nonetheless tend to blur the island image of Jewry, and the image of island Jewry.

A more erudite but no less unusual image of Judaism in Martinique is projected by the Kabbalistic School of the Caribbean whose dean, A. D. Grad, has been teaching kabbala to a general, that is, mostly non-Jewish, audience since 1996. Grad, a seventh-generation direct descendent of the Gaon of Vilna, born in France of White Russian parents in 1916, dispenses a combination of rudimentary Hebrew with "scientific" philosophy in weekly evening classes at the Annanda bookshop in Lamentin. The classes are faithfully attended by a core of fifty to sixty adepts from all walks of French West Indian life, with some sessions attracting twice that number. The Kabbalist of Martinique eschews any remuneration or honorarium for his pedagogic activities.

Many of "Master" Grad's twenty-six published works are available at the Annanda bookstore, which specializes in religious, spiritual, and mystical literature of all types. They include one written specifically for a French West Indian readership.[46] Founder of the World Kabbalist Movement (MKM-MAKOM) in Paris in 1967, the internationally renown Grad has taught philosophy at the University of Chile and psychology at the Pedagogical Institute of Valparaiso. According to Grad, many French West Indians have a special "sensitivity toward, and affinity for, original and solid sources of truth outside of the Church and sects."[47]

There are no ties between the Ecole Kabbaliste de la Caraïbe and the Association Cultuelle Israélite de la Martinique. Indeed, the Master Kabbalist is barely known to members of the island's organized Jewish community.

Theologically situated between the Hebrewistic Rastafarianism of the Martinican Manga and the Kabbalistic Zionism of the Jewish Grad is the currently dormant Consolation of Israel by the Islands of the Sea (CIIM). Founded by the French West Indian Dominique Bobi, the CIIM represents an uncommon combination of anticolonialism and philosemitism. Martinican society, according to Bobi, remains colonized by anti-Semitic Catholicism, no less than by French assimilationism. Jewish preservation of identity through ancestral religion and political emancipation through Zionism is an appropriate model for the French islands of the West Indies. Both peoples have been victims of slavery and racism, but only the Jews have found an adequate theopolitical solution.[48]

Such unorthodox views have put the members of CIIM at odds with both pro-French and pro-Palestinian elements of Martinican society. Monsieur Bobi has relocated to Metropolitan France and awaits a more auspicious moment for organizational reactivation.

Martinican–Palestinian Solidarity and Anti-Semitism

Anti-Israeli, pro-Palestinian sentiment is especially keen in far left and pro-independence circles in Martinique. This may be attributed in part to the limited popularity for outright sovereignty for the island: liberation for Palestine becomes a surrogate for the independence struggle in Martinique. Demanding statehood for the Palestinians is a salve for those not prepared to wrest it for Martinique. At times of intense conflict in the Middle East, anti-Israel sentiment has smacked of anti-Semitism. This has particularly been the case during the Israeli incursion into Lebanon in the early 1980s and the second Intifada that began in September 2000.

Israeli military offensives into Lebanon triggered a series of anti-Zionist articles in one of the far-left mass circulation periodicals of the French Caribbean, *Antilla*. A good number of these articles, mostly written by Pierre Davidas, unequivocally crossed the line between anti-Zionism and anti-Semitism. In "Israel, an Accursed People and Country," Davidas wrote that "all those who have had the opportunity to read Mein Kampf . . . must . . . recognize how right Hitler was in his judgement against the Jews."[49] At the request of the ACIM, judicial action was brought against Davidas and *Antilla* on grounds of defamation and "incitement to racial hatred."

The defendants retaliated by publishing further attacks that now associated Israelis in the Middle East with Jews in the West Indies. Martinican Jews were characterized as a "detachment of international zionism." "Today there are only about 400 Sephardic Zionists but when there are a thousand of them they will dominate Martinique and enslave us in our own country."[50] Already, claimed Davidas, local Jews had infiltrated the national and local governments; controlled the island's construction, insurance, and tourist industries; and sabotaged a pro-independence ecological movement by planting marijuana on its property and having a member of that same group accused of rape.

In 1983 the court decided in favor of the ACIM, fined the defendants, and ordered them to pay court fees. For its part the ACIM demanded indemnity – *pour l'honneur* – of a single franc.

Antilla is far from representative of French West Indian sentiment as a whole. It bears repetition that most ordinary islanders are barely conscious of the presence of Jews within Martinican society. Of those few who are, the sentiment is often positive. When France as a whole was scandalized by the vandalism of the Jewish cemetery in Carpentras in 1990, a spontaneous demonstration outside the synagogue included West Indians displaying family heirlooms with Jewish motifs.[51]

The second Intifada of 2000–2002, by which time the Martinican media had been thoroughly globalized by television satellite and cable, has brought the Israeli–Palestinian conflict into the French West Indian foyer as never before. Inevitably, it has affected the general image of the Jew. To appreciate the importance of the second Intifada for French Caribbean consciousness, it is necessary to briefly revisit Martinique during the first Intifada of the late 1980s.

In 1988, the Collective of Martinican Solidarity with the Palestinian People was created. In its letter to the "Jewish Community of Martinique," the Collective, spearheaded by a Ramallah-born businessman, stressed that its actions were not directed against either the island's Jews as individuals or as a community, "nor against the right of the State of Israel to exist." The letter, which was never answered, invited the community to join forces "to contribute to the urgent task of bringing PEACE to the Middle East by replacing the destructive logic of balance of power with the logic of the future, of respect for the interests of all."[52]

Not all of the members of the Collective, it appears, embraced the moderate stance as officially articulated. More extremist elements, mostly among "anticolonial" West Indians, rejected Israel's very right to exist and rode the same fine line between anti-Zionism and anti-Semitism that *Antilla* had incontestably crossed. As a result, the Collective fractured, only to reemerge in July 2001 in response to the second *Intifada*, as the Martinique-Palestine Solidarity Committee for a Just Peace in the Middle East (CSMP). Its president is now the French West Indian poet and playwright Daniel Boukman.

On March 24, 2002, Palestine Day was organized by CSMP in the youth center of Lamentin. The program included lectures, videos, poetry in Arabic, and Martinican folk dances. A pro-Palestinian demonstration on April 6, 2002, in Fort-de-France included placards, one with a swastika, characterizing Israeli premier Sharon as a Nazi and equating him with Hitler. Committee president Boukman declared that "there is great emotion on the part of . . . the Martinican people who recognize a great injustice . . . [M]assacres, destruction, and genocide are going to continue against the Palestinians." Among the groups taking a visible part in the demonstration was the Martinican Democratic Central of Workers (CDMT), whose medical-social branch had a few weeks previously voted a motion "call[ing] on the entirety of Martinicans to participate in the international movement of solidarity with the Palestinian people." The rally concluded with a reading, in creole, of the 1970s "Speech on the Unemployment Market" by Palestinian poet Samih El Qasim.

In the wake of the reoccupation of the West Bank in 2002, letters to the editor published in *France-Antilles* were uniformly critical of Israel, expressing scant recognition of the suicide bombing that precipitated the Israeli offensive.[53] Given the prominence of his position, those of the deputy to the National Assembly Camille Darsières are worth citing.[54] In an open letter to then prime minister Lionel Jospin, Darsières castigated the French government for not putting greater pressure on Israel: "I am among the numerous overseas French citizens whom History has sensitized to the struggle of peoples for their emancipation, who expect from the France of Human Rights a clear position, disassociating itself from cowardly abandonment of the universal values of which the big powers boast." For this Martinique representative to French parliament, all acts of Palestinian militancy apparently constitute "legitimate resistance . . . to occupation and should not be thought of as terrorism."[55] Three and a half months later, in the wake of fire bombings and other vandalism of synagogues in metropolitan France, Darsières wrote the following: "[W]e do not approve of these attacks . . . against the Synagogues . . . but we will not explicitly condemn them until Jewish associations, in France and elsewhere, have explicitly condemned the State of Israel for not respecting the U.N. Resolutions, notably those calling since 1967 for the withdrawal of the occupied Palestinian territories."[56] At no time, it ought to be noted here, has the synagogue in Martinique, either in its present or former location, been the target of politically or religiously inspired vandalism or anti-Semitic graffiti.

The second *Intifada* happened to coincide with a political event of great local importance: the extraordinary Congress of 2002 that brought together elected representatives to deliberate on the future status of Martinique *vis-à-vis* France and to recommend an alternate administrative framework for the local government. One of the most hotly contested motions was one that would recognize Martinique as a nation. In favor of the motion came this declaration by Louis Boutrin of the Construct the Martinican Country Party (BPM): "There is only one people . . . that does not constitute a nation, even as it lives on its own territory. That is the Palestinian people. I hope, dear colleagues, that you are not going to assimilate us with the Palestinians."[57]

It is impossible to measure the influence of these expressions of elite opinion upon the populace at large, a populace that generally displays little interest in international politics, excluding, of course, that of France. There is no doubt, however, that among at least the intelligentsia and political leaders of Martinique the security policy of the Sharon government – who, as its elected representatives, willy-nilly incarnate the Jewish State – have diminished residual post-Shoah francophone philo-semitism.[58] Given that the Jewish community of Martinique does not respond publicly when Israel is attacked, the fuzzy image of the Martinican Jew – the ever silent marrano, ostensible citizen but social stranger – remains blurred.

Conclusion: The Psychically Wandering West Indian Jew

A Jewish documentary broadcast in France on the 1996 inauguration of the "Ends of the Earth" synagogue in Martinique playfully puns with the French phrases for "Jewish French West Indies" (*Antilles sémites*) and "antisemitic" (*anti-sémite*).[59] Such wordplay is acceptable to the extent that Jewish life in Martinique is today a free one, and that royal, Vichyist, and pro-Palestinian expressions of anti-Semitism are either dépassé or marginal. For nearly four centuries Jews have periodically settled on the island, flourishing between periods of expulsion – from Brazil in 1654 and from Martinique in 1683; natural disaster – the years preceding the volcanic explosion of Pelée in 1902; and outright persecution – the local Vichy regime from 1940 to 1943. French gendarmes are nowadays dispatched to the Jewish community center on the high holidays and other major gatherings, such as Israeli Independence Day, not to intimidate the community, but to protect it. Likewise, an intelligence agent stays in touch, not to spy, but rather to reassure. More than at any time in history, the island's Jews are in a position to emerge from the sidelines and claim a place in the famous Martinican melting pot: to leave behind social marronage and the religious fear of the marrano.

Yet planting firm roots in Martinique has never been the Jewish way. Rare is the Jew who feels this French overseas department to be a true and permanent home; rare is the Jew who is actually buried on the island. Is it because the legacy of colonial, including Catholic, assimilation includes French anti-Semitism, in both pseudo-intellectual and theological forms? Is it because the Jews' own liturgy, stressing that they are "a nation apart," mixes ill with a culture of hybridity, *métissage*, and *créolité*?

Martinican Jews are either "passing through," even for spells lasting decades, or melting into the cultural scenery. Like the local fish that is named for them, *poisson juif*, they swim in the local waters, but are never featured on the Martinican menu.[60] To leave and reappear – this has been the life of the *juif martiniquais*. Or, to invoke Césaire,

> To leave.
> As there are hyena-men and leopard-men,
> I would be a jew-man . . . [61]

Acknowledgments

The author wishes to express his gratitude to the Stotsky Professorship of Jewish Historical and Cultural Studies, under whose auspices this work was conducted and presented at the Caribbean Studies Association annual meeting on May 29, 2002, in Nassau, Bahamas. A Northeastern University sabbatical leave, during which he was affiliated with the Research Center for Local Powers in the Caribbean (CRPLC) at the Université des Antilles-Guyane (Martinique) made the fieldwork for this chapter possible. Special thanks go to Amram Riboh, Roger Toumson, and, as always, Roland Suvélor, for their insights, suggestions, and assistance.

Notes

1   Jean Bernabé, Patrick Chamoiseau, and Raphaël Confiant, *Eloge de la Créolité* (Paris: Gallimard Presses Universitaires Créoles, 1989).

2   This section draws heavily from Abraham Cohen, "Les Juifs dans les Colonies Françaises au XVIIIe siècle," *Revue des Etudes Juives* 4–5 (1882), and "Les Juifs de la Martinique au XVIIe Siècle," *Revue des Etudes Juives* 2 (1881), 93–122; Zvi Loker, *Jews in the Caribbean. Evidence on the History of the Jews in the Caribbean Zone in Colonial Times* (Jerusalem: Institute for Research on the Sephardi and Oriental Jewish Heritage, 1991); Jacques Petitjean-Roget, "Les Juifs à la Martinique sous l'Ancien Régime," *Revue d'Histoire des Colonies* 43 (1956), 138–58; Amram Riboh, "Les Juifs de la Martinique," *Kenaf Haaretz. Le Journal de la Communauté Juive de la Martinique* 5 (5762, Nissan; equivalent of March 2002), 4; and Cecil Roth, *Histoire des Marranes* (Paris: Collections Histoire, 1932). See also Mordechai Arbell, *Spanish and Portuguese Jews in the Caribbean and the Guianas. A Bibliography* (Providence: John Carter Brown Library, 1999), especially chapter 10. For an earlier synthesis in English see William F. S. Miles, "The Jews of Martinique," *Midstream* (February 1986), 31–3.

3   Others of the Recife refugees settled in New Amsterdam, becoming the first Jews of what later would be called New York.

4   The expression comes from Roth, *Histoire*, 229. In some circles the term *marrano* is pejorative; readers may wish to mentally substitute *converso*.

5   Petitjean-Roget, "Les Juifs." Letter of Governor D. Baas (August 1, 1669).

6   *Ibid.* Letter to the King (November 19, 1680).

7   Loker, *Jews.* Letter of March 13, 1683.

8   Louis Sala-Molins, *Le Code Noir ou le calvaire de Canaan* (Paris: Presses Universitaires de Paris, 1987). Code Noir of 1685, Article 1 (author's translation).

9   Loker, *Jews.* Letter of August 28, 1695.

10   Judith and Rebecca themselves lived in France. The case was complicated by the fact that one of Abraham's brothers-in-law, Coustault, a lawyer for the parliament, claimed the estate for himself, on the basis of "difference of Religion." Indeed, one of Abraham's sisters had married Coustault, a gentile, and had converted to Christianity.

11   Still standing, a Star of David graces the main habitation. Origins of the Depaz family lie in Livorno, Italy.

12   While Jean-François Depaz was formally baptized nine years before arriving in 1770, like most conversos his family retained palpably Jewish customs and symbols. Another prominent béké family believed to be of Jewish origin are the (Wielle) de Reynald. Eugène Bruneau-Latouche and Philippe Cordiez,

209 *Anciennes Familles Subsistantes de la Martinique* (Aix-en-Provence, Fort-de-France, Paris, 2002).

13 Visits and telephone calls to most of the more than two dozen West Indian households bearing the name Lévy, Levi, and Lévi (as listed in the Martinican phonebook) revealed scant consciousness of the presumably Jewish origin of their name.

14 The Meyers came to Martinique in 1848 from Denmark. Even during the Dreyfus Affair (observation of Léo Elisabeth), advertisements for their high-quality rum included the Star of David. Genealogical research conducted by the couple Rossignol for the centenary of the eruption of Mount Pelée unearthed, in the context of applications for assistance by survivors of St. Pierre, three familiar family names: Levy (Joseph in Carbet and Léontine in Marin), Gradis (Raoul, on behalf of the company in Bordeaux), and Depaz (Louis Alexandre Victor). The latter's application was rejected on the grounds that, though an orphan, he "can take care of himself; has retained resources" (*www.stpierre1902.org*). A number of Polish Jewish families apparently came to the island at the beginning of the twentieth century, one founding the Loewinsky (or Loewenski) quarter in Rivière Pilote and all melting into the general population (Christine Clément, personal communication).

15 In his memoirs of the era, Robert does not acknowledge any role in promulgating official French anti-Semitism in the Antilles. See Georges Robert, *La France aux Antilles* (Paris: Librairie Plon, 1950).

16 See Richard D.E. Burton, "Vichyisme et Vichyistes à la Martinique," vol.1 *Les Cahiers du CERAG* (dedicated to *La Martinique sous l'Amiral Robert*) (1978): 17, 30 note 81.

17 The quote is from the local anti-Vichy journal *Tristes Tropiques*, as cited by Fitz A. Baptiste, "Le Régime de Vichy en Martinique: l'Application des Mesures d'Ordre Public," vol.2 *Les Cahiers du CERAG* (1979): 71.

18 *Journal Officiel de la Martinique* (January 18, 1941), Actes du Gouvernement Local, 41, Décision portant internement administrative.

19 Archives Départementales de Tartenson (Martinique) (M4612).

20 Vichy authorities in Martinique were correct to suspect Guthmann, but for other reasons. His name later appears in a police report among those participating in a Gaullist, that is, Free France, demonstration in Saint-Pierre on June 18, 1943. Police Report from Carbet Canton (reproduced in Marie-Hélène Léotin, *La Martinique Pendant la Second Guerre Mondiale, 1939–1945* [Martinique: Centre Régional de Documentation des Antilles et de la Guyane, 1993]), 101. Less than one month later, on Bastille Day (July 14, 1943), the Gaullist Martinican Committee of National Liberation (CMLN) staged an uprising, compelling Admiral Robert to depart Martinique the next day.

21 *Journal Officiel de la Martinique* (June 28, 1941): 697, 699.

22 Coincidentally, twenty-three is the same number of Jewish families recorded in 1683, at the behest of Jesuit persecutors. In 1683 the total population of Martinique was 14,000; in 1941, it was 220,000. Liliane Chauleau, "Départements d'outre-Mer," in Gildas Bernard, ed., *Les Familles Juives en France. XVIe siècle–1815* (Paris: Archives Nationales, 1990).

23　Archives Départementales. Captain Delpech's letter of November 21, 1941.

24　Unable to procure the materials necessary to continue her chosen profession because the US navy imposed a blockade, Madame Gold turned to haberdashery (M. Calvy, personal communication, May 9, 2002). Dr. Stern is remembered for accepting barter from patients too impoverished to pay cash, and for teaching illiterate peasants to read and write, from his remote practice in Morne Rouge (Dr. Pierre Petit, personal communication, June 26, 2002). After the war Sussfeld would nevertheless testify on behalf of Admiral Robert. Though not mentioned by name, he is certainly the "Israelite" cited in Pierre Zizine, *L'Amiral Robert devant La Haute Cour* (Paris: Imp. Emmanel Pourtout, 1947).

25　Interview with Aimé Césaire (April 25, 2002). Césaire recalled Professor Salanski as an "eminent mathematician" who taught at the Lycée Schoelcher and was eventually reintegrated into the French ministry of education after the war. During the hiatus Salanski was employed by the Catholic high school in Martinique, hired by its principal Father Droch.

26　Lazareff's mother was arrested in Paris and deported to Auschwitz where she died. One of the Clément-Lazareff children, recounting family lore, relates that her mother Sarah voluntarily presented herself to the Vichy authorities in Martinique and, "out of solidarity" with the other Jews, demanded – over the objections of the reluctant officials – that she too be listed as Jewish and issued *l'étoile jaune*. There is no evidence, however, that in Martinique Jews were ever actually issued the yellow star.

27　A fourth couple, the Bercovici, better known as Maïer, from the store that bore their name, died childless. The list of declared Jews was partially reproduced as part of the high school entrance examination (*brevet national*) in Martinique in June 2002. Middle school students were asked to describe the Vichy regime and its application in the French West Indies. Inclusion of the list represented a rare recognition of a Jewish presence (and anti-Semitic legislation) within official Martinican historiography.

28　The first Jew buried in Martinique in modern times was the three-month-old son of the family Nahon, who died in the mid-1970s.

29　This is the figure compiled by ACIM. It includes both Jews who have self-identified as such by their active contact with the Jewish community as well as those who have come to the attention of the community by word of mouth. There is also an unknown number of Jews, mainly Ashkenazi, who are not known to the community.

30　The town of Sétif is especially well represented.

31　The figure is per the calculation of the resident rabbi.

32　Among the several Jewish families in Martinique who had lost family members in the Shoah, and were invited to light memorial candles, was one of the rare "mixed" Sephardic-Ashkenazi couples.

33　Christine Clément, personal communication. Clément is well sensitized to the phenomenon of hidden Jewishness: only as an adult did she discover that her French mother, the daughter of immigrants from Algeria, was born Jewish and had converted to Catholicism only after World War II. It was in Martinique that the psychotherapist eventually reclaimed her Jewish identity.

34　Katia Smadja, personal communication.

35 Aimé Césaire, *Return to My Native Land* (Paris: Presence Africaine, 1947; English translation, 1971), 56.

36 Aimé Césaire, *Œuvres complèts*, vol. 3 *Œuvre historique et politique. Discours et communications* (Paris: Editions Désormeaux, 1976).

37 *Pour regarder le siècle en face. Hommage à Aimé Césaire. Exposition itinérante internationale présentée par le Conseil Général de la Martinique* (Fort-de-France, Martinique: Conseil Régional, 1998), 6. (Author's translation)

38 William F. S. Miles, "Aimé Césaire and My Jewish Question," *Wadabagei. A Journal of the Caribbean and its Diaspora* 6 (2003): 179.

39 Simone Henry-Valmore, "Oreilles de Juif, Oreilles de Noir," in *Portulan. Mémoire juive, mémoire nègre. Deux figures du destin* (Châteauneuf-le-Îles Rouge: Vents des Îles, 1998), 21. The commentary of this West Indian writer and "ethno-analyst" is well worth quoting: "The symbol is king. 'Ears of Jew, Ears of Black.' Encounter of two worlds. Convergence of destinies. In the two-sided mirror the positive image of oneself is projected with difficulty, deformed by the vision of others, their cultural and religious prejudices and all the archaic myths. In the eyes of the Christian West, Jew and Black are subject to the same suspicion. For the one as for the other, the Devil profits from the disturbing strangeness."

40 See Fanon's chapter "The So-Called Dependency of Colonized Peoples." See William F.S. Miles, "Negritude and Judaism," *Western Journal of Black Studies* 21 (1997): 99–105, for a fuller treatment of anti-Semitism by Frantz Fanon.

41 "Mémoire juive, mémoire nègre. Deux figures du destin," *Portulan. Littératures, sociétés, cultures des Caraïbes et des Amériques noires* (Châteauneuf-le-Îles Rouge: Vents des Îles. 1998), 9.

42 Two authors are African.

43 A "middle-brow" exception may be the serialized novel, set in postwar France, published in Martinique's sole daily newspaper during the first three months of 2002 entitled *Zielmann the Jew*. Michel Dussauze, *Zielmann le juif. France-Antilles* (Fort-de-France, Martinique: 2002; serialized version January 28–March 20).

44 According to Dr. B. I. Feldman, who served in Martinique as the unofficial honorary consul of Israel and its emissary for immigration in Martinique from 1983 to 1988, this anti-Israel portrayal in the media is orchestrated from the Quai d'Orsay, the French ministry of foreign affairs. Feldman's Israeli view of West Indians and Martinique represents an interesting counterpoint of Martinican views of Jews and Israel: "How can French West Indians resolve their identity malaise? By divorcing from France, rejecting Islamicist advances, and establishing legitimate links with another, complementary people – one itself sensitive to suffering, which knew how to recover its freedom, but which needs them: the Jewish people" (Bernard-Israël, *L'Ile Aux Fleurs ou La Dernière Colonie*, fc).

45 For a scholarly treatment of the so-called Syrians, see Isabelle Dubost, "Les 'Syriens' Martiniquais: une alternative identitaire exemplaire," in Jean Bernabé et al., eds, *Au Visiteur Lumineux. Des Îles créoles aux sociétés plurielles* (Petit Bourg, Guadeloupe: Ibis Rouge Editions, 2000).

46 A. D. Grad, *La Kabbale Universelle* (Monaco: Editions du Rocher, 1994).

47 Interview with A. D. Grad (June 21, 2002).

48 Interview in Feldman, *La deuxième étape du Sionisme*, fc.

49 Quotes (my translation) are reproduced from the extensive analysis by Michel Giraud, "Crispation identitaire et antisémitisme en Martinique: Le cas d'Antilla," *Traces* 11 (1985): 129–151. Giraud explains Martinican anti-Semitism in terms of psychological and political paranoia that emerges, among a fringe of identity politics nationalists, from an actual legacy of colonial repression.

50 *Ibid.*

51 Didier Lévy, personal communication (May 9, 2002). Monsieur Lévy, of North African origin, has lived in Martinique for over two decades.

52 Shafik Ibrahim. Letter of March 22, 1988.

53 Dates of the letters are: December 22–23, 2001; March 23–24, April 10, April 11, April 20–21, May 29, June 22–23, 2002.

54 Martinique sends four representatives to the parliament in Paris. Darsières was elected under the ticket of the Progressive Martinican Party (PPM), founded by Aimé Césaire.

55 Letter is reproduced in *France-Antilles* (December 28, 2001).

56 *Ibid.* (April 16, 2002).

57 Congrès de la Martinique, February 20, 2002 (televised broadcast of Overseas French Radio [RFO]).

58 Roger Toumson, personal communication.

59 José Esbete, *L'Emission Hébraïque* (weekly French television broadcast), TF1.

60 Nocturnal fish whose zoological name is Priacanthus (perciformes order).

61 Césaire, *Return*, 56.

Mexico

10

The Rise and Fall of Yiddish

Ilán Stavans

> In Yiddish the boundary between comedy and tragedy,
> and between fact and fiction,
> is always a thin and wavering line.
>
> Irving Howe

Bela Stavchansky, a small, imposing old lady known among her grandchildren as Bobe Bela – and, in the jargon of Mexico's Ashkenazic Jews, as *La Bobe* – utters delicious Yiddish sentences to herself in the dark. She is not alone in her one-bedroom apartment. María – aka Mari – her tempermental maid, is around. But the two are always fighting: in polite Spanish, Bobe Bela asks for something – a glass of hot tea with a sugar cube, a Tylenol, her daily dose of vitamins; Mari, in a terrible mood, won't answer though. So Bela switches languages. This is a recurrent strategy: when in distress, return to your homeland: your first tongue. Bela talks to herself, and thus, to the ghosts of her past. Or else, she calls her beloved second child, my father Abremele. Generally, it is an answering machine she gets on the other end. "*H-o-l-a, h-a-b-l-a B-e-l-a . . . Abremele, quiero hablar contigo. Háblame.*" Is her voice on tape already? Must she press a particular number? Will her Abremele listen to her? These machines are magic. How do they work? Do they have a genie inside? She might simply wait until somebody answers the phone, for she surely prefers a living person. Why should she talk to a machine? She needs company, a voice to listen to. So she calls again hours later. "Abremele *chulo*," she says, carefully avoiding Mari's name so as not to announce her intentions, "*vos ken men ton mit di goye? Zi redt mir nisht.*" The maid is driving her crazy, she says. She does not answer her queries and is always in a bad temper. And then again an hour later. And again. Soon Abremele will listen patiently to her complaints, first on tape, then live through the miracle of phones from Bela's apartment in Colonia

Polanco. He can't avoid them. He is used to them. "You've had her for almost twenty years, Mami," he replies. "Will you finally fire her? Who will help you? You're alone. Your three children are too busy . . . Do you want to move to the *heischel?*" he wonders, referring to the Jewish Home for the Elderly in Cuernavaca, Morelos, also known as *moishe-zkeinim*, some fifty-five miles south of Mexico's capital. "I will take you whenever you want."

Bela isn't ready. She is eighty-four but looks at least a decade younger. Her buoyancy is her most admirable quality: wrinkled as a prune, but with a drive as spirited as an Olympic champion. No, life is not finished yet. There is still more, much more to see, to read, and to appreciate. Her eyes are tired all right, and her bones are heavy. She has lost her hearing, so Abremele must shout on the phone for her to understand. "What? I don't understand," and he tries again, but she doesn't register. "*Zog es mir in Yiddish?*" switch to Yiddish, she suggests, for Yiddish is *der mame-loshen*, the language of stomach and soul. It is also the language of the dead. And if the dead can understand it, why shouldn't she? My father complies, only to realize what he has known all along: Bela is really not interested in conversation; dialogue is too exhausting an enterprise for her, too demanding. Three, four fixed ideas are all she has in her mind, and nothing in the world, not even a major catastrophe, will change them. Mari is not her problem. It's her restlessness, the isolation that comes with old age. "*Ya he pasado de la tercera a la cuarta edad. No sirvo . . . Estoy descompuesta,*" she tells him: I'm useless, I'm damaged, I have reached a point of no return. She isn't, obviously. She might be losing it, but she is as vigorous as a horse: every day she walks a few blocks to the supermarket, in the afternoons she plays poker with friends, on Friday nights she attends services at a nearby synagogue, and on weekends she visits her children and grandchildren.

"*Abremele, zug mir, main liebe kind: ¿Y que con Ilán?* Has he written back?"

"What do you mean 'what is with Ilán'? *Está ocupado.* He is busy, Mamá, just like all of us. He has a family to attend, and . . ."

Not always have I been a jewel in Bela's crown. For years I wasn't good enough. What kind of money does a writer earn? Isn't it like acting? Can he support a family? Look at your father. Didn't he have problems raising his family? Your cousins in Israel and Philadelphia, ah, they do have solid professions, don't they? Nevertheless, since my essays have begun appearing in national newspapers, since my name circulates among her friends – *Dain liebe einikel*, Bela! – I'm the grandchild she thinks about.

"Did he get my package? You haven't told me . . ." she wonders.

"Of course I did," he replied impatiently.

More than a month ago, she sent to my New York address a package that included some correspondence and a tightly wrapped bound notebook. *MI DIARIO*, she titled it, my diary, though it has no daily entries to speak of. She also calls it, in broken Spanish, *un chico relato*, a brief tale. It has a total of thirty-seven pages, all typed in capital letters. My mother did the secretarial work: Bela would give her a pile of handwritten pages; my mother transcribed it meticulously and sent it back; then Bela revised the typed version once, twice, until fully satisfied. She began writing it around 1980 and finished thirteen years later.

"So, has he read it?" Bela is anxious to hear my reaction, for I am, as of late, the literary genius in the family and whatever I say goes.

"He has it, Mamita, he has, believe me. I'm sure he'll write you directly. In due time."

And I do, of course, in a matter of days. I cannot cherish her diary enough, so important is it for me. I have reread it three, four, five times, trying to find meaning between the lines. The style is undeliberately loose, chaotic, repetitive, ungrammatical; and it pays no attention to accents and punctuation. Nevertheless, it is invaluable in its warmth, conviction, and clarity of vision. Bela is overwhelmed by nostalgia, uncritical of her past. How could she not be? What else could one expect from a self-made woman whose schooling didn't reach beyond second grade?

Why did she write her *diario*? So as not to waste her memory, I tell myself at first. So as to turn her life into an asset for future generations. What if all of a sudden she became an amnesiac? Or is this a gimmick to manipulate the family's collective memory? The more I think of it, the better I realize that the 'why did she write it' is the wrong kind of question. Don't all of us want to leave a mark, set the record straight before time runs out? Don't we all dream of changing the world at least a bit by solidifying our place in it? History (with a capital "H") doesn't claim her as a hero. She grew up, escaped Poland shortly before Hitler invaded, settled in Mexico, prospered, had children and grandchildren . . . Nothing intrepid about it, except for the feeling, so deep in her heart, that we are what our words say we are, and *tsuzein* is different from the Polish *byc*, the Hebrew *leiyot*, and the Spanish *ser*.

Bobe Bela dedicates her diary not only to me but to my wife and one-year-old son as well: "*Dedico mi [diario] [o un chico relato] de mi juventud a mis queridos nietos, Ilan, Alison y Josh, como recuerdo de Bobe Bela.*" She dedicates it in Spanish, though. I wonder why. And not only is the dedication in Spanish but so is the entire narrative. This, in fact, is the most urgent question I have, the one I would love to discuss with Bela. Why not in Yiddish, her mother tongue, the tongue in which instinctively she sobs and screams? I know the answer, of course: she wants to be read, understood, appreciated; she is eager to reach not only me but my wife and, sometime in the future, my children as well. I don't for a second doubt the truthfulness of her diario. But her words have been modified – or, shall I say, betrayed – , have they not? And yet, I won't raise the issue in my letter. First, because as susceptible as she is, my remarks will surely be misunderstood. She might suspect that implicit in my query is a censure of her written Spanish, although that is the last thing I would dare to imply. Her Spanish is pidgin all right – broken, ungrammatical – but it is hers all the same: it has style, it has pathos, it has power. It is the tongue of an immigrant – embryonic, wobbly, in constant mutation. It came to her at age nineteen, when alone, scared to death, she crossed the Atlantic and settled in Mexico. She appropriated the language so that I, thirty years later, could make it my own. So I don't dare to question her. Who am I to dispute her choice of language? A guardian of der mame-loshen?

Háblale, Ilan . . . *Orale*. She wants to know what you think!

And what do I think? I treasure the text, for sure. I have read segments of her diario to Joshua. As I wander through its descriptions, I seize, with amazement, the scope of her existential journey, for Bela is a natural polyglot: aside from Yiddish she was fluent in Polish and Russian, and with time she learned a broken English and a bit of Hebrew as well: seven languages, including Spanish. She was born in 1909, in Nowe Brodno, now a suburb of Warsaw. When she emigrated to Mexico in 1930, she made a conscious decision never to use Polish and Russian again. Astonishing, I tell myself: most people have trouble even pronouncing a second tongue, but Bela was verbally so rich, she could afford to give up two languages. Rich, obviously, is the wrong adjective, for her rejection of Polish and Russian didn't come as a result of a surplus of words. Instead, it was a matter of survival, a brusque but healthy attitude she forced herself to take so as to achieve the only available peace of mind she could dream of: she was a youngster, ready to begin her new life, her past needed to be overcome, even erased, if survival was to be achieved. Not only a new country and a new culture but a new language was on the horizon when she left Nowe Brodno.

Poverty was not a curse, but a state of mind. "When you don't know what you're missing," she once told me in broken Spanish, "you aren't really missing it, are you?" Bela's maiden name, Altschuler, means in German "old-synagogue attendee." Perhaps the family originated in Provence in the thirteenth century and later on moved to Prague and from there on to Galicia in the Austro-Hungarian empire. They were lower-middle class. Her father, Yankev Yosef, owned a garment store with a pretentious English name: Sklep Manufactory. It was a two-story building, with wooden floors, that also functioned as the family's home. I visualize its pallid colors, not unlike the settings of an Andjei Wajda film. Every time a customer entered through the front door, a bell would announce his arrival. A little window allowed Bela's mother to see from the kitchen who it was. On the first floor was the kitchen, separated from the store by a door through which entering customers could be seen and heard, as a small bell announced anyone stepping in. At the kitchen's center was a charcoal oven. Dovidl, Bela's younger brother, whom I would later on hear about as Tío David, would sleep next to the oven, for there was never enough room upstairs for two adults and eleven children. A back room behind the store functioned as a bunker: preserves, blankets, and extra clothes were stored in case an anti-Semitic attack occurred, and I also conjecture a sharp ax often used to cut wood. (A pistol might have been of use, of course, but Polish Jews were not allowed to possess weapons.) In the back of the building was a kitchen, with a small furnace and a bed for one of the seven children. Bela and her sister Reisl slept on the second floor.

Fear, *el miedo*, is the unifying message throughout Bela's diario. In the first part alone the words *el antisemitismo* appear a total of seventeen times, more than any other proper noun. Nowe Brodno was infested with it. I picture the town through Bela's childish eyes, artificially, realizing it is but a figment of my imagination, a hazy marketplace of noise and odor, silhouettes shuffling around, orthodox Jews confabulating in a corner, automobiles gaining attention, horses carrying milk and butter. Nowe Brodno was divided in half by Bialolenska Street, a commercial road, wide, newly asphalted by the Polish authorities, on which Sklept Manufactory was located. The street reminds me of Isaac Babel's Odessa in "Story of My Dovecot," a haunting tale I've reread a thousand times if only to evoke a past I'm convinced I had a share in, a story where el miedo is described in such a subtle, indirect way, the reader is left thinking after the last line is over if life for the Jews on the banks of the Baltic Sea and in Central Europe in general was ever about anything else.

The Altschulers were urban dwellers. The women, it seems, were much more cosmopolitan and enlightened than their male counterparts. They took care of business while their husbands prayed at the synagogue. I'm tempted to describe them, anachronistically, as *maskilim*, a term that traditionally referred to the enlightened male Jewish establishment from the eighteenth century onward. Perhaps not full-fledged intellectuals, but attentive listeners to the voices of the mind. While the men believed the universe is filled with angels and demons, the women were hard-nosed and utilitarian. They looked down at the *shtetl*, as most others in Nowe Brodno did, approaching it as too parochial, too confined to a medieval superstition, the *Haskalah*, as the Jewish "age of reason" is called in Hebrew, had painstakingly struggled to overcome.

I confess to feeling insecure. Am I portraying them as more educated than they really were? Was superstition not an essential element in their husbands' daily lives? When, as a child, I would visit Bela at her previous apartment, in Colonia Hipódromo, I would hear more than I could ever digest about fanatical beliefs: on a dinner table, the salt shaker should not be passed from hand to hand, as the devil thus spreads his influence, as he does, too, when Jews whistle, so *nunca chifles* . . . ; and if a sibling is ever lying flat on the ground, never jump over him, for *la muerte lo condenará* . . . , the Angel of Death might quickly follow . . . I am still perplexed at the way in which Bela, along with other women of her generation, conveyed these superstitions to me. Was there not a hint of irony in their tone? Or were they convinced evil forces, *Yetzer ha-Rah*, could suddenly overwhelm us all? Is this too literal an approach: females as practical, males as somewhat fanatical? In the Mexico of my childhood, Jewish men were out making money to support the family, whereas women stayed at home. But this was only a superficial division, for women had the upper hand when it came to family business. Even after a discussion occurred, *di yiddishe mame* ruled, never through easy-to-understand sound bites but through forceful persuasion that left no room for doubt.

Gender issues might not have been aired, but morality was and in a way that turned it into the sine-qua-non topic of conversation: Does the individual bring on his own downfall or is everything predestined? Are we free to battle the forces of darkness? Are they a test the Almighty lays out for us? The Altschulers were not a conflicted crew: society was moving forward toward a less mystical, more scientific future; religion played a role in their daily routine, but it was clear, from the children's various interests, that ideology could soon replace it as the next generation's idol worship. Nowe Brodno, I read in Bela's *diario*, was some forty miles away from Warsaw. To get there one took a train to cross Prague, a small district, and then crossed the Vistula River. The trip could take hours, but the closeness of the capital, with all its financial and cultural attractions, made life in provincial Nowe Brodno bearable. This proximity to the center of Polish culture allowed for a sense of superiority, a kind of distinction nurtured by the modernity that surrounded them. And it marked Bela's views: in spite of the tricks destiny held in store for her, she would strive to educate herself, to elevate her soul, to be above others, particularly above the gentile peasantry, whose illiteracy she perceived as a prison.

On Friday night, when the cleanup was over, a white tablecloth was spread on the table by Reisel and Bela. It was *shabes*. The candlesticks would be placed at the center, surrounded by *khales*, the traditional bread rolls. Bela's mother was short, obese, and blue-eyed. She knew arithmetic, which made her a *khukhem*, a wise woman. She took care of the store's finances and often traveled with her son Gil to Warsaw to buy merchandise. In Warsaw she also bathed in the *mikveh*. Bela's father, on the other hand, was a Hasid belonging to a mystical sect tied to the emanating glory of the *Ba'al Shem-Tov*. He prayed twice a day and spent long hours reading the Talmud. But he was a family creature, just like my own father: he woke up early every morning to prepare tea for his wife, which he took to her bed; next he cooked breakfast for the entire family; in the afternoon he fixed tea with chicory. A loyal husband, it seems, and a trusted father.

The Altschulers didn't last long in Nowe Brodno. A pogrom convinced Shaul to move, and he took the family to nearby Pultusk, apparently a more protected and peaceful town, where one of Bela's older siblings had established himself with his wife and newborn baby. But the general sense of insecurity – el miedo, yet again – soon reached Putulsk as well and both Bela and her older brother Gil were victims of physical attacks. By then Bela was already an ardent Zionist and often spent her free hours disseminating propaganda at public meetings. Once, a gang of young Poles had caught up with her after school. They pushed her aside, ridiculed her in public, rudely pulled her long pony-tails, and screamed at her: "Pig Jew. Why don't you move to Palestine, where you and your putrid friends belong, and help in the cleansing of Poland?" This scene is conveyed in Bela's diario with enormous pathos but without embellishment, in a matter-of-fact fashion. The words "pig Jew" – *puerco judío* – seem written in fire.

I can see why Bobe Bela would become a Zionist. She has never really talked to me about her adolescent ideologies, and her narrative is silent on this issue. Abraham, my father, has told me her Zionist dreams were short lived. "I don't believe she ever truly considered moving to Palestine, like some of her friends did," he says. It wasn't only a matter of emigration though. For her, Palestine was not, I trust, a Jewish state in the future, but an alternative in the present: an escape, a safe haven. Many years later, in the late seventies, her oldest grandchild would emigrate to Israel. With time she would go visit him. But Israel, in her eyes, was too rough, too ironbound. Could she ever have moved there for good? She is, she always was, a diasporist – a guest, a renter of someone else's property. Still, she paints herself as a restless, committed feminist whose family poverty made it impossible for her to enter institutions of higher learning and thus become a leader of her own people. An accurate picture? Impossible to know. Other women of not so dissimilar backgrounds did excel: Emma Goldman, Golda Meir, Dvora Baron. Bela's father hired a *lerer*, a Yiddish teacher, whose responsibility it was to instruct the children in religious and secular subjects. But she was ambitious, she wanted more – to the point, as she puts it, of ingratitude. In one scene, Bela has a terrible fight with her parents, which she soon after regrets, for not allowing her to study in a respected Warsaw school. In another, she suggests a number of possible plots for novels she could have written, had she received the proper education. Memoirs are subjective, manipulative, driven by our desire to improve our prospects in human memory, and as rudimentary as it is, Bela's is no exception. Her flattering self-portrait is in sharp contrast with the domineering, exploitative, conservative lady she has always been, at least within family circles.

True, her literary interests are obvious. She is, and has been since I can remember, a voracious reader, if not a versatile debater. An avid borrower of library books from the Centro Deportivo Israelita (CDI), the Jewish sports and entertainment center in Mexico's capital, the librarians know her simply as Señora Stavchansky. They see her regularly and are even ready to send her titles home on request, should she be unfit to make the journey from Colonia Polanco to the northern edge of the city. She reads everything, in Yiddish, Spanish, and, with difficulty, English: from the weekly *Der Shtime* to Chaim Potok's novels, from Sholem Asch to Saul Bellow, even though, as she confessed to me once, *Humbold's Gift* made absolutely no sense to her. I once gave her a Spanish translation of *My Life as a Man* by Philip Roth as a birthday present. She hated its open sexuality, its condescending tone. "Too dirty," she announced as she returned it to me. She was not an enthusiastic fan of Bashevis Singer, but in her eyes Singer was a champion of the Yiddish language in a post-Holocaust era, and thus needed to be read, even in translation, if only to pay homage to a culture that is no more. In private, though, she believed him too erotic as well. (She didn't know, nor did I tell her, that Singer was publishing stories in *Playboy* at the time.) Bashevis's older brother, Israel Joshua, was more akin to her spirit. She adored *The Brothers Ashkenazi*, which she read in Yiddish, as well as *The Family Carnovsky*, a novel we were made to read in junior high. When in 1978 Isaac Bashevis Singer was awarded the Nobel Prize for Literature, Bela was thunderstruck by excitement, as if she herself had been the recipient of the Stockholm honor. She immediately called me: "What joy, Ilancito!" she said.

Deep inside, she is sentimental and even melodramatic, and her descendants are well aware of it. The most beloved present she ever received was a 75-minute video – kitsch in its most tangible incarnation – made by her three children, Tío Isaac, my father, and Tía Elenita, on the occasion of her eightieth birthday. A sequence of stills, first in black-and-white and then in color, juxtaposed to real-life sequences of Bela having breakfast, Bela at the beauty salon, Bela in the park, Bela smiling to – and for – her grandchildren, is accompanied by chewing-gum music. I wasn't present when she received it, at a sumptuous fiesta, but heard all about it: Bela wept inconsolably, her life parading before her toward the happiest of endings. Her love of melodrama was revealed in her one and only icon: Danielle Steele. She has read every single one of Steele's sagas of love and money. For a time, she would try to persuade me to read at least one. What Bela liked about them was their emphasis on feelings and the conflicted passions they described; and the fact that the sex scenes were never too explicit. So infatuated was she with Danielle Steele that, much as her father, a G-d-fearing Hasid at the turn of the century, sought the helpful advice of erudite rabbis in time of trouble, so did the vulnerable Bela turn to Steele. When Galia, her youngest granddaughter, suddenly ran away with a gentile, a *sheigetz*, in Bela's Yiddish terminology, she wrote a long tortured letter to Steele asking for guidance. She asked me if this would be proper. She was eager to know if novelists of her stature occasionally responded to their fan mail. And she asked if I could provide her with Steele's address. To me, the whole situation was painfully comic. I was torn: I loved Bela with all my might, but I felt she was doing herself a disservice by seeking help from so cheap a writer. Still, all she asked for was an address, not my own advice. Did my sense of intellectual superiority need to intrude? Who was I to stop her? Had not Bela succeeded in rebuilding her life from scratch? In the end, I gave her the address of Steele's publisher in New York and told her not to expect too much: authors of her stature responded to their mail, but not directly; they did it through a secretary, who probably had three or four standard letters sent out to millions all over the globe. In the end, I was wrong, of course. Not only did Danielle Steele write back to Bela, she actually composed a long and detailed letter about Galia's escapade. She asked Bela to be patient and, more important, to allow the young of today to seek their own path without intrusion. Steele obviously took my grandmother's pain quite seriously, and in her reply, made her the happiest woman on earth.

The other icon she worshiped, and wished she had corresponded with, was Sholem Aleichem – Pan Sholem Aleichem, about whom I heard her talk at considerable length while growing up. No doubt my own passion for *Tevye the Dairyman* was a result of her influence. Several times Bobe Bela took me to see, in 1974, *Violinista en el tejado*, the Spanish adaptation of *Fiddler on the Roof*. The lead actor was the legendary Manolo Fábregas, a megastar on the Mexican stage and the child of refugees of the Spanish Civil War. The melodies of the syrupy show still cling in my mind: "*Si yo fuera rico, yaddah, yaddaaaah daddah daddah daaaah* . . . " Bobe Bela obviously thought we would all get a strong dose of *Yiddiskeit* by listening to an imposing gentile actor portray Sholem Aleichem's character in a way that recalled Anthony Quinn in *Zorba the Greek*. I wasn't as attuned then to the delicacies of translation as I would later become, but even then it struck me as fanciful that a completely gentile cast would talk about *dybbuks* and *shlimzals*. Could a goy teach Yiddishkeit?

Bobe Bela often reminisced about public readings by the author of her favorite characters – Tevye himself, as well as Motl Peyse, Penachem Mendle, and Shayne Shayndl – delivered to cheering crowds in Warsaw and all through Galicia. In Nowe Brodno, these gatherings were a catalyst of sort for the Jewish community, illuminating moral values in a rapidly changing time. Sholem Aleichem, in a way, was a rabbi, a spiritual leader: in an age of secularism, wherein hordes of Jews abandoned tradition, he, more than any other Yiddish fabulist (Isaac Leib Peretz, Sholem Asch, Itzik Manger) articulated the dilemmas of ideology and faith with the kind of humor people found utterly irresistible. He died in 1919, around the time when Bela turned ten years of age, and was buried in Brooklyn. The last years of his life had been marked by dislocation, as World War I exiled him, first in Denmark, then in the United States. She was sorry not to have attended a reading, for as her *diario* silently acknowledges, she nourished the dream of one day becoming a writer herself: a prestigious one, capable of hypnotizing big audiences with enchanting tales of love and treason. Truth is, she had neither the imagination nor the verbal dexterity to accomplish this goal. I cannot recall a single occasion on which she told me a story. Nor can I remember her having a disposition toward the "plotlines of our convoluted world," as Charles Dickens once put it. Her dream, I think, was a result of a distinguished career as reader: Bela, after all, would devour full books in a matter of days, although she hardly reflected on them with others; it was, clearly, her way of escape, of inhabiting a reality far better than the one fate had bestowed on her. And well, if she only had the talent and opportunity to shape that imaginary reality, to make it her own, she would be a far happier person.

For Bela in essence was sour and unforgiving. The strategy of abandoning Polish and Russian in order to begin a new life is, at first sight, a survivor's triumph. But it also denotes an uncompromising approach to the past: pain and unpleasantness ought to be ignored, eliminated from memory, nullified. This approach permeated her whole existence. My father would often complain of not having the chance to discuss anything remotely painful with his mother. When he was a boy, she had several miscarriages. Or most probably, they were abortions. He and Tío Isaac would be given money and sent out to the movies in a nearby theater. They knew, of course, their mother was undergoing some sort of operation – in my mind, I picture buckets of blood – but after returning home, not a word would be uttered about it. Silence reigned. Can I blame Bela for censoring her past? Isn't immigration, by definition, a search for a different self? History, in her view, was a cruel monster ready to obliterate everything in its path. Of Bela's six siblings, three perished under the Nazis. Their individual stories are heartbreaking. I invoke them frequently, puzzled by the way human affairs are ruled by accidents. What else, if not randomness, explains her survival?

Herschel, her oldest brother, managed to emigrate to Rio de Janeiro with his young wife Javche and their little children. Brazil had opened its doors to the Jews, and Herschel saw prosperity ahead and even prophesied that the entire Altschuler family would soon be transported to the New World. It was not meant to be. Javche died tragically while giving birth to their third son. Herschel returned to Warsaw with the children and they were all killed in Auschwitz. Bela's mother died shortly before Herschel's return and is buried in Putulsk, but almost everyone else ended in the gas chambers. Three siblings, Gil, Moishe, and Dovidl, emigrated to the New World at various times: the former in the early twenties to Tampico, a busy coastal town on the Gulf of Mexico; the second to Paris around the same time, where he miraculously survived the Holocaust hidden on a farm and became a partisan; and Dovidl remained near his parents and Bela until she was already resettled in Mexico. From Tampico, Gil sent letters back to Putulsk – in Yiddish, all of them lost – promising to send money to bring his parents, Bela and Dovidl. But saving enough money for the travel expenses, and gathering all the necessary legal documents, proved to be a most difficult task. She waited for long months as the bureaucracy moved at turtle speed. Finally, at the age of twenty-one, she was ready. Luck was on her side: *"Me saqué la lotería,"* she once told me in Spanish. It was mid-1930 and the outbursts of anti-Semitism were becoming more common. The prospects of freedom and a solid education, especially for women, were almost non-existent. Also, Poland embraced laws drafting Jewish cadets into the army, many of whom were subjected to the cruelest of regimes and were not seen alive again. I remember Bobe Bela telling me once, for example, how a male friend of hers had cut off the fingers on his right hand so as to avoid the draft. "Better an invalid than a conscript for the Czar, *¿no es cierto?*" I asked her if the Czar was Poland's ruler. "No, he ruled Russia, but it was all the same."

This portion of Bobe Bela's past feels like a horror tale by H. P. Lovecraft. I see it as if through a veil, with a bizarre sense of suddenly having been invited into a medieval landscape, filled with witches and wolves. Is this a deliberate feeling she wants to provoke? Dates are confusing, historical figures appear in anachronistic settings, people's lives are reduced to a single harrowing incident, and rumors prevail. As an adolescent I remember her talking about the accusation against Jews for killing gentile children and using their blood to bake matzah. And about the incessant question: Did Jews kill Jesus Christ? This feeling of bewilderment, of course I realize, not only pertains to her universe; I experienced it during my Yiddish schooling, in scores of books and movies. The Jewish past in the Old World, the message was, oscillates between laughter and fear: on one side is Sholem Aleichem's enchanting universe of miserable yet gentle, compassionate souls, all tied together by tradition; on the other is a terrifying atmosphere where Jews are worms.

When Bela's papers arrived, her mother packed one single suitcase with all her belongings – "they constitute your only dowry," she said – and, in deep sorrow, the girl said good-bye. *"Zai gezunt . . . Shreibm undz a bribele, Bela main tayerer."* Did she know it was the last time she would see her parents? She claims she did, but her parents nurtured the dream of following her. The trip lasted a total of thirty-five days. Her diario lists October 29, 1930, as the date she left Warsaw's railway station. Her siblings and their in-laws came to wish her happiness. Her father, his hands on Bela's head, said the Hebrew blessing: "*Baruch Atah Adonai, Eloheynu Melej A-Holam* . . . " The train took her to Berlin, where she spent time with an old boyfriend, of whom, I believe, she still keeps a yellowish photograph taken in Alexanderplatz, then to Amsterdam. Her brother Gil had sent her a ticket for the Sparndam, on the Holland-America Line. Hitler would be elected German Chancellor three years later.

As it turned out, she severed the only connections to her past. With Gil she continued to have relations, but Gil didn't like Bela's husband, Srulek. He thought of him as a failure, a businessman with neither vision nor guts. And Bela, in his view, was over-sensitive. So it was mostly connected to finances that Gil's name was invoked. Bela's other two siblings in the New World fared better, but only slightly. Her brother Moishe had married a French woman. One of his children, Tío Marcel, joined the resistance and eventually moved to Israel, where he was enlisted in *Tzahal*, Israel's army, during the War of Independence. But once the Jewish State was established, in 1948, Israel lost its appeal; he then moved into Bela's home in Ciudad de México, where his relationship with her was tense and quickly deteriorated. He regularly complained she treated him unfairly, like a servant, sending him to do errands like buying chalah at Señor Burakoff's store. Soon he moved to Guadalajara, a prosperous metropolis. Tío Marcel married a Sephardic Jew, brought his father over from Paris, and became a shoemaker and eventually a very prosperous entrepreneur. Ironically, for decades the family in Mexico's capital – Bela's three children and their progeny – knew next to nothing about him and his descendants in Guadalajara. The reason, it seems, is a fight Bela had with Moishe, most surely about money. Perhaps he wanted to borrow money from my grandfather, Srulek, Bela's husband, when he was dying of stomach cancer. Moishe wanted to buy a house in Guadalajara, but the Stavchanskys had no money. Medical expenses were high and Zeide Srulek's ruinous business deals had engulfed the family in debt. Moishe was offended and never spoke to Bela again . . . ever. She dealt with it by erasing his name from the family's memory. I, for one, don't remember her ever uttering it, in spite of the fact that my father occasionally made an elusive reference to his Tío Moishe.

How was it possible, to this day I ask, for Bela to ignore her remnants of her past? I found out about the Guadalajara connection the day Marcel's oldest daughter, Sandra – aka Sany – , arrived unexpectedly in the late seventies, announcing an end to the feud. "Enough," she said in a rather confident tone. "The quarrel is so old, nobody even seems to remember what the feud is about." And she challenged my father and others to recall what had sparked the anger between her grandfather and Bela. Nobody did; and if they did, it was time to forget, for a new generation had been raised, the sins of the parents are not to be inherited by their children. In time, everyone came around. Only Bela herself remained silent, trapped for years in her bitterness, even after my parents and uncles happily traveled to Guadalajara and back to spend precious time with their rediscovered relatives.

To me Moishe's story is hard to fathom but the one about David Altschuler is a testament to Bela's astonishing instinct to survive but also of her fierce destructiveness. My father, brother, and I all see it, each in his own way, as a symbol of the kind of tragedy always looming ahead of us. Dovidl was the youngest of Bela's siblings, the most fragile and investive. His was a bohemian, sensitive spirit. He immigrated around 1938 to Mexico's capital, also helped by Gil but landed in Bela's house. My father was five years old. It is mostly through him, my father, that I've learned the details of the story. My father turned Tío David into an idol. He sided with him when Bela harassed him. Was he really a talent? It is impossible for me to know, for, beyond the myths my father constructed, Dovidl's odyssey is buried in secrecy. Bela doesn't talk about him. Nor does my own uncle, Tío Isaac. And there is no one else alive to be asked.

Tío David dreamed of becoming an artist (a painter, perhaps a writer), of devoting his days to the appreciation of the beauties of nature, but he was trashed by Bela's conservatism. He would spend the entire morning at home, wandering from one room to another in pajamas, with a tea cup held in his hand, reflecting on the immortality of the soul and awaiting artistic inspiration. His hours were devoted to avid reading: first in Yiddish, then – slowly – in Spanish. Perhaps he hoped to become the writer I would become half a century later. Or he might have pondered the opportunities that lay ahead of him in the Americas, wondering, as I often do, if success is not a product of sheer and absolute chance, for talent is crucial but surely secondary as one shapes a career by throwing the net as wide as possible and hoping an abundance of fish will fall into it. But Tío David was not given to fair chance. His sister Bela, at first a friend, rapidly became an enemy – in a matter of weeks. She disliked him thoroughly, and apparently so did Gil, probably under her influence. A hoodlum, they said, *bueno-para-nada*. They believed their younger sibling was too vulnerable. He could easily fall into the wrong circles. So they decided that Tío David would move to a form of internal exile in Tampico, far from the immediate family, where Gil had a furniture store. He would name David its general manager. In Tampico, if he wanted, he could pursue his artistic and literary passions.

Their fears became a reality. At the store, Tío David got involved with one of the workers, a gentile of course, whose name, I believe, was Nelly. I have never known any details about her. Nelly in Mexico's Spanish is a shortened version of Nélida. But I prefer to call her Nelly, for the name rings truer to the legend. She obviously saw in him – he was, by then, David and no longer the alien Dovidl – a sensitive soul and a promising Jewish husband. Who was Nelly? Where did she come from? Was she able to provide the love Tío David lacked from his immediate family? At any rate, soon Nelly was pregnant. The Altschulers in the nation's capital could not tolerate that of course. His involvement with a *shikhse* deserved excommunication. He was a *desgraciado*, a scoundrel, exiled once again from the Altschulers, this time to the newly-formed State of Israel, where Bela and Tío Gil sent him, *huyendo*, throwing him away so as not to have to deal with him anymore. If he could not be saved from himself, at least the family could be spared the embarrassment.

Ysröel, as Bobe Bela always pronounced it: the Promised Land, sure, but also a safe haven for philanderers and bankrupt businessmen of the diaspora. Tío David and my father loved each other dearly. The elder was unconventional, irreverent, rebellious, and my father emulated these qual-ities as much as he could. And as an ancestor who shared my father's insurgent *élan vital*, and as Bela's antithesis, he was a hero of mine and my brother's as well. In Israel, David was even more unhappy. *Un malparido*, a born loser. Did Nelly give birth to a child? Yes, it was *un secreto a voces*, a widely-known secret, for everyone was aware that Tío David had added a bastard child to the family constellation, even though no one wanted to openly recognize the baby. Not surprisingly, Nelly had such anger for the Altschulers that relations quickly broke apart and the child, a little boy, never saw his father. *Más vale olvido que pena*, better to forget than to suffer. As for the whereabouts of Tío David in Israel, they remained a mystery: Was he in Haifa or Tel Aviv? Did he have an address? News was sparse. At some point, he got involved with another woman, a Romanian Jew, but somehow this liaison also received the disapproval of Tío David's siblings in Mexico and collapsed. By the time my father, in 1960, on his honeymoon, met him one last time, he was psychologically unstable, a ruined soul incapable of remembrance. Not much later, he was institutionalized in a psychiatric asylum, paid for by the Mexican family. That, as far as I have been able to gather, is the end of his story, for when and how he died nobody knows. To be left to oblivion, is there a worst ignominy?

The story has an unpalatable coda, one with an even more calamitous conclusion. I thought, for a while, of adding it in parentheses, but doing so would diminish its echoes and affront, yet again, Tío David's blessed memory. More than two decades later, very soon after I had emigrated to New York, a beloved family friend, the journalist Golde Cuckier, died with her three children – the youngest, Ilan, still a toddler, had been named after me – in a preventable AeroMéxico plane crash en route to Manzanillo. A day or so after the accident, overwhelmed by sadness and spending half of my days reciting *kaddish* in synagogue, I read in the *New York Times* the list of passengers. Not only were Golde and her children in the plane but so was David's son, along with his wife and children. Was it an act of divine will, to eliminate all traces of Dovidl's steps on this earth? I often ask myself this question, knowing, of course, that I'll get no answer.

Aboard the trans-Atlantic ship Sparndam, Bela found few other Yiddish speakers, but when she landed in Tampico, the verbal, social, and natural landscapes changed dramatically. Mexico: How did she end up in such an alien, exotic, "uncivilized" locale? How were these ports of entry chosen? What made Herschel, Bela's older brother, travel to Rio de Janeiro? And what made their sibling Gil choose the ancient land of the Aztecs? How on earth did they know about these unlikely places in the misnamed *Nuevo Mundo*? At that time *shtetl* dwellers and other Eastern European Jews were emigrating to North and South America, especially to New York, and, to a lesser extent, to the Argentine Pampas, thanks in large degree to the encouragement of philanthropist Baron Maurice de Hirsh. But other nations of the Americas were also actively seeking immigrants at the turn of the century. In Buenos Aires since the mid-nineteenth century, a debate on the backwardness of the countryside had established that the only way to "civilize" the nation was by developing cosmopolitan urban centers as much as possible. Immigrants were perceived as agents of progress and capitalism and, in spite of a strong feeling of anti-Semitism sponsored by the Catholic Church, the doors were opened to the Jews. They settled in small communes in central Argentina, such as Moisésville and Rajíl. By the second generation though most of them had moved to Buenos Aires and other major cities. Brazil too had opened the doors to Eastern European Jews. By 1915, Argentina had around twenty-six thousand, whereas Brazil had approximately eighteen thousand. In the southern hemisphere, these were the largest magnets for Yiddish-speaking immigrants, followed, in descending order, by Mexico, Cuba, Colombia, and Peru.

It is next to impossible – *un acertijo*, a puzzle – to track down why Bela ended up in Mexico. Or so it seems to me. Was it because it was close to the United States, and a different destination at a time when Yiddish-language Eastern European dailies were wondering, in loud editorials, how many immigrants America could really digest? Or was it a comment by a forgotten friend, a chance encounter, or a small newspaper advertisement, perhaps, in the corner of the section devoted to opportunities abroad? What is unquestionable was that the US immigration quota was restricting entry for Jewish immigrants and an alternative needed to be found. This quota, in fact, made Bela and her descendants Mexican, did it not? At the heart of her rebirth across the Atlantic was a negation: *Thou shall not be American.* Whatever it was, I cannot avoid describing it as *ain tzufal, un accidente*; the enigma of arrival as an accident of fate. In her memoir, Bela's arrival in Tampico is described in astonishing detail. As the vessel approached the port, she saw from afar the many shanties, *las chozas y casuchas.* The town was rustic and primitive. Nothing like Warsaw in sophistication. She disembarked from the Sparndam and was exposed, for the first time, to a different type of *mujik*: the mestizo. Repeatedly, I have tried to visualize these first few minutes – the shock, the disquieting confusion. It appears, at least at first sight, as if Bela's past, tense and miserable, was replaced by a destiny equally tense and miserable.

She would often invoke the wise Ecclesiastics: *nada hay nuevo bajo el sol*, there is nothing new under the sun. Often she thought of returning to Nowe Brodno and her parents and friends. How could she not? The chaos, the anxiety came to her in the syncopated rhythms of Spanish, a language that at first overwhelmed Bela. It was too guttural. But it was hers: to survive, she would need to master it, to make it her own. One day, she would need to feel as if Polish was nothing but a loose thread in her past, a memory. One day she would think: What is "nostalgia" in Polish? And she would not be able to come up with the right word, for it had receded to depths she would no longer be capable of reaching.

In only a few weeks she realized Tampico was unworthy of her, and so she decided to move into Ciudad de México, *the* commercial and cultural magnet for the entire region. The railway system had been built more than thirty years before but the revolution of 1910 impeded its updating, so it took her twenty-eight hours to reach the capital by train. She quickly found room and board and soon felt embraced by the vigor and enthusiasm of a thriving, Yiddish-speaking Jewish community. Bela quickly realized her potential: she would marry and multiply, prosper and reign.

The Jewish presence in the city was limited to a handful of neighborhoods. A tour today through the downtown Calle Justo Sierra, near the Cathedral, where the Sephardic Temple Monte Sinaí still stands, not far from its Ashkenazic counterpart, Nidje Israel, on the adjacent Calle Revillajijedo, allows the visitor to stand on the sites where the Holy Office of the Inquisition publicly burned a handful of crypto-Jews who in 1492, when *Cristóbal Colón* found an alternative course across the Atlantic in his search for the Indies, sought to escape the intolerance of Spain. These Sephardic immigrants arrived some three centuries before the Ashkenazic newcomers. But is it right to describe them as *imigrantes judíos*? On the street, Bela and her peers were often described as *rusitos* and *polacos*. Their plainness stood out. In contrast, their Iberian counterparts blended more easily: they looked Spanish. The long and fruitful cohabitation of Muslims and Christians in the peninsula had darkened their skin, and in many cases had also lessened, if not altogether erased, their piety. Their fate was tragic though. Three hundred years later, what was left of their traditions and costumes? Could many still call themselves Sephardim? Were they familiar with Ladino – Judeo-Spanish, also known as *judesmo* – a dialect that recalls old Spanish and Portuguese but is written in Hebrew characters? How many conversos settled in *Nueva España*, or New Spain, as Mexico was known during colonial times, it is impossible to know. By most historical accounts, the number oscillates between three- and four thousand. A substantial minority among them were *marranos*, in Hebrew, *annusim*, that is, conversos whose devotion to the Jewish faith, kept in secrecy, was still strong.

The Inquisition was a mighty institution in the New World. Established in 1569, in Mexico its strength reached a height in 1596. So-called "Judaizers" had settled in the country undisturbed, especially in the northern sections. Round-ups began to take place. The most celebrated case against a marrano was that of Luis de Carvajal y de la Cueva, the Portuguese-born governor of the New Kingdom of León, whose arrest in 1589 was only the tip of the iceberg, for his whole family – including his sister Francisca, his brother-in-law Francisco Rodríguez de Matos, and his nephew Luis de Carvajal "el Mozo" – were tortured and in some cases burned in auto-da-fés. It is to governor Luis de Carvajal to whom the following famous Sephardic epigraph is ascribed: "*Adiós España, tierra bonita, tierra de la consolación.*" "Goodby to Spain, the tender land, the land of my consoling."

By the early years of the seventeenth century, such public cases diminished but didn't altogether cease. Between the time when Marina de Carvajal, one of Luis de Carvajal's sisters, already insane, was burned, and the independence movement, in 1810, led by a Catholic priest, Miguel Hidalgo y Castilla, himself a target of the Inquisition for *judaizar*, sprang, the crypto-Jews were totally assimilated to the Catholic environment. "Total," of course, is a strong word. Remnants still remain and are traceable to the savvy eye. When I was growing up, for instance, I remember visiting a gentile friend whose mother always swept dirt toward the center of the room for fear of passing near the *mezuzahs* hanging on doorframes. She would always change – automatically, I dare say – the tablecloth on Friday night. By the time Bela descended from the boat, the only vestige of their existence was in popular culture. During my childhood, the noun *judío*, in devout Catholic circles, was synonymous with stingy, abusive, treacherous. My own home in the Copilco neighborhood was half a mile away from Cerro del Judío, a neighborhood that at one point served as a marrano enclave in the eighteenth century. And a legend claims that cabalistic Jews from Spain wandered north to found Monterrey, and its inhabitants, the *regiomontanos*, are well known for their frugality and unscrupulousness. There is also a type of brown bean known in Mexican Spanish as *judías*.

The arrival of the Ashkenazim from Russia and Eastern Europe in the last couple of decades of the nineteenth century was seen as an altogether new beginning. The two waves couldn't have been more different. In the sixteenth century religious persecution and purity of blood – *la pureza de sangre* – brought them to this *refugio* far away from Europe, but while the marranos arrived in disguise and the conversos had already given up their Judaism, their successors, the Ashkenazim, also victimized as a result of their faith, never hid their religious affiliation. They didn't need to. An era of freedom and openness after the 1910 revolution, and peaceful, fruitful cohabitation of marginalized groups was the approach taken by the Mexican government. In fact, President Plutarco Elías Calles, in office during World War II, approached by the Alliance Israelite Universelle and other international organizations, publicly invited Jews to settle in Mexico. His rationale was simple: Jews were catalysts in emerging capitalist societies, and Mexico, in the first quarter of the twentieth century, after the bloody revolution of 1910, was hoping to leave behind its feudal past and become a stable and strong economy. But the groundwork for Mexico's Jewish community took place earlier, in distinct periods and from disparate geographies – between 1880 and 1930, when immigrants arrived from Eastern Europe, and in the sixties and later, when a wave arrived from the Mediterranean, from what once was the Ottoman Empire, that is, Syria, Lebanon, the Balkans, northern Africa, and the Middle East. By the time Bela set foot in Tampico and, subsequently, in Ciudad de México, a thriving community was already awaiting her. The first Ashkenazic synagogue and mikveh were built in 1890, and Bela discovered the much-needed refuge from her solitude, the hot Club Centro on Calle Tacuba #15, where community activities of all sorts – weddings, balls, parties, theater, poker, and so on – could be planned. Between 1910 and 1920, some three thousand arrived, and the number increased by three times during the next decade. Since most immigrants were socialists, communists, and Bundists, among their first projects was the building of a Yiddish-language day school, which they did in 1924, a Jewish committern (aka *Der Yiddisher Centraler Comitet*), and a number of philanthropic organizations that might allow Eastern European Jews to climb the social ladder. Their success was tremendous: in only a matter of decades, many shtetl dwellers opened a variety of businesses, from jewelry to leather, brewing, and clothing, and became quite wealthy. Culture flourished in every respect, and a couple of Yiddish dailies – *Der Shtime* and *Der Veg*, which I fondly remember reading – served as organs of cohesion.

Yiddish, *her* Yiddish . . . and mine: I remember Bobe Bela, already a widow, arriving at our home, most likely on Sundays, talking in beautiful Yiddish with my parents and, less consistently, to me. I would listen to

her attentively: her uncareful pronunciation of der mame-loshen, a
bastardized dialect already infused with Spanishisms, mostly culinary:
gefiltefish a la veracruzana, knaydlach en caldo, and *knishes mit mole;*
and also adjectivated expressions such as *portalishe nutniks* and
Indianishe mentshn. With most of her grandchildren, Bela would use an
ungrammatical, heavily accented Spanish with an occasional lapse into
Yiddish; but I always had a particular affection for the Jewish tongue and,
when it was appropriate, would respond to her in it. Yiddish, in fact, was
the mortar between the bricks of the community. In the forties, a nascent
Yiddish literary scene, with figures such as poet Jacobo Glantz – the father
of essayist Margo Glantz and a distant relative of mine, and journalist
Salomón Kahan, established itself at the forefront of Jewish letters in the
southern hemisphere. Some of these writers maintained correspondence
with members of *Di Yunge,* the Yiddish avant-garde in New York. But
literature was a small, almost insignificant token when seen against the
larger picture. The Eastern European settlers, secular in their manner,
understood language to be the conduit of tradition. They refused to give
it up at the speed of their siblings north of the Rio Grande – New York,
Philadelphia, Chicago, Detroit. Their offspring, to remain Jewish, needed
to be raised in the same verbal tradition. And so, language was a tool of
continuity, the mechanism through which Bela and her peers managed,
magically, to go on living, as it were, in Eastern Europe.

Bela's generation used to refer to the Jewish community as *der yishuv,*
the settlement, one not unlike the *shtetelech* in Galicia. In fact, it seems as
if they managed to recreate a shtetl in the metropolis, to reghettoize themselves in enclaves with little but business contact with the outside world.
Did she ever fully leave Nowe Brodno? Was she not, as were her peers, a
genius in reviving, across the Atlantic, almost the exact same environment
– *al pie de la letra,* as the Spanish expression goes, "to the dot" – she had
been exiled from? When time came to choose a career, my father, her
Abremele, became an actor in Yiddish theater, and also and more significantly, in plays translated from Yiddish and about the Jewish world that
was no more.

In her diario, Bela describes in emotional detail how she met, on Calle
Tacuba #15, her beloved Srulek Stavchansky, a *centavo*less Ukrainian
immigrant from Khaschevate, a small milling town southwest of Lwow,
and of course a Yiddish speaker as well. She remembers the first phone
call she received from him and the sunny Sunday afternoon in Alameda
Park, when Srulek asked to marry her and kissed her – in her Spanish, *se
me declaró.* In my imagination, Diego Rivera's painting "Sunday at the
Alameda Central" includes them both, next to each other, just behind José
Guadalupe Posada. The description of the kiss is narrated briefly, as if
Bela, at the time of writing, was conscious of the potential eroticism of
the scene, dirty in her eye, and thus decided to repress it as best she could.

Exactly four months after her arrival they became engaged. Their marriage took place in 1930, also at the Club Centro on Tacuba #15. Her brother Gil, still in Tampico, was unable to attend the wedding, but helped the young couple financially. Their poverty, nonetheless, was abysmal. They shared a house with another family and struggled to make ends meet. Zeyde Srulek had arrived with only his most basic belongings, but he was a lucky fellow: he borrowed money to buy shoelaces and shaving blades, and when he sold these, he bought a lottery ticket. He became a winner and used the money to buy a hardware store on the busy corner of Calles Academia and Corregidor. His luck did not last long though. Hardship forced him to sell it, and he became an employee. They moved to Tampico, where Gil, still on good terms with them, helped him open a children's clothing store. The couple prospered and multiplied. Tío Isaac was born. No *mohel* was available in town and one had to be brought in from Veracruz to perform the ritual circumcision. After a year the family returned to Ciudad de México, where Srulek opened an animal food store, Molino El Venado, the predecessor of the Forrajera Nacional, S.A., my father would inherit on his father's death. They moved to a newly built home in the eastern section of Colonia Anzures and then to another, more modern one in the nearby Colonia Portales, both Jewish bastions. It wasn't until Bela's children were married that the Jewish community as a whole gravitated north to more affluent neighborhoods like Polanco, Las Lomas, and Tecamachalco, where politicians and the nouveau riches settled.

Bela kept her children close to her. She trained them to be first Jewish and then Mexican, and exhorted them to embrace Spanish as their mother tongue while keeping Yiddish as "the Jewish, that is, intimate language." As was common, they met gentiles only in the neighborhood, for kids were sent to Jewish schools and after school programs. This separation generated in them – and in their entire generation – an ambivalent sense of identity. What made them Mexican? And how did they distinguish themselves from other Jews? This duality was, and still is, much more accentuated among Mexican Jews than in their counterparts in the United States and, I dare say, even in Brazil and Argentina. Yiddish, among Ashkenazim, was the umbilical cord with Europe, one never fully cut. Spanish made them native citizens with full civil rights, but mixed marriages were few and contact with Catholics and other immigrants was minimal. In short, it was an insular mentality.

All this, needless to say, was destined to change as I was growing up. The ambivalence persisted, the nostalgia for shtetl life, but the term *shmaltz* had become ubiquitous. It was clear the shtetl had not been a *paradise* after all. It was crowded with ruffians and criminals. Praying to G-d? Devoting one's whole life to tradition? Well, a portion of the population did, but the place was stern, miserable, cold. At first, the Holocaust, the fatal blow to Yiddish as a living vehicle of communication – how many languages in history have perished so suddenly, in the span of five to six years? – elevated the shtetl to the stature of lost kingdom. But the State of Israel emphasized the idea that Jews were not ethereal beings but flesh-and-blood citizens, militaristic, down-to-earth. And, as Mexico struggled to modernize by opening itself up to the world, it was clear Jews could no longer be aloof, unconcerned, apathetic. They were part of the nation, just like everyone else, with misgivings about their *mexicanidad* perhaps – what Mexicans call *malinchismo* – but fully responsible for their actions. None of Bela's children finished a college education, but others in their generation did, my mother included. And while the Jewish day schools, by definition private, kept a close eye on early education, college was the place where exposure to the outside world was inevitable. The result is clear: divorces increased, inter-religious marriages were more common – two of Bela's nine grandchildren, my brother Darián included, married gentiles – and the degree of Jewish participation in Mexican public life increased considerably. Whereas not a single Jew of Bela's generation held a high ranking government job, several did a generation after, and many more in my own.

The Colegio Israelita de México (aka *Der Yiddisher Shule in Mexique*), in Colonia del Valle, that I attended from kindergarten to high school – a total of fifteen years – embodied the views on history, education, and culture sustained by Bela's immigrant generation. From outside, nothing about the building signaled its Jewishness: it had no letter signs, no insignias. It must have had more than a thousand children enrolled. Its ideology was decidedly Bundist: secular in vision, embracing culture as the true religion. Rosh Hashana, Yom Kippur, Succoth, and other Jewish holidays were celebrated, but in a non-militant fashion. What made us Jews, we were told, was not G-d but the intellectual and spiritual legacy carried along for three millennia. The immolation of the Jewish people was not stressed – suffering wasn't a ticket to superiority.

Yiddish class, our link with the past, was obligatory. It met every day, sometimes even twice. At a time when, in the Jewish world at large, the number of speakers whose average age was around fifty made it a language smaller than Serbo-Croatian, we were taught how to read, write, and speak fluently. Students attended lectures in Yiddish and were assigned history volumes in Yiddish too. I remember submerging myself in long novels by Israel Joshua Singer, Sholem Asch, and Sholem Aleichem. And I read innumerable Hasidic tales and Holocaust poems as well. Understandably, a majority of the student population saw this as a nuisance: Why study Yiddish, a dying tongue? They sat in their exams almost mechanically and quickly forgot what they had learned the moment they exited the classroom. But for me Yiddish was a passion: I loved its cadence, its hallucinatory beat. At fifteen or sixteen, I fervently reread passages from *Die Mishpokhe Carnovsky* and *Kiddush ha-Shem* at home and memorized poems. I especially recall a melancholy march by Hirsh Glik that became the hymn of the United Partisan Organization in 1943 and has become a memorial for martyred Jews:

Never say that you are going your last way,
Though lead-filled skies above blot out the blue of day.
The hour for which we long will certainly appear,
The earth shall thunder 'neath our tread that we are here!

From lands of green palm trees to lands all white with snow,
We are coming with our pain and with our woe,
And where'er a spurt of our blood did drop,
Our courage will again sprout from that spot.

From us the morning sun will radiate the day,
And the enemy and past will fade away,
But should the dawn delay or sunrise wait too long,
Then let all future generations sing this song.

This song was written with our blood and not with lead,
This is no song of free birds flying overhead,
But a people amid crumbling walls did stand,
They stood and sang this song with rifles held in hand.

I also sought out Yiddish films of the twenties, thirties, and forties. If a copy was available, I showed it in a cinema club I organized every Wednesday at the school auditorium. I loved watching Maurice Schwarz and Molly Picon. So feverish was my enthusiasm that I began to dream myself into Sholem Aleichem's stories.

Yiddish, for me, was truly the mother tongue, whereas Spanish, the street language, the one I most often used, was the father tongue. The duality was not artificial: Jewishness – though not Judaism, at least not then – was in my heart and soul. There was nothing cerebral about it: it was, I was taught, the source of endurance, the fountain of life. Spanish was also taught at school, of course, and so was Hebrew, although the latter was introduced fairly late. Zionism didn't become the predominant dogma until I was about to leave school. This brought along the slow demise of Yiddish and the triumphant embrace of Hebrew as the language of the Jewish people of today and tomorrow. But Hebrew felt constructed to me, artificial. On Monday mornings students sang the Mexican and Israeli anthems and pledged allegiance to the two flags. And yet, although I learned it fast, I couldn't quite feel comfortable with its cadence: Zionist patriotism seemed foreign. It wasn't really mine.

So . . . what was the purpose of my whole Yiddish education, its subtext? Was it not an anachronism to teach youngsters about a universe that had disappeared? I left school convinced Sholem Aleichem, I. L.

Peretz, and Theodor Herzl were essential figures of our country. How much did I know about Cuauthémoc, the last Aztec ruler, and about Benito Juárez? And about thinkers like Alfonso Reyes and Octavio Paz? How many poems by Mexicans like Ramón López Velarde had I read? Not enough, not nearly enough. I had been raised in a bubble, unconscious of the gentile environment around me. Not long ago, as I passed through Ciudad de México, I did what every memorist dreams of doing but should avoid: I revisited my old school. The dilapidated building was sold to the government in the mid eighties and houses offices for some unspecified ministry. A guard allowed me in through the back door and I wandered around the corridors, hunting for the ghosts of my childhood and adolescence. The shock was great: the bubble was empty, its pupils gone along with the ideals that shaped them. Whatever socialist dream was nurtured inside those four walls with us as its guinea pigs has been replaced by sheer individualism. My old friends, of course, are, like me, parents; they send their own kids to the new *Yiddisher Shule*, a flamboyant, architecturally innovative building in the northern section of the city. Bela's generation is no longer in command, so nostalgic Jewishness tied to Eastern Europe has been replaced by American pop culture. Yiddish – Bela's Yiddish, my Yiddish – has almost totally faded from the curriculum, replaced by English and French. On my way out, the guard told me the government is planning to tear down the place in the near future. I'm not surprised. Wasn't the school already scheduled for demolition in my last year there, when Israeli *shlikhim*, pedagogical envoys described it as "unfit for progressive education?"

Bobe Bela's journey parades slowly in front of my eyes, as if I was watching the long video movie made when she turned eighty. Smiles, tears, feuds – the melodrama of everyday life: Tío Isaac first became a travel agent, then a jeweler, and finally a respected painter; Tía Elenita, Bela's daughter, married a leather manufacturer; a grandson became a physicist in Israel's Weitzman Institute; a granddaughter had an early fight against cancer; two grandchildren divorced; one became a kabbalist. The turning point for her was Zeyde Srulek's death in 1965. The passages about it in her *diario* are the ones where fear – el miedo – is felt most tangibly. But her family brought her back to life and kept her busy. Srukel's death, in fact, is the closest Bela comes to addressing pain . . . pain and tragedy. There is no reference in her narrative to her lost siblings, killed by the Nazis, or to the memory of her parents. Each time I reread it, I experience the same ambivalence toward her. While Bobe Bela is an enviably active person, she remains a Pole in Mexico, one who refused to speak a single word of Polish ever, ever again but only half-heartedly adopted the Spanish language – a hybrid, an in-between. The last pages of her narrative are dry, tense, and undescriptive. There is a feeling of uneasiness to them, as if the reader has been prepared for a monumental revelation in them, but the revelation, the denouement is somehow evaded. Or is it? *"Mi último deseo,"* she writes, her last wish: to leave behind a financial legacy – real estate – in three equal shares, one for each of her children. No favoritism, she suggests. And, more importantly, she begs her heirs not to fight but to be in peace, with themselves and the others. She lists her properties: three lots and one apartment. "Be honest," she says. *Sean honestos.*

Honesty: a most elusive word. Can we be honest about what we *don't* see and understand? As time went by, Bela struggled to keep up with the pace of changes around her. *Ya pertenezco a la vieja guardia*, I remember her telling me while still in her late fifties, implying she was already a mummy, a relic of an age long defunct. The twentieth century had moved faster than she was able to digest. A clear sign of this, in my memory, was her refusal to alter her hairstyle or wardrobe: she always wore the fluffy, lacquered spray-due, which, at nighttime, she protected with a delicate, almost invisible net. She would put on her elegant wool and silk dresses à la Golda Meir, her high-heeled black shoes, and her cat-shaped, plastic-frame glasses. A stoic, she neither smoked nor drank. And she wasn't interested in sharing the sexual and intellectual energy in the sixties, emanating from the United States. It wasn't for her. Though she tried repeatedly to learn English and, less vehemently, Hebrew – her youthful Zionism never diminished, even if she never truly contemplated *aliyah*, she was always more attuned to the past.

Ilan, por favor, escríbele . . . Quiere saber qué piensas de lo que te mando, my father tells me again by phone. And what do I really think? *Sé honesto*, my father adds. What can I write to her? Any attempt at criticism would be misplaced, for Bela is my grandmother; objectivity is obviously not within reach. Besides, I have not been asked to critique her diary but to inherit it, to digest its memories and to make them mine, to be a link in the chain of generations, to pass along the torch. I should wholeheartedly applaud her effort. I should write to thank her, should I not?

I struggle to draft my first words of reply. Isn't there an element of comedy and tragedy in her? After all, she survived the xenophobia of her native Poland, emigrated to Mexico, and thrived; but she also helped build a community on the margins of history, one unconcerned with *lo mexicano*, things Mexican – an anachronistic enclave, disdainful of the rest of the world. Once again, I think of Yiddish, her portable ghetto. What am I going to say when I see her?

It strikes me, suddenly, that Bobe Bela's *diario* is a control mechanism specifically directed at me, that she is anxious to get my response, to hear – not from her Abremele, but from me directly – that I have read it conscientiously, processed it, and have no qualms about its main storyline. In the past year or so, I have been telling my family about my desire – or better, my "intention" – to write a memoir about my own upbringing in Mexico and emigration to Amerika. How soon it is likely to happen, I do not say. The English-language readership that surrounds me is infatuated with autobiography as a literary form: to shape one's life into narrative has become a sport of sorts. My aim, although I dare not say it too loud, is to produce one in a few years where accuracy as such, objective truth, is questionable. For how much of what we are, what we know about ourselves is really *true*? We are merely a sum of viewpoints, and human memory is treacherous and inconsistent.

Life is experienced through language, isn't it? Gestures, voices, words. As I read and reread Bela's *diario*, time and again, the word *inauthentic* comes back to me. I try to imagine how Bela would have written to me in her true tongue: Yiddish. I conjure the warm, gentle sounds articulated in its sentences, the magic of recreating Nowe Brodno as it felt to her. By translating it for me, has she injected it with a dose of nostalgia? In seeking words absent from her childhood – simple forms: se me declaró, un malparido, Puerco Judío – has she amended her own past? I think of the challenge ahead of me. I'm aware that crafting my memoir in English will, in and of itself, be a form of treason. For shouldn't it be written in at least three if not four languages – Yiddish, Spanish, Hebrew, and English – the four tongues in which – and through which – I've experienced life? But no publisher in his right senses would endorse such an endeavor. It is perhaps an unrealistic dream, and ridiculous too. My aim, nonetheless, is to convey not my nationality but my *translationality*. To succeed, the original ought to read as if written already *in* translation – a translation without an original. I think of the segments in Englishized Yiddish in Henry Roth's *Call It Sleep* and those in "transliterated slang" in Richard Wright's *Native Son*; they appeal to me because they are bastardized forms of language, polluted, uncompromised. And an illegitimate language is exactly what I seek.

Bela, of course, has no clue about my thoughts. She simply knows I'm ready – or getting ready – to write a memoir: to reflect on the family's past and evaluate its present; to single out, as all autobiographers do, members of the family not only through a hierarchy of anecdotes but by means of what Martin Buber once called a "comparative morality," e.g., the standing each member has *vis-à-vis* the rest of the group. And she knows – how can she not? – that she, Bela, is likely to share center stage with my father, *her* Abremele, as well as with my brother Darián, the Stavchansky trio whose influence on my *weltanschauung* is most decisive. And so, before memory fails her, before it is too late, she makes up her mind: modestly yet decisively, she will write a memoir herself. Not a full-scale, multi-volume one, like the one shaped by Sholem Aleichem, *In the Country Fair*, or the one by Israel Joshua Singer, *Iron and Steel*. No, Bela's will be a plain, simple narrative whose main objective is to set the record straight.

Straight? As I try to compose my reply to her diario, I realize she has produced it mainly for me – and through me, for the rest of the world – to get "the correct impression" of who she is. In all honesty, she is not the only one that has expressed concern. There is nothing to denounce in my life, no one to ridicule . . . except myself, of course. Still, the moment news went out that I was contemplating an autobiography, family members on both sides came to me with requests, people obsessed with their place in family history. But only Bobe Bela has gone out of her way to put down her version of the events, and to send it to me through my father. She is concerned about the record. Or is she? Am I imagining secret motifs behind the innocent memories of a mature woman? Am I falsifying her message? Who cares if the story in her diario is a pack of lies, where Tío David, to name just one relative on whom Bela directed her merciless fist, is not even mentioned? Whose autobiography isn't farfetched? Will I, when I'm finally courageous enough to speak my turn, be ready to face my own foibles, my own hypocrisies? Isn't the genre of autobiography about redefinition and redemption?

And so, I send her a quick note – in Spanish, how else? – via e-mail, to my father's address. I've done it before many times. Mexico's postal service is a disaster. Besides, Bela loves to be read messages by phone. Every Sunday, when she is brought to my parents' home in Colonia Cuicuilco, Insurgentes Sur, she asks to be connected to the Internet and without further delay writes to me. My mother usually types while she dictates. I've asked her numerous questions about Bialolenska Street in Nowe Brodno, about her arrival in Tampico on the Sparndam, about the Club Centro in Calle Tacuba #15. In fact, as she responds to me and my imagination is ignited, I feel the excruciating process of drafting my own memoir has begun.

"It's here, *suegra*," my mother tells her. "Ilan sent you a message."

"Really?" she smiles. Minutes later she sits in front of the screen. "The Internet . . . We could not have imagined it in our shtetl?"

You were never in a shtetl, Mamá," my father replies.

Soon after, my mother reads out loud.

Querida Bobe:
Mil gracias por tu hermoso diario. I admire you. Your memories are mine already.
Te amo, I.S.

Acknowledgment

Originally published in the author's *On Borrowed Words: A Memoir of Language* (Viking Putnam, 2001). Reprinted with permission of Viking Putnam.

Part III

Poeticizing, Painting, Writing the Pain

Traces of Memory

11

Translated by Laura Rocha Nakazawa

Marjorie Agosín

Traces

for Paul Nakazawa

More than a memory,
or the place where memory lives,
like texture,
more than a presence,
among the flickering spirits,
in the wandering heart of night,
among the flames
in that unsettled place,
I found traces, only traces,
cast-off, shipwrecked syllables,
shattered alphabets.

Fragments of memory,
vestiges and mute angels.
traces, spinning, wandering, murmuring,
traces.

More than a memory,
traces
of fiery portals,
of streets, of cities,
only traces,
sublime traces
of meaningless humiliation,
traces of wounded steps,
traces of pillaged suitcases and plundered souls,
traces of a blue suitcase.

More than memory,
in the trace of that memory,
I sensed a voice
that demanded sacred silence,
the silence of poetry,
the gravity of poetry.

Only a voice,
submerged,
a voice whose only purpose
was to remember,
the persistent tenacity
of remembrance.

And in this voice,
beyond the fragile bounds of memory,
and the cruelty of silence,
the dead and the living convened,
to dance around tombs,
and the living, moving deftly like wise dancers,
over those graves of dead
and dreadful cities.

In the midst of those walks,
they repeat names, the frozen edge of language:
Auschwitz, Dachau,
Treblinka
"Work will make you free."

And in those names,
the trace,
the omen, the sign of the burning eyelid
and in that trace, an obliterated civilization
in the most perverse of scandals.
It is the trace of the naked Jews,
of the neighbors mocking the naked Jews.

Here in Yad Vashem
look at the million traces we have left behind
in these grottos of death,
in these gardens of death.

More than peace,
here in Yad Vashem
they demand, they glare, they cry out for remembrance,
to the gesture of remembrance,
to the light of memory
that is one voice,
a singular walk among the barbed wires
and the forest of pale roses.

Humble, arriving at Yad Vashem,
silence is gladness, peace
a star,
the stillness of the abyss and the precipice.
Someone lights a flame,
someone picks a flower
they leave traces,
lucid testaments of history.
Someone walks among the rubble
and listens to a lament,
a cadence,
traces,
a name,
people who wail and recount,
people who pray and shine.

To imagine a ship

To imagine a ship,
rigorously dark,
silent, in pain
like borrowed steps
of unhappy fugitives.

To imagine the ship,
secret watchman,
leaving port,
behind, the fate of the dead,
decomposed Europe.

To imagine that ship,
and only that ship,
like a melody fleeing
an official death
a punishment for your origin,
for your birth condemned.

In this ship,
that will cross the nameless sea,
the landscapes of horrific memory,
are the Jews
barefoot, naked
their only belonging
the possibility of life
of being life
of living life.

They travel, audacious,

mute
Carrying candelabra of seven arms
and the memory of happiness.

To imagine the ship,
Hiding pale and sleepwalking women,
Dressed in garments of death
Dreaming of amber.

Eternal is the voyage
like a nameless abyss,
a bridge that does not span the shores,
the passengers imagine the departures.

Behind, Europe remains, feral and humid,
after the rains and ashes.

To imagine the ship
and a shroud of stars
a sky full of echoes and names
still to be named.

To imagine a ship,
Someone says:
Land and it is land,
Light,
a soft touch in the wind
a game of chance
tongue of a god
now present.

Santo Domingo,
Hispaniola,
Columbus and Juan de Torres.
Jews of old,
Jews of Sefarad,
Jews dreaming the sea,
and their seafaring raiment
rescue,
like an open palm
the land
opens
to receive,
palpitates.
They, men and women,
all of them
quietly sink their feet in the sand
and the pleasure is morning and night
and the pleasure is a pure wish.
Somebody sounds now,

alive,
looks at the sky,
sings.

To imagine the ship
on this Shabbat of glorious arrivals,
the wind murmurs syllables of our ancestors,
grandmothers return with challa from behind barbed wire.

To imagine that ship
1940
the Jews have arrived
on land,
they recognize each other
embrace their origins,
their right to live
amidst the clear waters.
Their hearts,
chambers that survived and waited.
To imagine a ship,
like a house
that floats in the light.

Cousins

My mother muttered
when she named them,
Julia, Silvia, Sonia
Sonia, Julia, Silvia.
They were the names of rivers,
the names of fairies.
They were my cousins,
women we knew,
with whom we shared a history.
I loved them from a distance
And close by.

We knew nothing about them.
Little was known about the obedient time of war,
only certain clues,
a murmur,
a sigh.
They sent us encrypted addresses,
never deciphered,
false trails,
invisible names.

On holy days
there were empty seats
and my father, with his sacred cup,
invoked them.
Julia, Sonia, Silvia.

I also came to love them,
happy just
to see their handwriting
in threadbare postcards
from Vienna, then
Prague and
later, the cities with austere names.

My grandmother Helena,
taciturn,
took out her photographs that
resembled amber-colored bones,
shining among absences.
Suddenly,
almost fifty years later,
the cousin from Sweden calls
and he can't help but remember.
He told us,
mute,
ethereal in the distance,
that he had seen them,
those cousins:
Julia, Sonia, Silvia.
He had found them
in the holy book of
the dead.
He had searched for
their last names,
and their crossings.

They had been transferred to those
trains of shadows
and shorn women,
singing in their blue clothes,
to Terezin,
later to be sent to
Auschwitz,
where there is no forgetting,
where there are no calendars,
where there is no memory,
where there is no voice,
where women keep silent,
are shorn,

are delirious
and carry on their heads the rituals
of dead birds.

The cousin from Sweden
found them.
They were dead and alive
or they had arrived in an afternoon of amber,
wounded and dead.

He tells me hurriedly
that they killed them with blue gas
and that is all he knows about them.
He asks me to tell this to my mother,
and also to Aunt Regina.

All of them
in Auschwitz,
and I don't know how to name them,
and I don't know how to remember them.

Anger blends in with my screams.
I recognize them
Sonia, Julia, Silvia.
I cannot name them anymore,
I see them severed in those forests
of dead butterflies
and I think I do not deserve this life
without them.

I tell my mother
and my grandmother, who has remained
forgotten in the South,
that we should not
search for them,
Not to imagine false
omens;
that they are there;
that upon their arrival
they made them burn;
their tiny bones were placed
without a name in the minuscule ovens
of death.

I feel distressed when I tell you this story
and I can only say it in a poem
because I cannot tell it to anybody.
I don't want to hear things like
"Again, the Jews and their memories."
"That happened years ago."

"I don't know anything about that."
That is how they talked when the neighbor,
the grandfather,
his small grandchildren
disappeared.
Tonight
all of this turns in my head
like a gathering of wilted
poppies.
I don't know where Julia, Sonia, Silvia are.
I shall navigate those meadows.
My passion will kiss the grass
waiting to meet their lips.

Julia, Sonia, Silvia,
you shall not die among barbed wires.
You shall no longer be the hidden Jews
without hair or language.

I will return to the fields
to sprinkle them with prayers and holy water.
I shall give you a notebook, Julia,
a fan, Sonia,
a breath of light, Silvia.
My cousins, my blood cousins,
family that could no longer be loved.
I don't want lies for your names.
I don't want anybody to speak
on your behalf.
I ask for a second, a century of peace
and memory
for all
the dead Jews,
the gypsies,
the women of Bosnia.
They are all named
Julia, Silvia, Sonia
and they are mine.

Unpredictable Northern Train

Like a traveler obscured by a severe darkness,
the train conductor
confident, precise,
checks that all the passengers,
including the shorn women,
those dressed like brides of death, and

the gasping elders,
climb the train
that will take them
to the place of certain
absence,
the place of nameless horrors
the most hidden secret,
the secret we all know.

The train conductor
is well respected for his work,
deserves a medal
for his punctuality.
He knows the destination of those trains:
the stations of blue gas,
the place of fog,
the silence beyond all silences,
the bodies burning like dead flowers.

The train conductor
considers himself noble in this obedience.
After all
it is only Jews who travel
in the trains
and it is his duty,
his passionate vocation
to make the Jews disappear.
Before it was Jehovah's Witnesses who had disappeared,
the sick, the old,
now even Jewish children,
a million and a half to be precise,
they must go.
And the conductor feels happy
when he sees them climb,
it is late at night
but clear enough to see.
They are beautiful and vulnerable
those children,
rhythmic and ceremonious
with translucent hair
they obey.
They are sincere,
they have passed their summer without haste
in this uncertain hour
they remain good
even though the train conductor
detests Jewish children.

The train conductor

loves the perfection of obedience,
the sound of the departing train
that ebbs and flows,
like suffocating fog.

The train conductor
knows when the doors of life
and death open
and he smiles.
He loves his work,
it is noble to kill Jews,
citizens of nothing,
insane children
empty out words of love and fear.

Today I pray for that train conductor
I demand an explanation
for those brides in mourning,
for the grandmother whose heart was split.
I demand justice for all the train conductors
who knew you reached that place alive
and you returned with
empty containers,
some dolls,
decapitated fairy tales,
dancing amid madness.
In that station, death appeared
faceless, with transparent heels,
a panting tongue
and the train conductor knew.

The train conductor
echoed the whistles of death
insisted that the trains
have their own schedules,
their arrivals and departures.
He loved the midnight trains
with sleepy, barefoot children,
weeping mothers, with ears like sad wells.

The train conductor smiled
as they arrived at Auschwitz.
His day was over,
heroic.
He had killed more Jews.

Traveling Bag

In a clearing
of the forest,
close to the precipices
of fallen night
and absences,
there was
a small girl's
traveling bag.
It could have been
that of your daughter,
full of charms,
small and wild
pebbles,
imagined jewels.
It could have been
the bride's bag
with her mauve clothes
like love
or rain on the soul
after love.

However,
it was the bag
of a Jewish girl
the one who sang at night
and perhaps lived in Prague,
or Amsterdam,
or in a snowy village in Romania.
Her crime was to have been born Jewish,
nothing more.
Suddenly, her bag is found
in the mist
and blue smoke,
drifting.
It had no destination
or owner and
it only said
"Auschwitz."

Is Auschwitz a city for
the dead or the living,?
asked the girl surprised.

It was a small bag
with the treasures of girls
and their longings of spring.
It was an abandoned bag,

without destination or
owner.
This little bag ended
in a place where,
upon their arrival,
children's hair turned white
and they no longer looked at the sky.

It is more than certain,
in the time of frost
without borders
some Nazi soldier
must have kept the loot:
perhaps a doll
or a diary,
maybe sunflower seeds
but only a memory.

My country

You tell me about your country,
daring in its minute geography,
you dream of its stars,
naming them like your cousins,
recognizing the meandering of its rivers,
the details of every corner.
Astonished you extol
the privileged horizon,
you believe in its landscape.

Your country,
a living legend,
everything is contained there:
the dead and the living
the insomniac disappeared,
the radiant whispering of water,
the first kiss,
shoes that hastily showed you
the dance of life.

Your parents
welcome you in the precarious returns.
You have already learned not to ask,
like a daughter who is also an outsider.

You love their routines
their gentle rituals,
they are your country,

permanent presence of woods,
they smell of sweet things,
of those habits that are nostalgia.

Your country,
mysterious history,
surviving history
now, so small,
before a giant,
in the fullness
of your childhood.

When you are away,
you become small,
nobody recognizes you,
you also inquire about
your lineage.
You close your eyes
to find yourself
in the constant movement of this deep wound.

You pronounce your name in your language,
the language of sun and bread,
the language of your mother
that today is not the one of your daughter

Your country,
resting next to the silence of your memory,
a dormant place,
a winter garden surrounded by gardenias.

Today you looked in the mirror
and saw it
in your face,
the rictus of your lips,
a dry island
in your skin
a fan of lights and shadows
in your eyes.

The southern seas,
a luminous lightning.

My city

I returned to her.
Once again,
my city held me in her arms,
guided my steps.

All dressed in moss, with depths of water and sky,
she gave me back the color of memory,
she watched over the wrenching pain of returning
without spying on me.
She was also celebrating,
triumphant after 27 years of darkness,
she did not have masks or funereal covers.

Once again I loved her,
like someone who re-encounters
a first love
with the timid and enveloping language
of lovers in summer.

Once again I loved her.
I was a light shimmering breeze,
texture of passions.
I gazed with her at the night
as I had done before with my parents
who, walking hand in hand,
exclaimed: how fresh the night of Santiago,
what sweet caress the wind pelting our skin.

It was summer.
Whispering voices whistled,
disappeared friends
were returning from oblivion,
fortune-tellers regained their voices,
children swam transparent in pools.

Once again I loved her
because she did not forbid anything,
bathed in sun and inebriated with words she sang.
I sang with her,
my voice regained the shape of a hummingbird river,
it obtained the silky feel of peaches.
Everything was summer, I looked at my hands,
they were covered with roots,
those I left forgotten in September.

I returned to my city.
Like Alice who returns from the land of sorrows,
now it was my turn to be in wonderland.
I recovered my memory,
the rhythm of a poem,
a song of pure truth.
She and I in summer,
night, like a music box,
the wind sending me back to the earth,
to the sediments of my history.

Joseph

You enter this day
luminous and peaceful,
all dressed in ancient
histories.
You resemble a child magician,
contemplating the marvels of
your people.

On your shoulders,
fragments of clear sky,
the tallit of your grandfather José,
a traveled and miraculous tallit,
like the covenant of your people,
daring and full of memories.

Beloved son,
small like the tiniest
of jewels,
great like the stories of a steadfast people,
in this, your day,
we come from near and far
to recognize you
as the travelers in the desert did before us.

We recognize you in the glory
of your effort,
in the humility of your innocence,
in the courage of your vulnerability
in the peace of your studies
in the wisdom that begins to unfold
before you
today and always.

On this holy day
you join with a people
and its living memory.
You carry the name of your great-grandfather Joseph,
who rescued his brothers and mother from a saddened
and burning Europe.
you carry the name Joseph, dreamer of dreams,
weaver of golden threads.
And the name of
your grandfather Moisés,
dignified and silent man.

And in these names,
you, Joseph, find yourself and bloom.
These are the names of those who have made

Judaism
a living memory,
a living commitment,
a living well.

Because being Jewish is:
to be a good man,
to mend the world,
Tikum Olan,
to take care of the neighbors,
to love the foreigners,
to honor the dead,
and listen to the light passing of angels
as if they were fireflies
in the night.

On this day, yours and ours,
you start in the path of beginnings,
amazed you recognize
what truth is
and you reject inconsequential words,
you choose to be among the vulnerable,
the forgotten,
those who need a word of encouragement,
a transparent prayer.
This is the meaning of being Jewish,
a man of the Torah.

Joseph is your name
a perpetual fire of hope
Jacob's ladder
populated with angels ascending and descending
sanctifying all the places on the earth
and the sky.

This day you receive in your hands and in your soul
the Torah
with the humility of the wise
the faith of one that contemplates
the peace of a man who knows how to love.

You understand your heritage,
the destiny of your origins,
a people condemned to exile and extermination,
a people destined to be a teacher to others,
a beacon in the paradise that is this unknown and severe land.

May faith and innocence
be with you,
may justice be your
true compass,

may you live among the angels
messengers of God over the earth,
may your gaze reach beyond all possible horizons.

In this day you enter in a perpetual alliance
with a people that share your history
but, above all, with your consciousness.

Joseph, small and great son,
we bless your presence
now that you have received the gift of the Torah and your history.
May you be happy
next to those who love you and that you love,
next to the history of a people that sings while it prays,
may your voice be a refuge to the dispossessed,
may your voice be always a chorus of angels.

Torah

Like living water
and fertile orchard,
I thread my hand
over your face
in the gestures of faith.

You dance gently over your loved ones.
You are a benign queen,
making little curtsies.
You are a bell announcing the sacredness of day,
fleeting carrier of rituals.

Confident in your itinerant life,
all dressed in colors,
you unfurl.
Like a wind
over the eyelids of God,
a breeze
over the olive trees.

I kiss your noble front.
All misty I flush before
our mutual presence.
You are Shabbat's bride
God's book,
men's book:
Torah,
golden and hesitant
in your alphabet
I am a believer dancing in a thousand mirrors.

Marjorie Agosín

The Address Books of Helena

You have put away your belongings,
the lilac lace blouse
that matches your hair
of wise and ancient fairy.
You have readied your suitcase
and the address book
is in your arms.
For whom are you searching, Helena Broder,
after the war?
Whom will you find in those
folded addresses,
in those houses that you cannot find?
What steps danced in
your garden?
What neighbor gave you away
while you trimmed the roses?
Who may have watered your geraniums?
Where are you going,
Helena Broder,
after the rain
and the deserted door of the wars?
A black wind protects you.
Mute voices await you.
The address book is burning.

Surviving Genocide

12

Raquel Partnoy

In 1995, when I first visited the Holocaust Memorial Museum in Washington, D.C., I realized that my series of paintings about the Jewish people was unfinished. I began searching the Internet for testimonies and images of Holocaust survivors for my "Surviving Genocide" series. While reading testimonies, I found these words: "I am now standing at the boundary between life and death. I already know for certain that I must die and that is why I want to bid farewell to my friends and to my work." They had been left by Gela Seksztajn, an artist born in Warsaw in 1907 and murdered in August 1942 in the Treblinka concentration camp. She had also written: "Farewell, comrades and friends. Jews! Do everything that such a tragedy will never be repeated!" There, on my computer screen and next to her words was her self-portrait. Looking at the strong lines of her face, the hard expression of her eyebrows, and the rage in her powerful eyes, I felt as if those eyes were staring at future generations, demanding of them that her wishes be fulfilled. Her message along with her watercolors were preserved underground in the Warsaw ghetto.

Reading her words I thought about the genocide committed by the military dictatorship in Argentina. "Do everything that such a tragedy will never be repeated," said Gela. "Never Again" are words that every survivor and every family member of a disappeared person in Argentina will repeat forever.[1]

As a mother of a "disappeared" child I experienced the horror of seeing how my family was gradually destroyed. From the day my daughter and her husband were kidnapped by the military forces, life was not the same for my husband, my son, or myself. Anguish, hatred, and depression overwhelmed us while we wondered if they were still alive, felt impotence because the military wouldn't give us any kind of information, spent endless nights without sleeping for fear that the evil ones would come to our house to take another family member. Those feelings were to destroy our lives forever.

After being disappeared for five months in a concentration camp, enduring all kinds of physical and psychological torture, my daughter and son-in-law were transferred to different prisons, where they remained for three years. Once in jail, political prisoners were treated more rigorously than dangerous criminals, while their families endured humiliation and discrimination from prison personnel, and were subjected to a severe visiting regime.

My little granddaughter Ruth was one and a half years old when her parents were kidnapped. Carlos, her father, was taken from his work place. The girl was with her mother at home when a large group of armed soldiers arrived. It was noontime. They did not allow neighbors to stay outside and the block was closed to traffic. After knocking at the door of their house insistently the soldiers began hitting it brutally, while shouting very loudly that they were the army. When my daughter heard them, she thought about the people who were being disappeared at the time and immediately began to run away, climbing a back wall. They shot at her from a neighbor's roof. While Alicia was caught, Ruth, who witnessed everything, was crying, terrified. Soldiers left her in a neighbor's house. Due to this sad episode, she remained vulnerable to loud noises for a long time. She also became frightened at the sight of people in uniforms. I still remember her voice while she wandered around our house knocking at every door, including the refrigerator's, and asking, "Mom, are you in there?" She would not leave me alone with my sorrows. When I went to my bedroom and closed the door, she used to call me and say, "Come on, let's play!" Ruth lived with us for three years until my husband and I, after presenting requests to many embassies in Buenos Aires, got political asylum for her parents in the United States. They were released from jail and traveled with her to that country.

At the beginning of our odyssey we did not know that we were not alone. Many parents, like us, were going through the nightmare of trying to find out where our children had been taken. We had gone to police stations and army posts; we had talked to priests and military chaplains; we had asked friends if they knew of contacts at the clandestine centers who would be able to say if our children were alive. But the army knew very well how to create a climate of terror in the family of the abducted victim. When Salomón, my husband, went to our city army headquarters to ask about our daughter, they denied she was there and showed him a paper, allegedly signed by her, stating that she was released. Where was she then? The scenario of the disappeared was in place, and the creator of this horrible concept, the manager of such horrendous drama was a terrorist state.

At that time, many families felt miserable, with thousands of young couples disappeared along with their babies or little children. Military forces murdered most of them.

Analogies

As I began to read survivors' testimonies, I noticed many similarities in procedures between the genocide committed during the Holocaust and that perpetrated by the military dictatorship in Argentina. In both cases the victims were taken from their homes or work places by the army or policemen in uniforms or by paramilitary forces in civilian clothes. The perpetrators mostly came at night, but oftentimes they acted during the day. While beating up the victims and screaming at them, the attackers destroyed or stole all their belongings. The victims were then kidnapped and murdered by their oppressors.

After losing everything – their families, their names, and their possessions – the victims were taken to concentration camps where they endured all types of physical and mental torture before being murdered. In the process of dehumanizing prisoners, the military forces did not allow them to use their names. Only numbers identified them.

Their family members remained for weeks, months, years, without knowing anything about their disappeared loved ones. Relatives entered a world of madness where it was impossible to get information from the authorities concerning the whereabouts of their son, their daughter, or their parent. Frequently, military forces abducted several members of the same family; this left the ones who remained at home absolutely helpless.

As in the Holocaust, the Argentine population remained in silence while the military government committed all kinds of atrocities. Nobody seemed to know what was happening, but when confronted with the facts, people used to say, "They must be guilty of something," as a way to justify such horror.

Most Argentinean newspapers became accomplices. While armed groups – military, paramilitary, and police forces – were capturing and killing students or defenseless citizens, the newspapers and magazines wrote articles and showed pictures reporting the events as "confrontations with security forces" (*enfrentamientos*), a consequence of the "dirty war." These were expressions invented by the military to mask the repression.

When the Inter-American Commission for Human Rights of the Organization of American States (OAS) requested a visit to concentration camps in Argentina to investigate denunciations of human rights violations, the military government dismantled torture centers or changed their appearance in order to make a good impression. This simulation did not prevent the murdering of the disappeared victims. Nazis had used Terezin as a model camp to show off to the Red Cross; they even encouraged the prisoners to develop their art skills and to have musical performances. After being visited by this organization, the prisoners, among them many talented children, were sent to the gas chambers.

Repression

Argentina shares with many Latin American countries a history of repression and silence. For many years the cruelest chapters of its history were erased. No names of the massacred people remain, no markers at the places where they were buried. The military forces took good care to hide information, delete any trace of their crimes, and avoid any attempt at criticism or judgment of their actions. Silence, impunity, the lack of punishment of those who committed such atrocities allowed similar episodes to happen again and again. Between 1976 and 1983, tens of thousands of people disappeared in Argentina in the name of national security, blamed for conspiring against the "Western and Christian way of life." Secret and open imprisonment, disappearances, torture, and murders committed by the military dictatorship to eliminate political opposition became the tools to fight against different ideas and beliefs. More than three hundred secret detention centers were operating throughout Argentina during the years of military rule. In these concentration camps the military government held around thirty thousand people in inhumane conditions, depriving them of all communication with their families. Most victims were young adults and adolescents. Not only political dissidents were kidnapped but also anybody suspected of "threatening state security": students, journalists, social reformers, human rights activists, and often times their spouses, family, or friends. Most of them were physically and mentally tortured, and eventually murdered.

Like much of the population in Argentina, the victims were first- and second-generation European immigrants from different countries: Spain, Italy, Russia, Ukraine, Poland, France, and others. They were Catholics, atheists, Jehovah's Witnesses, and Jews. The idea of the torturers was to exterminate the victims by destroying everything: their beliefs, their dreams, their families, their bodies. Unlike the Jewish Holocaust, the Argentinean genocide was not an attempt to eliminate a race. However if the victim was a Jew, the cruelty of the soldiers and torturers increased. Testimonies from Jewish and non-Jewish survivors presented before the law in the case titled "Terrorism and Genocide – Central Courtroom Number Five – National Audience – Madrid" tell in detail how the rage of the torturers intensified when the prisoner was a Jew. According to the report of the *Comision de Solidaridad con las Familias de Desaparecidos, Barcelona* (Commission of Solidarity with the Families of Disappeared People, Barcelona, Spain), there were more than two thousand Jewish victims during Argentine military rule. The commission describes this as the largest genocide against Jewish people since the Holocaust. In addition, they have evidence that in many cases Jews were detained only because of their origin, due to the Nazi and anti-Semitic ideology of the security forces that carried out the repression. They also state that in some detention camps the guards showed Nazi swastikas and painted them on the backs of prisoners.[2]

Anti-Semitism

Two dramatic assaults against Jewish institutions took place in the 1990s in Buenos Aires. On May 17, 1992, the Israeli Embassy suffered a terrorist attack. A bomb thrown at the building by unknown people caused the death of twenty-two people, many injuries, and destruction of the entire building. Two years later, on July 18, 1994, a car bombing of the Israeli Argentine Mutual Association (AMIA) caused tremendous damage: eighty-six Jews and non-Jews died, three hundred persons suffered severe injuries, and like the embassy attack, the building was totally destroyed. In spite of the intense pressure from both institutions and from the victims' relatives, demanding that the Argentine government investigate and bring the perpetrators to justice, until today, they have done very little to find out who committed such terrible crimes.

Argentina has a long history of anti-Semitism. In 1891 when a large number of Jewish immigrants from Russia arrived at the port of Buenos Aires, anti-Semitism already existed. Argentine newspapers published articles against this immigration. Thousands of Jews had fled the Czarist regime. After many years of persecution, injustice, and pogroms, they were looking for a better future for their families. They did not know that two decades later they would have to endure a similar kind of discrimination in their new country.

The Jews who remained in the cities became skilled workers. In Buenos Aires, they became strongly involved in union organizing and created their own national trade unions. In the ghetto-like neighborhoods of Once, Villa Crespo, and Caballito where they lived and worked, they created important cultural organizations, libraries, and a newspaper.

In 1910, under the government of President José Figueroa Alcorta, an extreme nationalist movement was born. That year Argentina also celebrated the centennial of its independence, which increased the fervor of nationalist groups. The government and police supported this movement and began to repress the labor ranks. Along with this anti-labor reaction, anti-Semitic actions began. Buenos Aires witnessed the first pogroms. Government troops, police, and paramilitary groups started to severely persecute trade unions, targeting Jewish neighborhoods first. Private homes were destroyed; stores, institutions, and libraries were burned; and many Jews were murdered. The cheering of many anti-Semitic people was heard, amidst the gunshots and the hunting of Jews. The victimizers wore the colors of the Argentine flag in their lapels and encouraged the police and the soldiers to protect the city from the "*rusos*," as the Russian-Jewish immigrants were called. In Argentina a Jewish immigrant was always considered a Russian, because of the large immigration from that country. Jewish people lived in the "Russian neighborhoods," and every ruso was suspected of being a Bolshevik, a communist. Because of the anti-Semitism that always prevailed in Argentina, they were nicknamed "filthy Russians."

Anti-Semitic propaganda was introduced in different ways. Elementary schools had textbooks like *La Tierra* and *La Argentina* where children learned that the Jews were thrown out of their countries because they used to "monopolize" other people's jobs. Some theater companies produced plays featuring anti-Jewish themes and characters. Ivo Pelay wrote *Judío*. Through its three acts and its outrageous anti-Jewish language, the play identified Jews with the devil. In one scene, the main character says, "Christians, watch out the Jews are entering the city!" *El barrio de los Judíos* (The Jewish Neighborhood), written by Alberto Vaccarezza, a popular Argentine playwright, satirized and made fun of Jewish characters. It was performed for the first time in April 1919 at the National Theater, three months after "Tragic Week," by a well-known theater company, and featured artists such as Luis Arata, Tomás Simari, and Eva Franco.[3]

Tragic Week took place in Buenos Aires during the government of President Hipólito Yrigoyen. The episode began on January 7, 1919, and left profound scars on the memory of some sectors of Argentine society. During Tragic Week the government used terrorism as a way to repress the labor movement and the Russian-Jewish immigrants. In the name of public security, military troops and armed civilians took over the city in order to repress a general strike. The government ordered its troops to control the working class neighborhoods of Buenos Aires. Police and groups of armed civilians joined the military forces to attack the population of these areas in a cruel and indiscriminate way. They fired on anyone who walked in the streets and burned houses and stores killing many persons, among them children and old people.[4]

During that week, the Argentine Nazi newspaper *El Pampero* published articles with very clear anti-Semitic references. The newspapers *La Epoca* and *La Argentina*, as well as the Catholic Church, justified the behavior of the government and the military forces. No one was ever tried or punished for those atrocities and, what is worse, a powerful movement was created that same week: the *Liga Patriótica Argentina* (Argentine Patriotic League), whose ideology was extremely nationalist and fascist. Its goal was to help the government keep public order and ensure national security. Firemen, policemen, navy and army officers, supported by conservative parties, the Catholic Church, the upper class, and national as well as foreign money played a substantial role in this paramilitary force.[5]

Since then anti-Semitism has persisted in Argentina. The country was a fertile ground for the seeds of fascist and Nazi regimes. Many organizations with these tendencies and strong anti-Semitic positions appeared. Among them were *Partido Fascista Argentino*; *Tres A – Acción Antijudía Argentina*; *Alianza de Juventud Nacionalista*; *Organización Nacional Argentina*; *UNITAS*; and later, *Tacuara*; *Operación Cóndor*; and *Alianza Libertadora Nacionalista*. In 1974, during the government of María Estela Martínez de Perón (Isabel), the *Triple A – Alianza Anticomunista Argentina*, a powerful and also anti-Semitic paramilitary organization, whose leader was José López Rega, executed hundreds of assaults and killings against people they considered political dissidents. This was the preface to the 1976 coup carried out by the military junta.

Argentine military training was inspired by Prussian brutality first, and the German doctrine of National Socialism later. However, the US School of the Americas was the military's principal source of instruction. By following the above influences the Argentine military justified its torturing and killing of people.

Argentina and the Nazis

Besides significant military relations, German and Argentine ties included a large number of important German businesses, especially import-export companies and banks. The Nazi influence started in the early 1930s and continued throughout World War II. The Nazis wanted to keep Argentina neutral for economic and strategic reasons; their goal was to transform Argentina into a secret western hemisphere platform for military operations, and also into a Third Reich intelligence center. The Argentine Blue Book, prepared by the US Department of State after the war, at the end of 1945, revealed that Nazi Germany had transferred large amounts of money to its embassy in Argentina. The money was used for German espionage, for purchasing materials for the Nazi war effort and for subsidizing press, propaganda, and an electoral campaign in Argentina.

When the archives were opened by the US, hundreds of documents confirmed the Third Reich's interest in Argentine political matters. They had closely followed Argentine elections believing that a faithful government in that country would provide a secure destination for looted gold. In 1996, the Argentine Central Bank opened vital accounting records for investigation by officials from the Simon Wiesenthal Center, which hunts Nazi criminals from the war. Five books listed four hundred transactions of funds transferred by Nazi agents between 1939 and 1949, through banks in the neutral countries of Spain, Portugal, and Switzerland. This huge wealth is supposed to have come from Holocaust victims.[6]

According to the report, "Argentina: Hitler's Courtesan" written by Uki Goñi, Argentina had also been interested in getting support from Germany.[7] In November 1942, nationalist leader Juan Carlos Goyeneche was sent to Germany to establish contact with high-level Nazi leaders on behalf of Argentine President Ramón Castillo and the nationalist groups. His purposes were fully accomplished, since he was welcomed by high-ranking SS leaders Joachim Von Ribbentrop and Heinrich Himmler and was able to set before them the concerns of Castillo, whose political situation was in danger. Goyeneche not only received economic help, but also political support. However, these demands were on condition of Argentina's neutrality. Himmler was the SS maximum authority and was in charge of the Nazi extermination camps. Von Ribbentrop was foreign minister; five months after his meeting with Goyeneche, he inaugurated the Auschwitz concentration camp.

Argentina was a safe haven for Nazi war criminals. They arrived between 1946 and 1949 during the government of President Juan Perón, who had facilitated their entry. The disclosing of information by the Argentine Central Bank showed a long list of Nazi criminals including Adolf Eichmann, Auschwitz doctor Josef Mengele, and former SS captain Erich Priebke. Eichmann and Mengele were put on trial in Israel and Priebke in Italy, after living undisturbed in Argentina for almost fifty years. Most of the Nazi criminals who sought refuge in Argentina lived, and many of them still enjoy, a long life as "honorable" citizens.

Holocaust Testimonies

The testimonies written by the survivors of the Holocaust told me about the horrors they both experienced and witnessed. Some were writers before being kidnapped by the Nazis, but many times they began writing after being liberated as a way to relieve themselves of the pain they had endured. Through their testimonial books, I was able to learn about the atrocities the Nazis committed against Jewish people, gypsies, homosexuals, and the handicapped. I also saw photographs taken in the ghettos and the concentration camps. Long lines of naked women, many of them holding their babies, on their way to be executed. Mountains of corpses of men, women, and children before they were buried in a mass grave dug by the Germans and oftentimes by the victims. Gas chambers, pipes, ashes . . . all these images speak very loudly about that massacre.

In 1945 when the survivors were liberated by the Allied troops, they learned that they had lost part of their families. In many cases, the only survivor of an entire family was a child. Their painful stories remained unspoken by the victims for many years; sometimes, thirty, forty, or more years passed until the stories were revealed to the world. Diverse reasons prevented them from talking or writing about their experiences. Sometimes they had promised themselves never to remember their past in order to survive. Sometimes, as children, they were obligated not to talk, as if their past had never existed.

Different circumstances in their lives compelled them to speak out and let people know about their memories. Such is the case of Edith Singer, a survivor of Auschwitz. Her father and brother were murdered at a concentration camp. After liberation, she came to the US and became a Hebrew teacher. Years later, when she was teaching at a school, a little boy asked her if the tattoo on her arm was her telephone number. From then on she decided to tell her history. Singer has been giving lectures around the US for many years. I met her at the Museum of Tolerance in Los Angeles where she was lecturing in 1999. Singer wrote the book *March to Freedom* where she recalls painful chapters of her past, including details she thought she had forgotten. She said: "It was not easy. Every story took me back to Auschwitz and Toucha [a labor camp]. After completing each story I stopped for a few months until I could write again."[8]

Elie Wiesel is a writer and the 1986 Nobel Peace Prize awardee. When he was liberated in 1945, he decided to wait at least ten years before beginning to write about what he had gone through when sent to a concentration camp at the age of fourteen. After writing his first book it was very difficult for him to find a publisher because "the subject was so depressing." Wiesel found himself alone, the only survivor of his entire family. He saw his father, who had always been a strong man, in painful agony before his death. While his father lay angry and exhausted, growing weaker with every day, the child made extraordinary efforts to keep him alive, but everything was in vain. He also saw his mother and three sisters, including one very young, taken to the crematories. He wrote in *Night*, a slim, very powerful book: "Never shall I forget that smoke. Never shall I forget the little faces of the children, whose bodies I saw turned into wreaths of smoke beneath a silent blue sky."[9] His book influenced survivors of the Holocaust to confront their past and start talking about it.

Rabbi Leon Thorne was born in Poland. He wrote *Out of the Ashes* in 1961, sixteen years after he was liberated. The book was more than a personal story; it documented the agony of an entire ethnic group. Rabbi Thorne wrote that there was "a forgetful and indifferent generation" who did not talk about the slaughter of the Jewish people. He also said that in spite of not being a professional writer and because Nazism was still alive, he had to share his memories with the new generation that was growing in a free world with the belief that the history of the Holocaust was unreal. He stated in his book: "I hope this book will help the present generation to comprehend the magnitude of the disaster that befell our people and gain a better understanding of the psychological problems which the surviving remnant had to overcome."[10]

"The reader may be surprised," wrote Primo Levi in his book *Moments of Reprieve*, "at this rediscovered narrative vein, thirty or forty years after the events. Well, it has been observed by psychologists that the survivors of traumatic events are divided into two well-defined groups: those who repress their past *en bloc* and those whose memory of the offense persists as though carved in stone."[11] Levi belonged to the second group. In his books he left testimony of one of the cruelest episodes in the history of humankind. As an Auschwitz survivor he had terrible memories and time had accentuated them. In 1987 he felt demoralized and was going through an episode of severe depression that ended with him committing suicide, throwing himself down the stairs of his aparment block. Levi had just finished writing his book *The Drowned and the Saved*.[12] He felt that he had written the last chapter of his life. The cycle was completed for him. Levi left testimony of his state of mind when he wrote in *The Truce*:

> A dream full of horror has still not ceased to visit me, at sometimes frequent, sometimes longer, intervals. It is a dream within a dream, varied in detail, one in substance. I am sitting at a table with my family, or with friends, or at work, or in the green countryside; in short, in a peaceful relaxed environment, apparently without tension or affliction; yet I feel a deep and subtle anguish, the definite sensation of an impending threat. And in fact, as the dream proceeds, slowly and brutally, each time in a different way, everything collapses, and disintegrates around me, the scenery, the walls, the people, while the anguish becomes more intense and more precise. Now everything has changed into chaos; I am alone in the center of a gray and turbid nothing . . .[13]

Nelly Sachs, the first Jewish woman to win the Nobel Prize for Literature in 1966, had all her family, except for her mother, killed in concentration camps during the Holocaust. She wrote: "If I could not have written, I could not have survived. Death was my teacher . . . my metaphors are my sounds." Her best-known poem is:

> O the chimneys
> O the chimneys, On the cleverly devised abodes of death,
> As Israel's body drew, dissolved in smoke, Through the air,
> As a chimney sweep a star received it, Turning black,
> Or was it a sunbeam?[14]

"I have written my story," wrote Gerda Weissmann Klein in her book *All But My Life* in 1957, "with tears and with hopes. As I finish the last chapter of my book, I feel at peace, at last I have discharged a burden."

"Survival is both an exalted privilege and a painful burden," she wrote in the epilogue to the 1995 edition, after looking back on what she had stated nearly forty years earlier.[15] She was born in Poland and lived there with her parents and brother when they were sent to a concentration camp. Gerda was twenty-one years old when she was freed, the only survivor of her family. Gerda married an American Jew who as a US Army lieutenant liberated her in 1945. In spite of having had a happy life with her husband and children, in spite of having written five books telling her life's experiences as a slave laborer of the Nazis and remembrances related to this subject, she was not able to overcome the shadows of her past. Still at the age of seventy, the burden of her ghosts appeared before her during commonplace events of daily life, awakening painful memories.

I am the Only Survivor of Krasnostav was written by Donna Rubinstein in 1982, on the forty-first anniversary of the annihilation by the Nazis of all the people who lived in Krasnostav, including Rubinstein's entire family: grandparents, parents, siblings, and also uncles, aunts, and their families. As the only survivor of Krasnostav, a small eastern Ukrainian town, she felt it was her duty to record her memories for her children and for future generations. She wrote: "I am still alive, a remnant of the Holocaust, and will not remain silent. As long as I live I will tell what I remember, so that at least one tiny part of the most horrendous catastrophe of the twentieth century shall never be forgotten."[16]

During the last two decades of the twentieth century many books and articles were written by the survivors of the Holocaust with the intention that the world not forget, deny, or ignore the annihilation of six million Jews during the years of Nazi rule. Children's testimonies are the most powerful. Through their innocent vision, existence in the camps seems even more inhumane. *I Never Saw Another Butterfly* is an anthology of poetry and art created by the children of Terezin concentration camp.[17] Of the fifteen thousand children sent to this camp for extermination, only one hundred survived. Many prisoners were talented artists and musicians, who not only developed the children's creativity, but also used their teaching as a way to relieve anguish and suffering. Tragically, both children and adult artists were sent to the gas chambers.

Argentine Genocide Testimonies

The history of genocide in Argentina has a living and powerful witness: *Las Madres de Plaza de Mayo* (Mothers of the Plaza de Mayo), an organization created during the dictatorship by the mothers of "disappeared" children. They have been marching every Thursday at the Plaza de Mayo, across the street from the Government House, since April 30, 1977, one year after the military coup. The women carry large signs with the photos of their children and ask for their whereabouts. As a consequence, some of the mothers have also disappeared. After so many years they have become a symbol of strength and courage around the world. Yet the large majority of the perpetrators of such human rights violations remain totally unpunished. In 1983, when democracy returned to Argentina, the government applied amnesty laws and pardoned all those responsible for the murders.

"Mothers of Plaza de Mayo"; series "Surviving Genocide,"
acrylic on canvas, 1994

Many witnesses' testimonies on Web pages, in novels, short stories, tales or poetry, lectures, and reports, teach people about the atrocities committed by the dictatorship against its political dissidents. There are testimonies about starvation, discrimination, and all kinds of torture in secret detention places; about mass murder of prisoners; about bodies burned and buried in hidden mass graves; and about lethal drugs and "death flights" where prisoners, oftentimes still alive, were thrown from helicopters or planes into the La Plata river or the ocean. There are testimonies regarding the babies who were born in captivity under the worst conditions and then given to military families, while their mothers were murdered. Some of those children, young adults now, were found by *Las Abuelas de Plaza de Mayo* (Grandmothers of the Plaza de Mayo), another strong organization. Most of the disappeared children, about five hundred, are still living apart from their real families, without knowledge of their true identity.

The military forces tried to hide the fact that they destroyed almost a whole generation. However, the survivor's personal memories, as well as the testimonies of family members of disappeared people who have had the strength, frequently at personal risk alerted international observers and allowed the world to learn the true history. Those whose testimonies were published were not always professional writers, but their need for justice made them write about the atrocities committed during the military regime.

Matilde Mellibovsky, mother of a disappeared child, Graciela Mellibovsky, is one of the founding members of the Mothers of the Plaza de Mayo. Her daughter was abducted on September 25, 1976, at the age of twenty-nine. Matilde wrote the book *Circle of Love over Death: Testimonies of the Mothers of the Plaza de Mayo* in 1990. This was her first book and also the first book of its kind. When a foreign writer approached her at a conference in Buenos Aires, looking for a book in Spanish with testimonies by the Mothers, she had to admit that no such book had been written. Mellibovsky decided then to face the hard task of interviewing the other mothers of the organization, taping or writing their painful experiences as well as her own. "I want to write this book so that the next generations can have an exact image of what happened, so that they know us, the Mothers, as if we were their contemporaries. So that they know how we felt and how we lived out this part of Argentina's history, which scarred our families forever," she wrote. In one chapter she discusses the difference between death and disappearance: "A disappearance places you in a very large, dense cloud from which you cannot escape, because in the unconscious a hope always survives, while you can rationally assume the absoluteness of death."[18]

Among the victims who did not survive, there were poets and writers whose works were preserved by their families or friends. Claudio Epelbaum was one of them; he disappeared in 1976. In 1985, *Desde el Silencio* was published in Buenos Aires, a moving anthology with poems and narratives by more than twenty young poets who, like Epelbaum, were killed by the military forces.

Agrego estas lágrimas secas
por el dolor,
mientras beso la tierra embebida
de rabia impotente
por el escándalo
del hombre asesinado,
de sus sueños violados.

The poet cries dry tears because of his pain, while he kisses the earth soaked with impotent rage, due to the terrible reality of people being murdered and deprived of their dreams.[19]

"The voices of my friends at the Little School grew stronger in my memory," wrote Alicia Partnoy in the introduction to her book, *The Little School: Tales of Disappearance and Survival in Argentina*. It was published in the US in 1986, seven years after she was released from prison and was granted political asylum in America. As a writer she has had the tools to express, through her tales and poems, her experiences as a survivor and a witness to the killings of all her friends. "By publishing these stories I feel those voices will not pass unheard," she wrote. The Little School was the name of the secret detention place where she was confined. By describing in her stories, and also in the appendix of her book, the guards and their behavior against the victims, the brief and hidden chatting with her friends, who were later murdered by the oppressors, she gives a precious testimony about torment and horror, life, and death at the secret detention places in Argentina. "I also paid tribute to the victims of repression in Latin America. I knew just one Little School, but throughout our continent there are many 'schools' whose professors use the lesson of torture and humiliation to teach us to lose the memories of ourselves," she added.[20] Alicia also wrote *Revenge of the Apple*, published in the US in 1992. When she was transferred to prison, she was not allowed to write new poems to describe the time she spent in the concentration center. Instead, Alicia tried to remember and write in a little notebook all the poems she had written since childhood. Later she realized that the recovery of her old poems helped her to survive, to recover her soul and her history.[21]

Rodolfo J. Walsh was a writer and journalist. He was murdered on March 25, 1977, on a street of Buenos Aires by paramilitary forces one day after he took the unusual and brave decision to send his *Carta Abierta a la Junta Militar* (Open Letter to the Military Junta), his last public word and a powerful testimony. His body was never found. Walsh wrote this letter "without hoping of being heard, with the certainty I am being persecuted, but faithful to the commitment of giving testimony in difficult moments."[22] The assassination of his daughter and best friends by the military forces; the persecution of intellectuals; the press censorship; all these events overwhelmed him with pain and desperation.

As a writer and research journalist, he had acted freely for almost thirty years; however, due to the repression he had to write clandestinely. In his letter, written just one year after the 1976 coup, Walsh denounced the disappearance of fifteen thousand people, the imprisonment of ten thousand, the killing of four thousand, and the expatriation of dozens of thousands. He also accused the military of maintaining hidden concentration camps, which allowed them to torture people indiscriminately and elude the inspection of judges, lawyers, journalists, or international observers. Walsh blamed the military for using the most horrific methods to torture and kill people, not only guerrilla members, but also trade union representatives, intellectuals, relatives of the armed opposition, dissidents, and suspicious or even innocent persons. Walsh blamed them for applying the same techniques used by the SS in the occupied countries during World War II.

In 1984 this document was added to a new edition of Walsh's *Operación Masacre*, originally published in 1957. In this book he had written about the June 9, 1956, clandestine shooting of fourteen innocent persons by a military firing squad at a Buenos Aires dumpsite. Two or three of those executed were suspected of being part of an uprising against the government. They were caught by the military forces at their house while they were listening to a soccer game broadcast on the radio, in the company of neighbors and friends. This human rights violation was crucial in a country with a history of more than thirty years of state murder and impunity. It was precisely this impunity that encouraged the repression applied by the military dictatorship during the seventies.[23]

Alicia Kozameh was imprisoned on September 24, 1975, and was released to freedom under surveillance in December 1978. She lived in exile in the US and Mexico until 1984, when she went back to Argentina. Her book *Pasos Bajo el Agua* was published in Buenos Aires in 1987, and as *Steps Under Water* in the US in 1996. Kozameh wrote: "After 1984 there were, for the most part, no disappearances or indiscriminate deaths in Argentina. A democratic government was in place. But the power still remained in the hands of the military, with everything this implies. My daughter and my writing were a source of great satisfaction for me during those years in Argentina, though I did experience pain, impotence, anxiety." After her book was published, she was threatened by the police of Buenos Aires; so she left this city to reside once again in the United States. Her book is partially autobiographical. By incorporating other prisoners' real stories into its main character, she describes the experiences of resistance in jail and the subsequent effects endured by political prisoners while resisting psychological as well as physical torture. The book is proof that when memory fails it is replaced by images and sensations.

I have been making serious efforts to remember certain episodes. But no such luck. It is like a sheet hung between my eyes and my brain. The reason for the memory loss is all right there: in the colors, the shapes, the greater or lesser clarity, the rhythms. The lethal potential of events.

Impossible to recall everything. Oh sure, certain moments of anguish . . .

Who were you cuffed to? I don't recall seeing anyone next to you at the time. But what I'll never forget, when we got to Devoto [a prison in Buenos Aires], was when Mercedes entered the ward we'd been assigned and promptly vomited her heart out.[24]

The introduction to the Internet report "24 Publications Concerning Traumatic Amnesia in Holocaust Survivors," compiled by Kathy Steele, says that most former inmates of Nazi concentration camps were not able to remember what happened to them when they first arrived at those places. Their experience was so overwhelming, the reality so tremendous, that they unconsciously blocked out their past as a way to protect themselves.[25] In *The Hidden Children: The Secret Survivors of the Holocaust*, Ava Landy, a child survivor of the Holocaust, describes her amnesia:

So much of my childhood between the ages of four and nine is blank . . . It's almost as if my life was smashed into little pieces . . . The trouble is, when I try to remember, I come up with so little. This ability to forget was probably my way of surviving emotionally as a child. Even now, whenever anything unpleasant happens to me, I have a mental garbage can in which I can put all the bad stuff and forget it . . . I am still afraid of being hungry . . . I never leave my house without some food. Again, I don't remember being hungry. I asked my sister and she said that we were hungry. So I must have been! I just don't remember.[26]

Nora Strejilevich, a survivor of the military regime in Argentina, began her book *Una Sola Muerte Numerosa*, with a poem she wrote:

When they stole my name
I was one I was hundreds I was thousands
I was no one.
NN was my face stripped
of gesture of sight of voice.[27]

Her writing is poetic even when she talks about the horrible times she went through. Her older brother, who was her friend and playmate, was disappeared and killed by the military forces. She was subjected to anti-Semitic insults even as they tortured her. In her testimony, we can sense her admiration for two strong women in her family. One was her grandmother, who struggled very hard to make a living for her family when she arrived in Argentina in 1900 from Warsaw, with no knowledge of the language and customs of that country. The other powerful model was her mother, who after her son's disappearance found strength in the company of the other mothers to walk around the Plaza de Mayo every Thursday for almost twenty years, as a silent denunciation for the dead and disappeared corpses of their children.

Like Elie Wiesel and other survivors who wrote about their Holocaust experiences, Argentine survivors of the dictatorship experienced difficulty finding a publisher interested in their testimonial writings. In fact, even after seventeen years of constitutional governments, Argentine publishers still show very little enthusiasm for such themes. Wiesel's publisher claimed his stories were "very depressing." When Mellibovsky took her manuscript to an editor, he rejected it saying: "All the Mothers say the same thing. They nostalgically exalt their children because they are no longer here." She left his office feeling very sad. While walking along the street she thought: "How bitter it is, they don't even leave us the right to scream! Perhaps he doesn't know that they were taken away . . . ? They took the best of a generation . . . They didn't even let us know why they took them away either, or let us look on at their burial, or give us a place where we could bring a flower . . ."[28]

Painting Experiences

While studying art in Buenos Aires I never thought that my teacher Demetrio Urruchúa, one of the best Argentine painters and muralists, was giving me powerful tools which I would use later to pull out pieces of pain from my inner self and put them on the canvas. Urruchúa was a born psychologist with the skills to develop the artistic expression of his students.

It was a very cold winter morning in Bahía Blanca, that August 8, 1983. I was in my studio working on one of the paintings of my series "The Brides," when my husband came in from the street with a very good friend of his, and told me that our son Daniel had committed suicide at his work place. Seven years before, on January 12, 1976, someone came to our house to tell us that military forces had kidnapped our daughter Alicia and her husband. During all those years my son had been suffering from depression. He had to abandon his studies at an engineering school, due to his lack of concentration. I helped him to open and run a small art picture and framing store. He felt happy for a while, but events surpassed him and he was not able to bear them. Daniel was a very sensitive person and suffered intensely from his sister's kidnapping as well as the family situation. He also felt that due to his illness he was not able to fulfill all his dreams: a career, family, children. Shortly before he took his life he said to me, "You know, mom, how I would like to marry and have children . . ."

Before his tragic death and since 1976, I have painted several series inspired by old family photographs: "The Dolls," "Inhabitants of Silence," "From Life," "Life's Windows," "The Brides," and "The Messages." While showing those paintings at art galleries in Buenos Aires, I would be asked, "Why the sad faces in your paintings?" I did not know the answer; but perhaps that was a way to express my own sadness. It took me all those years to be able to produce the series "Life's Experiences" in 1984, and "Clothes" one year later. It was a kind of catharsis. By painting memories of those times when I was wandering like crazy through the streets of the city looking for my disappeared daughter, or memories of Daniel using as models the empty clothes left by him, I felt as if I had unloaded an immense burden. Yet, looking back to that time I realize that I still had inside myself many things to tell, to paint. Perhaps that was the reason why after painting these series I fell into a depressive state that would last some years. In spite of that, I never stopped painting. To go to my studio and keep working required a tremendous effort from me. However, I think that painting helped me survive my nightmares. I figured I had to change not only my themes but also the materials I was using. In 1986, mostly during sleepless nights, I worked on the series "The Jewish Race," inspired by Jewish ceremonial art. I used the technique of relief collage, applying pieces of lace, tapestries, gauze, and acrylic painting on ply board. Later I painted "Women of the Bible," using the same technique but on canvas.

Surviving Genocide

When I realized that my series about the Jewish people was unfinished if I did not include works on the Holocaust, I also thought that I had to paint and write more about my experiences during Argentina's military dictatorship genocide. I could deeply understand the Holocaust survivors' testimonies I was reading. It was then that I decided to unify both subjects and paint "Surviving Genocide."

I chose a large canvas to start this new series. My first theme was "The Message," in which I tried to express how messages, any kind of message, can threaten or change our lives in a single minute. By painting a couple wrapped in themselves, large envelopes or small ones held by unknown figures, empty clothes almost flying over their heads, I wanted to portray the constant menace that surrounds individuals as well as family groups when they live under a totalitarian regime. Subsequent effects can also be dramatic for them. I took the idea for this painting from "The Message Arrives.., " an ink drawing I made in 1982. I see that drawing as a premonition, because it was done one year before I got the notice that my son had taken his life.

**"The Message"; series "Surviving Genocide",
oil on canvas, 2000**

The unpredictable existence during military rule in Argentina, when people disappeared every day, the uncertainty that many families experienced in their daily lives, created all kinds of horrible feelings, but above all, fear. In fact, fear and death were extremely closely related during those days. When the military forces, using large numbers of armed soldiers, brutally burst into houses, shouting and breaking windows and doors to grab people, they deliberately generated an atmosphere of terror. Knowing about all those murders and having experienced my daughter's disappearance, it was not strange to have the dream I translated into my painting "Dancing With the Death." I was dancing with my daughter very softly, but maybe because of my fear that she was already dead, suddenly I realized she was death on my arms. After twenty-three years I could never forget that dream and still have dreams related to those horrible days.

In her book *The Diary of a Young Girl*, Anne Frank wrote: "I simply can't imagine that the world will ever be normal for us again." She was only fourteen and this was more than a year after getting the message that would break her life. In 1942 she was living with her parents and sister in a Holland full of restrictions for Jewish people, when the SS sent a call-up notice to her father. Anne already knew what a call-up meant: to be sent to a concentration camp. While she, her family, and some friends were hidden from the Nazis in their "Secret Annex" for two years, she felt "in a little piece of blue heaven, surrounded by heavy black rain clouds."[29] In spite of her courage and hopes to become a journalist, she could not avoid panic when she envisioned that the circle between them and danger was closing. She died in 1945 during an Auschwitz death march, four days before the liberation. Anne Frank is remembered as a symbol of lost possibilities. There were tens of thousands of young people in Germany as well as in Argentina, Chile, Uruguay, El Salvador, and other Latin American countries, who could fulfill neither their dreams, nor their right to live, due to genocide. Most of the victims never got a chance to speak. However, some of them wrote diaries and poems, or painted and drew, to vent their daily torments. Anne's diary and all those writing and art works, oftentimes anonymous, became genocide survivors. My painting "Silent Witnesses" is about those silent yet precious and powerful testimonies.

"Silent Witnesses"; series "Surviving Genocide," oil on canvas, 2000

"Rebirth" is a triptych related to the children who survived the Holocaust. In spite of such a tragedy I wanted to express hope; in spite of the Nazis's desire to eliminate an entire race, those children would generate life. "Rebirth: From The Ashes" shows two boys playing in the bare ground of a ghetto and wearing yellow stars. A girl is playing her fiddle for coins to get some bread, while another child is wrapped in rags to protect himself from the cold. From the chimneys, instead of ashes birds are rising, as a symbol of the return of life. "Rebirth: From The Black Flower" alludes to the spotlight in the main tower over the entrance to the unloading ramp at the Birkenau concentration camp. Under its light rolled the trains taking the Jews to their death. People used to call it The Black Flower of Brzezinka. I painted a child who was able to survive by hiding in the forest. He stands between a butterfly's wings, which was in the camps a symbol of lost freedom. Above the child, there is a girl dressed in a communion gown. Some Jewish parents saved their children by leaving them with Christian families. In my canvas "Rebirth: From The Broken Wires," I tried to catch the bittersweet expression on the faces of young survivors, whose photographs were taken the day of the liberation by the Allied forces. Through the broken wires of that inferno, a promissory sun arises, while in the background there is a sad landscape, composed by a texture of brushes. Before murdering the victims in the concentration camps, the Nazis, applying systematic plunder, confiscated all their belongings. First they took money and other valuables and after that articles needed for daily living: clothes, shoes, glasses, and brushes, which were gathered separately and later sent to German settlers.

Dismembering or annihilating families was one of the Argentine dictatorship's goals. By painting "Fragments" I wanted to express how the methodology of state terrorism broke down my family as well as all those thousands of families who endured similar fates. At that time, during the night, we used to hear gunshots very often. Later, somehow, we would learn that some students had been murdered during simulated "confrontations," or that groups of people had disappeared. We also learned that seven army trucks, with more than two hundred armed soldiers, surrounded the block where the house of my brother-in-law was, and after climbing to the second floor balcony, broke the windows and entered the bedrooms where the couple, their baby girl, and a teenage son were sleeping. After destroying everything, they caught, handcuffed, and blindfolded my brother-in-law, José Partnoy, and his seventeen-year-old son, and took them away as if they were the most dangerous assassins.

While this sad part of our history was taking place, there were no available statistics about the numbers of persons who had been disappeared or murdered. However, we did know all about their armed "confrontations," as they used to call their schemes to catch people and make them disappear. They asked the population to collaborate with them in their search operations. The government used the media to let people know the telephone number they could use to call and denounce any "suspicious" or "strange" behaviors of their neighbors, roommates, or co-workers, in order to "protect" national security. This originated an atmosphere of panic and insecurity. Many innocent people, like my brother-in-law, suffered detention and humiliation because of false denunciations.

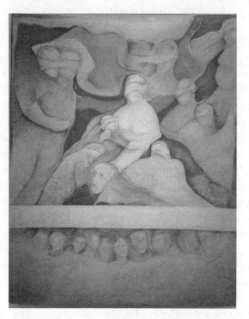

**"The Disappeared"; series "Surviving Genocide,"
oil on canvas, 2000**

Like Matilde Mellibovsky, many mothers or relatives of a disappeared person in Argentina have tried to explain how they feel, how the word "disappeared" can be rationalized. It is not an easy task. When I began doing sketches for my painting "The Disappeared," I could not avoid remembering my own experience. How could I portray images of persons who vanished without leaving a single trace? The criminal rulers had transformed young people, pregnant women, teenagers, children, into beings without names, without faces. Their Mephistophelian plan invented the concept of the "*desaparecido*" to create a haunting landscape of death. The word "disappear" is defined as to hide or to vanish a person or a thing from sight very fast. To cease to exist. State terrorism vanished people very fast, as the only way to eliminate their ideas, their dreams; however, they were not able to vanish their legacy, their beautiful faces. The disappeared are alive in the memory of their friends, relatives, family, and in the written testimonies, for generations to come.

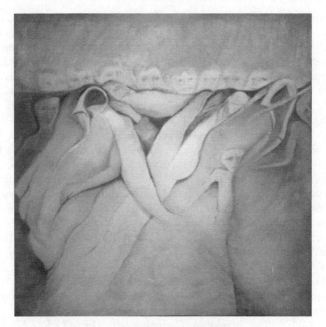

**"Still Landscape"; series "Surviving Genocide,"
oil on canvas, 2000**

My painting "Still Landscape" shows remains of human beings. When I began this work I thought of the remains of the millions of persons who were systematically slaughtered by the Nazis, echoed in the images of thousands of persons who were assassinated by military dictatorships in Argentina and other Latin American countries. Millions, thousands, hundreds of dead people, of disappeared bodies . . . these figures may sound like cold statistics, but we only need to hear a survivor's account, or to read a testimonial book, or look at a photograph of an innocent child, victim of genocide, to understand profoundly the magnitude of such outrageous crimes against humanity.

As individuals who survived genocide, writers, artists, sensitive human beings, we shall never forgive, we shall never forget. We have to raise our voices in order to alert humanity about what happened not only in Latin America and Europe but also in the rest of the world, so that such atrocities may never happen again.

Notes

1   *Nunca Más* (Buenos Aires: EUDEBA, Editorial Universitaria de Buenos Aires, 1984). Formed after democracy was restored in Argentina in 1983, the Comisión Nacional de Personas Desaparecidas (National Commission on the

Disappearance of Persons) was chartered to investigate the fates of the thousands who disappeared during the junta rule <http://www.nuncamas.org>. The Vanished Gallery <http://www.yendor.com/vanished/index.html>.

2 Baltazar Garzón, "Aplicaron los Métodos de Hitler," *Página 12* <http://www.pagina12.com.ar>. Spanish judge Garzón has charged ninety-eight military, police, and civilian members of the junta, who ruled Argentina from 1976 to 1983, with the kidnapping, torture, and murder of three hundred Spanish citizens.

3 Julio Nudler, *Tango Judío: Del Ghetto a la Milonga* (Buenos Aires: Editorial Sudamericana, 1998), 23–6. In the chapter, "El Antisemitismo: A Escena," the author describes how two important Argentinean playwrights, Ivo Pelay and Alberto Vaccarezza, expressed their anti-Semitic thoughts through the characters of their plays. Ivo Pelay, *Judío* (Buenos Aires: Editorial Argentores, 1936); Alberto Vaccaezza (also Vacarezza) <http://www. todotango. com/english/creadores/avaccarezza.asp>.

4 Eduardo J. Bilsky, *La Semana Trágica* (Buenos Aires: Centro Editor de América Latina, 1984), 63–84.

5 *Ibid.*

6 US Department of State, International Information Programs, NG: Argentina <http://usinfo.state.gov>; Simon Wiesenthal Center: Holocaust Assets <www.wiesenthal.com/swiss/index.cfm>.

7 Uki Goñi, "La Argentina Cortesana de Hitler," *La Nación* Line <http://www.lanacion.com.ar>.

8 Edith Singer, *March to Freedom: A Memoir of the Holocaust* (North Hollywood, CA: True Press Publishing, 1993), 10.

9 Elie Wiesel, *Night* (New York: Bantam Books, 1982), 32. Francois Mauriac wrote in the foreword of this 1986 Nobel Peace Prize-winning book: "The child who tells us his story here was one of God's elect. From the time his conscience first awoke, he had lived only for God and had been reared on the Talmud, inspiring to initiation into the kabbala, dedicated to the Eternal. Have we ever thought about the consequence of a horror that, though less apparent, less striking than the other outrages, is yet the worst of all to those of us who have faith: the death of Good in the soul of a child who suddenly discovers absolute evil?"

10 Leon Thorne, *Out of the Ashes: The Story of a Survivor* (New York: Bloch Publishing Co., 1961, 1976).

11 Primo Levi, *Moments of Reprieve* (New York: Summit Books, 1986).

12 Levi, *The Drowned and the Saved* (New York: Summit Books, 1988).

13 Levi, *The Reawakening (la tregua): A Liberated Prisoner's Long March through East Europe* (Boston: Little, Brown, 1965). Interview with Levi, photos: <http://www.inch.com/~ari/levi1.html>.

14 Nelly Sachs, *O the chimneys; selected poems, including the verse play, Eli* (New York: Farrar, Straus and Giroux, 1967).

15 Gerda Weissmann Klein, *All But My Life* (New York: Hill and Wang, 1957, 1995), 247.

16 Donna Rubinstein, *I am the Only Survivor of Krasnostav* (New York: Shengold Publishers, 1982, 1988).

17 Hana Volavková, *I Never Saw Another Butterfly: Children's Drawings and*

Poems from Terezín Concentration Camp, 1942–1944 (New York: Schocken Books, 1993).

18 Matilde Mellibovsky, *Círculo de Amor sobre la Muerte: Testimonios de las Madres de Plaza de Mayo* (Buenos Aires: Ediciones del Pensamiento Nacional, 1990); *Circle of Love Over Death: Testimonies of the Mothers of the Plaza de Mayo* (Willimantic, CT: Curbstone Press, 1997), 26–8. The Mothers of the Plaza de Mayo have always made claims for justice. Unfortunately, impunity left free the assassins responsible for the disappearance and subsequent killing of thousands of persons during the years of dictatorship, as well as the corrupt people guilty of the disastrous economic situation that Argentina's population endured in 2001–2002.

19 Mariana C. Belli, *Desde el Silencio* (Buenos Aires: Sudamericana/Planeta, 1985).

20 Alicia Partnoy, *The Little School: Tales of Disappearance and Survival in Argentina* (Pittsburgh: Cleis Press, 1986), 18.

21 Partnoy, *Revenge of the Apple=Venganza de la manzana* (Pittsburgh: Cleis Press, 1992).

22 Rodolfo J. Walsh, "Carta Abierta a la Junta Militar," Literatura Argentina Contemporanea <http://www.literatura.org>.

23 Walsh, *Operación Masacre* (1957; Buenos Aires: Planeta, 1994).

24 Alicia Kozameh, *Pasos Bajo el Agua* (Buenos Aires: Editorial Contrapunto, 1987); *Steps Under Water* (Berkeley: University of California Press, 1996).

25 Kathy Steele, compiler, *24 Publications Concerning Traumatic Amnesia in Holocaust Survivors* (http://www.brown.edu/Departments/Taubman_Center/Recovmem/25holocst.html).

26 Jane Marks, *The Hidden Children: The Secret Survivors of the Holocaust* (New York: Ballantine Books, 1993), testimony of Ava Landy.

27 Nora Strejilevich, *Una Sola Muerte Numerosa* (Miami: North South Center Press, 1997); *A Single, Numberless Death* (Charlottesville: University Press of Virginia, 2002).

28 Mellibovsky, *Circle of Love*, 1.

29 Anne Frank, *Anne Frank: The Diary of a Young Girl* (New York: Bantam Books, 1993), 115.

13 Poetry as a Strategy for Resistance in the Holocaust and the Southern Cone Genocides

Alicia Partnoy

> I feel
> in my bones
> the bones
> of those
> who once were.
> In me,
> they are
> skeletons,
> we are
> what I am,
> I am
> those who were
> yesterday.

These lines were written in prison by Mauricio Rosencof, who spent eleven years in isolation under the military dictatorship that ruled Uruguay from 1973 to 1985.[1] Rosencof, better known as an accomplished playwright, has left us a legacy of prison poetry and some invaluable reflections on writing as a tool for resistance. He drew poignant connections between his experience and that of Holocaust victims, "(m)y paternal grandmother had been killed with an axe by the SS while refusing to turn over her two infant grandchildren. In my mother's family, nobody survived and a number died resisting. And so whenever it was my turn to be tortured, I thought about my daughter, but also about my relatives who fell in the Warsaw ghetto or fighting with the partisans in the forests of Poland, or who perished in the gas chambers and crematoria of Auschwitz."[2]

As a political prisoner of the military dictatorship that killed my closest friends and devastated Argentina in the late 1970s, I too thought about my daughter Ruti during my years in captivity between 1977 and 1979. However, unlike Rosencof, I was not really aware of certain chapters of my family's history: my grandfather had chosen to remain silent about his own ordeal. Not that I lacked the will and the inspiration to resist because of his silence. Anywhere I looked, brave *compañeros* were risking their lives for freedom. Movements for social change were strong in our Latin American countries and, for both Rosencof and myself, it was not our family background, but our participation in those movements that triggered torture, disappearance, and subsequent imprisonment. We are among the few to survive the genocidal extermination of political dissidents conducted by the military dictatorships in Argentina (1976–1983), Chile (1973–1990), and Uruguay (1973–1985). In our region, known as the Southern Cone, secret detention camp torturers and prison authorities drew their "inspiration" from the Nazis and from the training camps at the US-sponsored School of the Americas, based, back then, in the Panama Canal Zone. National Security and Regional Security doctrines gelled in the criminal Condor Plan, sought to install a US-supported economic and political system in our region. The supremacy of capitalism was at stake. Therefore, the "final solution," concocted by the dictatorial regimes to safeguard that system, called for the extermination of every individual and organization suspicious of political opposition.

In June 1977, after my five-month ordeal as a "disappeared" in a place called the Little School, my grandfather Mauricio Partnoy came to the jail to visit.[3] He sat on a narrow bench in front of me and just looked into my eyes with deep sadness and the deepest tenderness. He did not say a word. I held tightly his bony hand and sat there, pretending I understood. I was twenty-two. The look in his eyes haunted me until my late thirties when I found out from both my father and my uncle that the Nazis had killed my grandfather's family. After puncturing his eardrum to avoid forceful recruitment into the Czarist army, he feared that his injury was not enough to resist the draft, and left Besaravia in his teens. He settled in Argentina. His closest relatives were spared the pogroms, but news from the Red Cross reached him after the war. They confirmed his worst fears.

In my highly politicized family, my grandfather participated in lengthy *discusiones de sobremesa* (after meal talks), where none of these events were talked about. The silence of my grandfather has puzzled me. In the United States, I learned from children of survivors that this silence is the norm rather than the exception. I also learned about the resistance movement during the Holocaust, and about the victims who had been targeted not because of their religious or cultural backgrounds, but because of their political beliefs. I learned that survivors might choose to be silent, but that too often they fail to speak out fearing nobody will listen: their voices have been shattered, their agency destroyed.

My work as a human rights activist, an educator, a poet, and a survivor has been to highlight the victims' resistance to silence. Carefully avoiding oversimplifications that would trivialize both the Holocaust experience and the Latin American genocides, I explore the similarities between Holocaust literature and the testimonial texts produced by victims of the Southern Cone dictatorships. Scholars in my field and Latin American literature have gone as far as to deny such similarities. From their perspective, Holocaust testimonies emphasize the destruction while their Latin American counterparts focus on the politization of the witness and the process of raising consciousness. I believe that the failure to see how Holocaust writings share those very same features with Latin American testimonial texts stems from neglecting the study of the literature produced in the ghettos and concentration camps. There, as well as in the Southern Cone prisons and torture centers, writing has contributed to preserving victims' moral and emotional integrity. Writing, and – for the purpose of this particular study – poetry, have helped victims recover their voices, fragmented by the pain of torture, and have served as instruments to chronicle those events for future generations.

Drawing from both my experience as a disappeared poet and from Frieda Aaron's *Bearing the Unbearable. Yiddish and Polish Poetry in the Ghettos and Concentration Camps*, I reached the conclusion that testimonial poetry in both situations was frequently born from the impulse of easing the pain of others as one of the ways to mitigate the poet's own pain.[4] Those writings were nourished by the notion that the only way to survive morally and politically was to construct a discourse of solidarity against the messianic discourse of power generated by the Nazis and the Latin American dictators. Once the poems are rescued and disseminated, they move their readers to act on behalf of the victims, thus continuing the labor of resistance initiated *in situ*, when the crimes were taking place.

Although writing the pain is a powerful resistance strategy, poetry produced under such extreme circumstances is seldom self-referential; it tends to avoid references to the act of writing. Therefore, the writers' motivations and possible perceptions of writing as a tool for resistance are rarely, if ever, discussed in the poems. However, if the authors survive and publish their work, they will preface it with helpful reflections, mostly for the benefit of readers who did not endure the same torments. The Uruguayan poet Miguel Angel Olivera recorded his torture sessions in poems that were smuggled out of prison. He wrote in the prologue to *Los que no mueren en la cama – Poética de la tortura* (Those Who Don't Die in Bed – The Poetics of Torture), "I introduced a concept . . . applied by the victims of the concentration and extermination camps in the Second World War. It involved bearing testimony of how they lived and how they suffered; to write it down and whenever they could, to get it outside of the prison and hide it in a million and one ways, so that one day, when the horror came to an end, some of these testimonies patiently left by the victims as if sowing the seeds of future, would be known, and the barbaric cruelties will be documented so they would never happen again."[5]

While Latin American survivors like Olivera, Rosencof, and myself see obvious connections between testimonial writing in the Southern Cone and that of the Holocaust, scholars of Latin American testimonial texts tend to highlight the differences between the two cultural productions. Georg Gugelberger and Michael Kearney posit that Holocaust literature focuses on destruction while testimonial writing in the Americas highlights the consciousness-raising process that the witness embraces when telling his or her stories. In their article, "Voices of the Voiceless: Testimonial Literature in Latin America," they state, "As for Holocaust testimonies they are characterized by a shocking laying bare of the traumatic tortures and killings inflicted by imperial powers, be they Nazi Germany or American atomic bombs over Hiroshima and Nagasaki. Most of the Holocaust documentaries differ by not emphasizing the learning process and the politization, or what Paulo Freire has called "*conscientização*" which makes Central American testimonials so significant and so different."[6]

I am convinced that this failure to see Holocaust survivors' texts as consciousness-raising tools is grounded in the types of texts whose study has been privileged in the US, that is, written and oral testimonies produced in this country, often through an interviewer.[7]

If we examine the background and agendas of interviewers it becomes apparent that in Latin America they tend to be left-wing intellectuals who support social change, whereas US documentary producers and interviewers are at the center of the political spectrum, have no interest in highlighting the victims' political participation in the Communist Party and other resistance organizations, and generally stress ethnic or individual moral values over political considerations. Consequently, Holocaust testimonial works privileged in this country are presented from a depoliticized standpoint, whereas Latin American testimonial texts produce the opposite effect. However, when the reader is confronted with works produced within the ghettos and concentration camps, as opposed to post-factum works filtered through an interviewer, the political intention of the testimonial witness, Freire's conscientização, is apparent.

To the multiple examples discussed by Aaron in her book, I would like to add a jewel of resistance literature, a poetry collection published by the Museum of Tolerance and produced in 1996 by the French Consulate in Los Angeles. *The Enduring Spirit: Art of the Holocaust* includes poetry and drawings created within concentration camps by French citizens.[8] Although the book's preface downplays the fact that members of the resistance movement produced most of the works, the poems and illustrations are a carefully organized exercise in solidarity and political consciousness raising.

Even when most readily-available texts focus on the post-traumatic experience, we must be alert to signs of the trait highlighted by Terrence Des Pres when he argues that, "the will to bear witness, oral and written, was the primary incentive to survival for many camp inmates who have subsequently become the self-appointed historians of the Holocaust."[9] For Des Pres, the urge to testify implies an appropriation of reality, an act to recover agency. In *Pedagogy of the Oppressed*, Paulo Freire states that, "A deepened consciousness of their situation leads men to apprehend that situation as an historical reality susceptible of transformation. Resignation gives way to the drive for transformation and inquiry, over which men feel in control."[10]

One could argue, as George Yúdice does, that the testimony of the Holocaust experience "destroys any rational basis for understanding" and focuses on the passage from life to death, whereas in Latin American testimonial texts, the life of the witness "has undergone irreversible changes" but "is in the process of reconstruction and the testimonial mode is precisely one of the privileged vehicles for that reconstruction."[11]

It is true that we find in most Holocaust testimonies widely disseminated and studied in the US, an unquestionable element of desperation, of fatalism in the face of a reality beyond control and impossible to transform.[12] However, a wide range of testimonial works, including poetry produced in ghettos and concentration camps, were conceived as instruments to preserve the victim's moral and emotional integrity while the crimes were perpetrated upon them. In that sense they are similar to most Latin American testimonial texts. In the words of Frieda Aaron: "Literature produced in the ghettos and concentration camps may not reflect the dramatic or tragic irony exemplified in *post factum* writing."

Aaron, a survivor of the Warsaw ghetto and several Nazi concentration camps, analyzes in her book *Bearing the Unbearable* "the impact of the immediacy of Holocaust experience as a formative influence on perception, response, and literary imagination."[13] Working with an extensive corpus of poetry written in Yiddish and Polish, Aaron concentrates on subjects that are also at the core of testimonial poetry produced in Latin America: moral, political and even armed resistance, solidarity, the protection of *all* collective cultural creation, and the need to testify for the future, to set a historical record that would prevent the same atrocities from happening again.

The absence of self-referentiality observed in Southern Cone testimonial poetry is shared by the corpus examined by Aaron. Poets Abraham Sutzkever and Wladyslaw Szlengel are as exceptional in this respect as Miguel Angel Olivera in South America.[14] The three refer in their work to writing about pain. In Sutzkever's "Chant of a Jewish Poet in 1943" the poet asks "Am I singing for corpses, am I singing for crows?"[15] The answer stresses the need for poetry in order to construct a discourse of solidarity that transcends the borders of the destroyed ghetto and outweighs sorrow: "Be open, my heart! And know that the hollowed hours/Sprout forth in the thoughts of posterity/ . . . /And sing from swamps, and sing from netherworlds,/ . . . /So that your voice will be heard by the skeleton like/brothers, the burning ghetto and the people beyond the seas."[16]

The desire of the victimized poet to project a prophetic verse toward the future and toward people "overseas" illustrates his need to testify. The lyric speaker summons his own heart to sing its testimonial song. Psychologist Dori Laub discusses this device, the use of an "internal inter-locutor," as a strategy that allows the witness to accept himself as such. "The testimony is, therefore, the process by which the narrator (the survivor) reclaims his position as witness: reconstitutes the internal 'thou,' and thus the possibility of a witness or a listener inside himself."[17]

The liberating role of testimonial literature is addressed by Chilean political prisoner Arinda Ojeda in "Barco anclado" (Anchored Boat), "I write, because that is/my small space for freedom/and my wish to write to you/is an invitation to share it."[18] Ojeda, who spent several years in isolation after her detention in 1981, offers us another rare example of self-referentiality, this time in the form of an "*ars poetica*." Her reader, not a prisoner, is deprived of something that the victim, on the other hand, treasures, "the wealth to conquer/a small space of freedom/through every written line."[19] Ojeda is no longer addressing an internal interlocutor: the reader participates in building a discourse of solidarity, a task that has been initiated by the victim who is therefore empowered in a process that helps her regain agency.

As in some of the poetry produced in ghettos and concentration camps during the Holocaust, the poet's intention to chronicle the atrocities as a defense against oblivion is present in the works of Latin America's victims. Another Chilean political prisoner, Ignacio Vidaurrázaga wrote, "We will be chroniclers/we will be present/describing, recording/what we will not forget."[20] The same approach is taken by Uruguayan poet Miguel Angel Olivera in his poem "Ciclo de la palabra" (Cycle of the Word), "to redis-cover oneself/ . . . a spokesperson/a witness as far as it is possible . . . "[21]

Striking and significative as these examples are, most of the poetry produced in the ghettos and concentration camps, in South American jails, and at the homes and literature workshops attended by the relatives of the disappeared, does not respond to an initial impulse to testify "outwards." The immediate role of testimonial poems is to contribute to survival in the most basic and raw of its meanings, that is, to empower the victim so he can make it to the next day, the next hour. Paradoxically, even those poems that refer to the act of bearing testimony, are initially a tool to reconstruct the moral integrity of the victims, constantly thrashed by their tormentors. Subject to isolation and to permanent physical and psychological punishment, deprived of their place in history, the victims reconstruct their identity writing poetry that links them to those willing to hear their testimony.

In short, the construction of the discourse of solidarity in testimonial poetry collections originates in the initial action of the victimized poet who writes to resist his or her spiritual annihilation. The first reader is more likely to be another victim. Poetry written in concentration and torture camps is therefore conceived, as Aaron has brilliantly observed, "less as a means of self-expression than as succor, a vehicle of mitigating daily disasters."[22] This intention explains the lack of self-referentiality in most testimonial poetry produced while its author is being tormented.

To "mitigate" those daily disasters, the prisoners attempt to recreate the elements of everyday life that help them maintain a sense of normality amidst our alienated daily life. I recall that even in the Little School, blind-folded, hands tied, under the constant vigilance of guards, I would exchange ironic comments and silly jokes with Zulma Izurieta, my best friend from college who was later executed by the army. Laughter, humor, irony, helped both of us deal with the cruelty of the situation.

Likewise, parodic poetry amuses and therefore contributes to preserve the prisoner's psychological integrity. Olivera recounts, "Many of these minute daily life details have gone unrecorded. Not everything was dramatic; there was joking, satire and above all, a concerted effort to fuel resistance, to uplift our spirits . . ."[23] Aaron calls these writings "poetry of humble fact," and reminds the reader of the famous Rubinsztajn, clown of the Warsaw Ghetto, who would stand on the streets of the ghetto reciting his comic stanzas.[24] In one of the harshest prisons during Argentina's dictatorship, the inmates rejoiced listening to "Las diez décimas del Tenemismo" (Ten Stanzas to Tenemismo).[25] This short excerpt clearly exemplifies the use of irony, while showing in a very dramatic light the switch from parody to the painfully pathetic effect the stanzas produce on the reader once they are removed from their initial context:

> Sports are prohibited
> same with radio and TV,
> with books and the heating plate:
> as they have come they have left.
> This is really bloody awful
> and it gets worse every day
> and there are those who, insane,
> in their maddest delirium
> tell us: "Soon, very soon,
> the prison system will break."

Neither the warm Spring sun
shining on plazas and gardens
Nor the scent of jasmine
Neither the sight of first roses
Nor the sweet swinging of hips
Along the finest of streets
Not even one of these things
Do I like I swear as much
as looking at this thick wall
from my lousy prison hole.[26]

When a poem that was written to "mitigate everyday disasters" emerges from its original context transformed into a testimony for the outside world, explanations abound and prologues elaborate on the ancillary nature of the works. In his preface to *Los que no mueren en la cama*, Olivera explains, "in my case, the insignificant little verse, the humble poetic form and my will to embark on the small but difficult act of writing, to transfer my thoughts and ideas to the page, gave me strength, kept me trained and alert, helped me endure the pain."[27]

Victimized poets write for everyday survival. In confinement, poetry is an instrument to provoke laughter, raise morale, exorcise pain, and exercise the intellect. Poetry's immediate function is then to help the authors recover their integrity as human beings in control of their history, individuals who belong to a world community that will in the future listen to their account of atrocities. Therefore, this profoundly testimonial poetry works at several levels building a discourse of solidarity inside the ghetto, the concentration camp or the prison, and afterwards, amidst the human rights movement.

This poem written by Mauricio Rosencof and tapped on the wall – via Morse telegraphic code as a birthday present to his prison neighbor of ten years, dramatically illustrates the solidarity impulse at work.[28]

And were this my last,
Threadbare yet whole poem,
. . . .
just
    a word
I would write:
Compañero.[29]

I have chosen to retain the word "compañero" in Spanish since many US English speakers understand that it means companion in the struggle and in life, as "comrade/*camarada*" would do for those active in the Communist Party. However, both terms (compañero and camarada) stress the privileging of the collective experience over the individual drama. According to Aaron, "Although by no means all, much of this poetry eschews the narrow concerns of private struggles and subordinates them to the problems facing the community."[30] This focus on the collective that is naturally shared with the first reader, the prison inmate, is one of the most moving features of testimonial poetry. When the poems are taken out of their first environment and published, prefaces often refer to this trait as indicators of the "triumph of the human spirit."

A clear example of the nature of prefaces can be seen in this enlightening introduction to the poetry anthology *Desde la cárcel* (From Prison).

> But the prisoner's humanity survives . . . by a miracle of which only humankind is capable: the miracle of solidarity, of love that connects those who suffer together down to their roots; . . . and along with the miracle of brotherhood, comes that of the written or graphic expression. Pencil and paper are the tools of dignity and integrity . . . They confirm the existence of the power, targeted for destruction by the jailers, to speak out, to elaborate from the bottom of one's own truth and with the strength born from an appreciation of life, a message to the rest of humankind, perpetuated forever on a piece of paper.[31]

The author of this preface, identified only as "a former Argentinean political prisoner," explains the dynamics behind building a discourse of solidarity within the prison and subsequently widens its reach to add the "rest of mankind." That presumably includes us, the new ideal readers for these texts.

Similar concepts preface the Uruguayan anthology, *Escritos de la cárcel* (Prison Writings).

> The creative impulse allowed even the most tormented of victims under the most critical circumstances to create and memorize a few verses, to find a sheet – even a tiny cigarette paper leaf, and a bit of pencil lead and write a sentence, a page, a story . . . or just a word to break the isolation, the seclusion, the marginalization imposed by the forces of prepotency and terror. Today we recover those works so they do not remain lost back in time, so that they may be testimonies to that historical period, so that you may access them, pick them up, make them yours to share, so they may belong to everyone. In a jail for political prisoners the protagonist is the entire people and its cultural products will belong to the collective realm.[32]

While the Nazi regime and the Latin American dictatorships conducted their genocides, they built a Messianic discourse of power. We have observed in this array of works written under terror, that the most effective tool to resist that destruction is the construction of a discourse of solidarity inside the torture and death camps. When the poems born to mitigate the pain of others as a way of soothing the poet's anguish survive and are collected in testimonial books, the building process continues, seeking the readers' support and essentially continuing the resistance work started by the victims while the crimes were committed. If the victimized poet survives, she never ceases to tell her story, a collective one. In the words of Dori Laub,

> This imperative to tell and to be heard can become itself an all-consuming task. Yet no amount of telling seems ever to do justice to this inner compulsion. There are never enough words or the right words, there is never enough time or the right time, and never enough listening or the right listening to articulate the story that cannot be fully captured in thought, memory and speech. The pressure thus continues unremittingly, and if we are not trustworthy or adequate, the life that is chosen can become the vehicle by which the struggle to tell continues.[33]

As a survivor of the Argentine secret detention camps, I believe that the only way to tell the story so that it neither consumes the life of the witness nor is perceived by her as a futile, desperate act, is to tell it within the context of the discourse of solidarity. Such a discourse will continue its building process in every interaction with our multiple readers, multiple realities, multiple texts, and will in turn trigger countless acts of resistance to state terrorism.

Yet, there are those, like my grandfather, who chose not to tell. When my father informed him of my disappearance at the hands of the army, he sighed and uttered, "Why our family again?" Our family is large indeed: it includes the oppressed of the world, the persecuted, those massacred because of their political and religious beliefs. My mother, Raquel Partnoy, feels that those connections nurture her art and writings. Her series of paintings, "Surviving Genocide," comes to mind. She traces her cultural roots back to her Jewish identity. I, however, choose not to focus on my Jewishness.

When feminist scholar Myrna Goldenberg befriended me and supported my writings fifteen years ago, she was doing pioneer work by finding relevant connections between my experiences in Argentina and those of Holocaust survivors. However, she did not ask me to discuss my Jewish identity. It was not necessary. We all know that for the Nazis, for the perpetrators of the pogroms that destroyed my grandparents' families and forced the four of them into exile, my last name would have sufficed to target me. It would have been enough to observe the way I lean on the trunk of my family tree, not with the anxiety the shipwrecked embraces a life board, but with the serene demeanor of she who knows that this tree is part and parcel of the woods she calls her history.

Acknowledgments

This chapter originally appeared in Spanish as part of my dissertation, *The Discourse of Solidarity in Testimonial "Poemarios" from Argentina, Chile and*

Uruguay. El discurso de la solidaridad en los poemarios testimoniales de Argentina, Chile y Uruguay (Ann Arbor: UMI Dissertation Services, 1997). My gratitude to Mario Rojas for his feedback and support while writing it, to Myrna Goldenberg and Jan Hokenson for encouraging me to explore the connections between the Holocaust and the Latin American experience, and to Amanda Hussey and Shonda Buchanan for their help in the translation process.

Notes

1 Mauricio Rosencof, "On Suffering, Song, and White Horses," in Saúl Sosnowski and Louise Popkin, eds, *Repression, Exile, and Democracy – Uruguayan Culture* (Durham: Duke University Press, 1993), 130. "Siento/en mis huesos/los huesos/de aquellos/que fueron./En mí/esqueletos/son, /somos/lo que soy,/soy/los que ayer/fueron."

2 *Ibid.*, 131.

3 As one of the few lucky survivors, I have discussed my experiences as a "disappeared" – somebody kidnapped by the authorities, kept in a secret detention center, tortured, eventually killed and whose body is never returned to the family – in *The Little School: Tales of Disappearance and Survival in Argentina* (San Francisco: Cleis Press, 1986). Thirty thousand Argentines, including about five hundred children, were assassinated this way.

4 Frieda Aaron, *Bearing the Unbearable. Yiddish and Polish Poetry in the Ghettos and Concentration Camps* (Albany: SUNY Press, 1990).

5 Miguel Angel Olivera, *Los que no mueren en la cama. Poética de la tortura* (Montevideo: CIC, 1988), 8.

6 Georg Gugelberger and Michael Kearney, "Voices for the Voiceless: Testimonial Literature in Latin America," *Latin American Perspectives* 70 (1991): 9.

7 The authors refer to concepts in Paulo Freire's *Pedagogy of the Oppressed* (New York: Seabury Press, 1970). Freire's validation of the experience of those marginalized by society, and his embracing witness storytelling as a way of articulating political awareness, are at the roots of the vast production of testimonial texts in Latin America. Although both the scope and forms of these texts are diverse, most critics have in mind the book by Rigoberta Menchú and Elisabeth Burgos-Debray, *I, Rigoberta Menchú. An Indian Woman in Guatemala* (New York: Verso, 1984).

8 The book, subtitled "Literary and Artistic Practices in the Concentration Camps in Europe During World War II," was published in conjunction with an exhibit of the drawings at the Museum of Tolerance. Veronique Alemany-Dessaint from the Musée des Beaux-Arts de Reims and Jane Tessa Ten Rink, Curator of Temporary Exhibits at the Museum of Tolerance, curated the show, and Anne Leroy-Saltzman designed the book. The limited distribution of this poetry collection, and the fact that it was an effort mostly funded and generated by Europeans, highlights my previous observations on material widely available in the US.

9 Barbara Foley, "Fact, Fiction, Fascism: Testimony and Mimesis in Holocaust Narratives," *Comparative Literature* 34 (1982): 334.

10 Freire, *Pedagogy*, 73.

11 George Yúdice, "Testimonio y concientización," *Revista de Crítica Literaria Latinoamericana* 36 (1992): 214 (author's translation).

12 Elie Wiesel's *Night* (New York: Bantam, 1986) comes to mind as the paradigmatic text, while the astonishing work of Sara Nomberg-Przytyk, *Auschwitz. True Tales from a Grotesque Land* (Chapel Hill: University of North Carolina Press, 1985) is a book remarkable for highlighting not only the destruction, but also the spirit of resistance among inmates, but which sadly remains largely ignored.

13 Aaron, *Bearing the Unbearable*, 2.

14 The work of Paul Celan is another exception. Shoshana Felman has made an in-depth analysis of his testimonial poetry, written after the poet's experience in Nazi forced labor camps where his parents were exterminated. Shosana Felman and Dori Laub, *Testimony: Crises of Witnessing in Literature, Psychoanalysis, and History* (New York: Routledge, 1992), 25–42.

15 Aaron, *Bearing the Unbearable*, 78.

16 *Ibid.*, 79.

17 Felman and Laub, *Testimony*, 85.

18 "Escribo porque ese es/mi pequeño espacio de libertad,/y al querer escribirte/te estoy ofreciendo compartirlo." Arinda Ojeda, *Mi rebeldía es vivir* (Santiago: Ediciones Literatura Alternativa, 1988), 19, from "Barco anclado."

19 "la riqueza de ir conquistando/un pequeño espacio de libertad/en cada línea . . . " Ojeda, "Barco anclado," 19.

20 "Seremos cronistas/estaremos presentes/describiendo en acta/lo que no olvidaremos." Ignacio Vidaurrázaga, *Se vive para darse* (Santiago: Ediciones Literatura Alternativa, 1987), 17, from the poem "Tu Frente" (Your Forehead), dedicated to Nelson Herrera, who was killed by a bullet to his forehead in a "staged/fake" confrontation with the army.

21 "uno se redescubre/ . . . vocero/testigo hasta que pueda . . . " Olivera, *Los que no mueren*, 47.

22 Aaron, *Bearing the Unbearable*, 3.

23 Olivera, *Los que no mueren*, 11.

24 Aaron, *Bearing the Unbearable*, 98.

25 Presos Políticos Argentinos, *Desde la cárcel* (Mexico: CADHU and other Human Rights Organizations, 1981). In the Coronda prison in Santa Fe province, "Tenemismo" was a tongue-in-cheek philosophical approach to life that painted the future of the prisoners in the gloomiest tones.

26 "Los deportes están prohibidos/la radio, el televisor,/los libros, el calentador/por donde entraron se han ido/esto está más bien jodido y empeora cada día,/y hay quienes en su insanía/y en sus delirios más locos/nos dicen: -Ya falta poco/se quebró la taquería./Ni el sol de la primavera/en las plazas y jardines/ni el olor de los jazmines/ni el de las rosas primeras/ni el vaivén de las caderas/en las calles primorosas/no ninguna de esas cosas/me gusta se lo aseguro/como mirar ese muro/desde esta celda piojosa." Presos, *Desde la cárcel*, 95.

27 "En mi caso, el insignificante versito, la humilde formita poética y el montar y realizar la pequeña pero difícil acción de escribir, de pasar a la hojilla lo pensado, lo elaborado mentalmente, me fortaleció, me mantuvo entrenado y

alerta, me ayudó a bancar lo que estaba soportando." Olivera, *Los que no mueren*, 13.

28 Rosencof, "On Suffering," 124.

29 "Y si este fuera/mi ultimo poema,/ . . . /raído pero entero,/tan sólo/una palabra/escribiría:/Compañero." Rosencof, *Conversaciones*, 70.

30 Aaron, *Bearing the Unbearable*, 20.

31 "Pero la humanidad del preso sobrevive . . . por un milagro del que solamente son capaces los hombres: el milagro de la solidaridad, del amor que enlaza hasta las raíces a quienes sufren juntos . . . Y junto con el milagro fraterno, el de la expresión escrita o gráfica. El lápiz y el papel son las herramientas de la dignidad y de la integridad . . . Afirman la vigencia de esa facultad que es, precisamente, la que sobre todo se quiere destruir: la de decir, la de elaborar desde el fondo de las verdades propias y con todo el vigor del aprecio por la vida, algo para comunicar al resto de los hombres, fijado para siempre en un trozo del papel." Presos, *Desde la cárcel*, 6.

32 "El impulso creativo permitió que el hombre más verdugueado y en la condición más crítica consiguiera concebir y memorizar unos versos, hacerse de una hoja – una hojilla de fumar apenas – y un pedazo de grafo para escribir una frase, una página, un cuento . . . una palabra siquiera para romper la incomunicación, el encierro, el marginamiento impuesto por la fuerza de la prepotencia y el terror . . . Hoy vamos rescatando todo eso del paso del tiempo para que sea testimonio de esa etapa histórica vivida, para que ustedes lo conozcan, lo recojan, lo hagan suyo y lo compartan, para que sea de todos, se socialice porque en la cárcel política el protagonista es el pueblo preso y el destino de la creación canera es la colectivización popular." Centro de Integración Cultural, *Escritos de la cárcel. La expresión poética de los presos políticos*, vol.1 (Montevideo: Centro de Integración Cultural, 1986), 8.

33 Felman and Laub, *Testimony*, 70.

The Contributors

Marjorie Agosin is a professor of Spanish at Wellesley College. She has published *A Cross and A Star*, a memoir of her mother's childhood as a Jewish immigrant in a German community in Chile. Among her extensive publications on Jewish Latin American culture and literature are *House of Memory: Contemporary Women Writers from Latin America* and *Invisible Dreamer: Memory, Judaism and Human Rights*. Her poetry and essays have appeared in many national journals and newspapers.

Ruth Behar is a professor of anthropology at the University of Michigan. She publishes on crossing cultural borders as a poet, essayist, fiction writer, editor, ethnographer, and most recently as a documentary film-maker of *Adio Kerida/Goodbye Dear Love: A Cuban Sephardic Journey*. Her books include *Translated Woman: Crossing the Border with Esperanza's Story* and *The Vulnerable Observer: Anthropology That Breaks Your Heart*. She has been awarded a MacArthur Fellowship and a Guggenheim Fellowship for her work. As a Cuban woman of the diaspora, Behar is committed to seeking reconciliation and a common culture and memory with Cubans on the island.

Beatriz Blanca Gurevich is a sociologist. She is a scholar-in-residence at the Hadassah-Brandeis Institute at Brandeis University for 2004–2005, and is a senior researcher at the Centro de Estudios Internacionales y de Educación para la Globalización (Center for International Study and Education on Globalization, CEIEG) at the Universidad del CEMA (UCEMA) and has been director of projects concerning the persecution and disappearance of Jews in Argentina. She was director of the research project Testimonio and a senior investigator for the Comisión para el Esclarecimiento de las Actividades del Nazismo en la República Argentina

(Commission of Enquiry into the Activities of Nazism in Argentina, CEANA) at the Ministry of Foreign Relations. She has published *Proyecto Testimonio* and *El Genocidio ante la Historia y la Naturaleza* (with C. Escudé).

Jeffrey Lesser is Winship Distinguished Research Professor of History at Emory University and director of the Latin American and Caribbean Studies Program. He publishes on immigration, ethnicity and transnational identity. His most recent books are *Negotiating National Identity: Immigrants, Minorities and the Struggle for Ethnicity in Brazil* and *Welcoming the Undesirables: Brazil and the Jewish Question*. He is also editor of *Searching for Home Abroad: Japanese Brazilians and Transnationalism*.

Robert M. Levine was a professor of history at the University of Miami and director of Latin American Studies. He authored *Tropical Diaspora: the Jewish Experience in Cuba, 1902– 1992* and three other books on Cuba, including *Secret Missions: Fidel Castro, Bernardo Benes, and Cuban Miami*. He also wrote extensively on Jewish communities in Brazil and responses to the Holocaust, Latin American photography, and race and ethnicity. He produced a number of documentaries, including *Hotel Cuba: A Historical Diary of the Pre-Castro Jewish Experience* (with M. Szuchman), and was a consultant for *Havana Nagila*.

William F. S. Miles is professor of political science and the former Stotsky Professor of Jewish Historical and Cultural Studies at Northeastern University. In addition to books on Africa, India and Oceania, he has published *Paradoxe au Paradis: de la Politique à la Martinique*. His Jewish-interest articles have appeared in *The Chronicle of Higher Education*, *Diaspora*, *The Journal of Genocide Research*, *Midstream*, *Transition*, *The Western Journal of Black Studies*, and *Wadabagei. A Journal of the Caribbean and its Diaspora*. Miles is also a frequent contributor to *Moment. America's Premier Independent Jewish Magazine*.

Alicia Partnoy is a professor and chair of the Modern Languages and Literatures Department at Loyola Marymount University in Los Angeles. Her testimony as a "disappeared" person in Argentina is found in *Nunca Más* and in her collection *The Little School: Tales of Disappearance and Survival*, illustrated by her mother, Raquel Partnoy. She is the author of *Revenge of the Apple* (poetry); the editor of *You Can't Drown the Fire: Latin American Women Writing in Exile*; and co-editor of *Chicana/Latina Studies: The Journal of Mujeres Activas en Letras y Cambio Social*.

The Contributors

Raquel Partnoy is a painter, art teacher, and essayist living in Washington, DC. Her solo exhibits include shows at the B'nai B'rith Klutznick National Jewish Museum; Parish Gallery; Embassy of Argentina in Washington, DC; Jewish Community Center; Studio Gallery; and Goucher College in Baltimore. She has been teaching mural art at the Latin American Youth Center in Washington, DC. Her essay "Silent Witness" was published in *Women Writing Resistance: Essays on Latin America and the Caribbean* edited by Jennifer Browdy de Hernandez. She has lectured widely on her experiences during the dictatorship in Argentina.

Raanan Rein is professor of history at the University of Tel Aviv and director of the Institute of Latin American History and Culture, and was recently elected a corresponding member of the Academia Nacional de la Historia de la Argentina. He is the author of numerous books and articles in various languages. His recent books include *Argentina, Israel, and the Jews* and *In the Shadow of the Holocaust and the Inquisition: Israel's Relations with Francoist Spain*. For the past ten years he has been the editor of the journal *Estudios Interdisciplinarios de América Latina y el Caribe*.

Kristin Ruggiero is a professor of history at the University of Wisconsin-Milwaukee and director of the Center for Latin American and Caribbean Studies. She has published two monographs: *Modernity in the Flesh: Medicine, Law and Society in Turn-of-the-Century Argentina* and *And Here the World Ends: The Life of an Argentine Village*. Her many research trips to Argentina both during and after the military government have acquainted her with the country's Jewish community.

Ruth Crawford Schwertfeger is professor of German at the University of Wisconsin-Milwaukee. Her publications include *The Wee Wild One: Stories of Belfast and Beyond*; *Women of Theresienstadt: Writings from a Concentration Camp*; and *Else Lasker-Schuler: Inside this Deathly Solitude*. She is currently working on "German Jews in the Dark Years: Narratives of Exile and Internment 1933–1945."

David Sheinin is professor of history at Trent University and is an associate at the Martin Institute for Peace Studies and Conflict Resolution at the University of Idaho. He has published on Pan Americanism, inter-American relations, US–Argentine relations, and human rights. He is the editor of *The Jewish Diaspora in Latin America* (with L. B. Barr). He has published *Searching for Authority: Pan Americanism, Diplomacy, and Politics in United States-Argentine Relations, 1910-1930* and is currently working on Argentine nuclear policy during the Cold War.

Rosalie Sitman is coordinator of Spanish language courses at the University of Tel Aviv. Her book *Victoria Ocampo and SUR: Between Europe and America* was recently published by Ediciones Lumiere, Buenos Aires. She is linguistic and associate editor of *Estudios Interdisciplinarios de América Latina y el Caribe*. Her fields of interest include Latin American history and culture. She has published extensively on the use of the internet in teaching the Spanish language.

Ilán Stavans is the Lewis-Sebring Professor in Latin American and Latino Culture at Amherst College. His books include *The Hispanic Condition: Reflections on Culture and Identity in America*; *Art and Anger: Esssays on Politics and the Imagination*; *The Inveterate Dreamer: Essays and Conversations on Jewish Culture*; and *Spanglish: The Making of a New American Language*. His work has been translated into half a dozen languages. He edited *The Poetry of Pablo Neruda*; the three-volume set of *Isaac Bashevis Singer: Collected Stories*; and *The Schocken Book of Modern Sephardic Literature*. The piece in this volume is from his best-selling *On Borrowed Words: A Memoir of Language*. In 2000 Routledge published *The Essential Ilán Stavans*. And the University of Wisconsin Press published *Ilán Stavans: Eight Conversations*, by Neal Sokol, in 2004.

Index

Index

Index

Index

Index

Index

Index

Index

Index

Index

Index

DATE DUE

The Jewish diaspora in Latin
America and the Caribbean